Fourth Grade

Basic Skills

Curriculum

PLAIN

and
not
so

PLAIN

ACADEMY

A simpler approach to
home based schooling

To the home educator,

I am very happy that you have chosen to purchase our products. We believe that our world is way too complex and that it can be simplified to avoid the chaos and confusion. Learning at home should be an enjoyable time between you and your child. Not something that they dread because they have hundreds of repetition problems to do over and over again. Plain and not so Plain Academy's approach to schooling is to concentrate on the basics and then fill in with real life learning. This approach to schooling is meant to take the stress and fear out of teaching your child at home. Your child's entire elementary schooling is going to be one big repetition, year after year. We take all the extra complexities out of schooling and get back to the basics of reading, writing, and arithmetic. By approaching schooling this way, your child will be more confident as they work through the worksheets. This allows extra time to pursue other areas of interest.

If you find that your child is struggling with a particular concept in Plain and not so Plain's curriculum, do some extra problems until they understand it. Make it fun. If they struggle with getting each worksheet done all at one time, have them do part of it and then take a break. No stress.

This 4th grade basic skills curriculum is enough to do 36 weeks of school four times per week. I would recommend doing four days of "worksheet schooling" and then one day of real life schooling. That would give you 180 days worth of record-keeping schooling. Do four pages each day. The workday begins with spelling words, a page for math concepts, a page for practicing math facts, and one for English and individual reading. This year's major focus is math facts. This will make math a more enjoyable experience for them if they learn these. Also included are 21 weeks of vocabulary words every 4th grader should know. Instructions are included as how to implement these into their week.

As you see your child doing well in printing letters, you can begin implementing cursive writing into their daily lessons. Due to space allowance, I am unable to include cursive writings. That book is available separately. As they grow confident they will gradually switch from print to cursive.

Explore learning through a variety of books and learning DVD's available at your local library. I have many recommendations that we use for history and science on my site. Read "living books" to your child. Let them gain an understanding about the world around them through these type books.

If needed, an answer key is provided on my blog under the homeschooling section. I was unable to put it in this book due to the size.

Be blessed,

Amy Maryon

founder and owner of www.plainandnotsoplain.com a simpler lifestyle in our complex world

week 1 copy your spelling words

ache

admit

animal

April

bacon

bathroom

camera

flap

grateful

happiness

manage

navy

plane

radish

waste

Add

5+6=   6+5=   8+0=

4+8+6=   4+5+6=

Jim ran 5 laps in the morning. He ran 8 laps in the afternoon. How many laps
did he run in all?

Find the missing addend:

7 + n= 10   a +8=12

$$
\begin{array}{cccc}
5 & 8 & 6 & 9 \\
5 & 0 & 5 & 9 \\
+5 & +7 & +4 & +9 \\
\end{array}
$$

3+2+5+4+6=

4 +4	7 +5	0 +1	8 +7	3 +4	3 +2	8 +3	2 +1	5 +6	2 +9
0 +9	8 +9	7 +6	1 +3	6 +8	7 +3	1 +6	4 +7	0 +3	6 +4
9 +3	2 +6	3 +0	6 +1	3 +6	4 +0	5 +7	1 +1	5 +4	2 +8
4 +3	0 +9	0 +7	9 +4	7 +7	8 +6	0 +4	5 +8	7 +4	1 +7
9 +5	1 +5	9 +0	3 +8	1 +9	9 +1	8 +8	2 +2	4 +5	6 +2
7 +9	1 +2	6 +7	0 +8	9 +2	4 +8	8 +0	3 +9	1 +0	6 +3
2 +0	8 +4	3 +5	9 +8	5 +0	5 +5	3 +1	7 +2	8 +5	2 +5
5 +2	0 +5	6 +9	1 +8	9 +6	7 +1	4 +6	0 +2	6 +5	4 +9
1 +4	3 +7	7 +0	2 +3	5 +1	6 +6	4 +1	8 +2	2 +4	6 +0
5 +3	4 +2	9 +7	0 +6	7 +8	0 +0	5 +9	3 +3	8 +1	2 +7

The noun

A noun is a word that names a person, place, thing, or idea.

name three nouns that have to do with a car	wheels	engines	seats
name three nouns that have to do with a forest			
name three nouns that have to do with a library			
name three nouns that have to do with a garden			

READING

Your other task for the day is to read a book. At this point you should be able to read for ½ hour to 1 hour each day. Look online for a variety of book lists. You can also check out my site www.plainandnotsoplain.com and see all of the books that we have enjoyed at this grade level.

Write the title of the book you are reading and how long you have read for.

_____

_____

```
T  E  W  C  Y  V  H  K  B  R  Q  U  Y  F  O
H  I  Y  U  G  P  Z  U  N  R  V  C  D  K  I
L  B  M  V  Y  R  B  X  Y  V  Q  Q  P  C  T
Y  P  T  D  V  U  A  B  F  M  Z  F  H  P  M
N  U  C  K  A  B  A  T  H  R  O  O  M  L  G
Y  S  T  I  N  H  S  S  E  N  I  P  P  A  H
N  C  Z  O  Y  H  N  T  L  F  M  Q  Q  N  Z
D  L  W  F  V  Z  Q  W  L  E  U  F  R  E  A
N  I  S  U  R  N  A  H  M  P  A  L  F  C  I
O  O  U  F  A  S  C  A  S  R  H  M  H  A  Q
C  Q  S  J  T  R  N  B  I  L  E  P  S  H
A  N  Y  E  L  A  E  I  M  Z  D  R  T  C  J
B  U  C  S  G  A  V  M  J  Z  I  A  W  A  X
X  M  I  E  A  O  U  A  A  L  F  O  R  X  S
F  D  Z  P  Z  W  R  L  C  C  P  T  Z  K  A
```

ACHE	ADMIT	ANIMAL
APRIL	BACON	BATHROOM
CAMERA	FLAP	GRATEFUL
HAPPINESS	MANAGE	NAVY
PLANE	RADISH	WASTE

Find the missing addend:

8 + a + 2=17

b +6+5=12

1+b+4=8

c+4+5=11

My rabbit ate 5 carrots in the morning, 6 carrots in the afternoon. How many carrots did he eat in all?

I ate 10 jelly beans in the afternoon and 5 more at night. How many did I eat altogether?

Which number is _____ in the following sentence?

6 + _____=10

a. 4   b. 6   c.10   d.16

100 addition facts

4 +4	7 +5	0 +1	8 +7	3 +4	3 +2	8 +3	2 +1	5 +6	2 +9
0 +9	8 +9	7 +6	1 +3	6 +8	7 +3	1 +6	4 +7	0 +3	6 +4
9 +3	2 +6	3 +0	6 +1	3 +6	4 +0	5 +7	1 +1	5 +4	2 +8
4 +3	0 +9	0 +7	9 +4	7 +7	8 +6	0 +4	5 +8	7 +4	1 +7
9 +5	1 +5	9 +0	3 +8	1 +9	9 +1	8 +8	2 +2	4 +5	6 +2
7 +9	1 +2	6 +7	0 +8	9 +2	4 +8	8 +0	3 +9	1 +0	6 +3
2 +0	8 +4	3 +5	9 +8	5 +0	5 +5	3 +1	7 +2	8 +5	2 +5
5 +2	0 +5	6 +9	1 +8	9 +6	7 +1	4 +6	0 +2	6 +5	4 +9
1 +4	3 +7	7 +0	2 +3	5 +1	6 +6	4 +1	8 +2	2 +4	6 +0
5 +3	4 +2	9 +7	0 +6	7 +8	0 +0	5 +9	3 +3	8 +1	2 +7

Write a sentence for each of the following compound nouns.

sunflower

_____

highway

_____

suitcase

_____

toothpick

_____

sunlight

_____

READING

Your other task for the day is to read a book. At this point you should be able to read for ½ hour to 1 hour each day. Look online for a variety of book lists. You can also check out my site www.plainandnotsoplain.com and see all of the books that we have enjoyed at this grade level.

Write the title of the book you are reading and how long you have read for.

_____

_____

Write a sentence for each of your words

Skip counting: Count by 10s

10	20	30							

Figure out what the rule is for this counting series:

30	27	24	21		15				

How many DIGITS are in 64,000?

What Is the last digit of 2001?

How many digits are in each number:

18_____   5379_____   8,344,087_____

What is the last digit of each number:

18_____   7655_____   7,987,098_____

Brooklyn has 5 dollars, Mayama has 6 dollars, and Blessing has 7 dollars.
Altogether, how much money do the three girls have?

Find the missing addend:

5 + m+4=12   8+2+w=16

100 Addition facts

4 +4	7 +5	0 +1	8 +7	3 +4	3 +2	8 +3	2 +1	5 +6	2 +9
0 +9	8 +9	7 +6	1 +3	6 +8	7 +3	1 +6	4 +7	0 +3	6 +4
9 +3	2 +6	3 +0	6 +1	3 +6	4 +0	5 +7	1 +1	5 +4	2 +8
4 +3	0 +9	0 +7	9 +4	7 +7	8 +6	0 +4	5 +8	7 +4	1 +7
9 +5	1 +5	9 +0	3 +8	1 +9	9 +1	8 +8	2 +2	4 +5	6 +2
7 +9	1 +2	6 +7	0 +8	9 +2	4 +8	8 +0	3 +9	1 +0	6 +3
2 +0	8 +4	3 +5	9 +8	5 +0	5 +5	3 +1	7 +2	8 +5	2 +5
5 +2	0 +5	6 +9	1 +8	9 +6	7 +1	4 +6	0 +2	6 +5	4 +9
1 +4	3 +7	7 +0	2 +3	5 +1	6 +6	4 +1	8 +2	2 +4	6 +0
5 +3	4 +2	9 +7	0 +6	7 +8	0 +0	5 +9	3 +3	8 +1	2 +7

Circle the nouns in the following sentences

1. Kim swims on a team.
2. Nicole and Ramen formed a committee to clean up the park.
3. Eliza rides her bicycle to the library after school.
4. Her favorite author is Bee Smith.
5. Mrs. Maryon visited the White House in April.

READING

Your other task for the day is to read a book. At this point you should be able to read for ½ hour to 1 hour each day. Look online for a variety of book lists. You can also check out my site www.plainandnotsoplain.com and see all of the books that we have enjoyed at this grade level.

Write the title of the book you are reading and how long you have read for.

_____

_____

quiz

Place value		
hundreds	tens	ones
5	2	3

This means that I have 5-100's and 2-10's and 3-1's

Use some toothpicks to demonstrate this.

How many hundreds are in the number 432?

How many tens are in the number 432?

How many ones are in the number 321?

The digit 6 is in the tenths place in which number?

362   632   756

Count by 5's

5	10								

How many digits are in each number

4,321,643_____   54_____   87,986,999_____

If I had 4 hundreds, 3 tens, and 2 ones. What number would I have?

Find the missing addend:

2+5+3+2+3+1+n=20

100 Addition facts

4 +4	7 +5	0 +1	8 +7	3 +4	3 +2	8 +3	2 +1	5 +6	2 +9
0 +9	8 +9	7 +6	1 +3	6 +8	7 +3	1 +6	4 +7	0 +3	6 +4
9 +3	2 +6	3 +0	6 +1	3 +6	4 +0	5 +7	1 +1	5 +4	2 +8
4 +3	0 +9	0 +7	9 +4	7 +7	8 +6	0 +4	5 +8	7 +4	1 +7
9 +5	1 +5	9 +0	3 +8	1 +9	9 +1	8 +8	2 +2	4 +5	6 +2
7 +9	1 +2	6 +7	0 +8	9 +2	4 +8	8 +0	3 +9	1 +0	6 +3
2 +0	8 +4	3 +5	9 +8	5 +0	5 +5	3 +1	7 +2	8 +5	2 +5
5 +2	0 +5	6 +9	1 +8	9 +6	7 +1	4 +6	0 +2	6 +5	4 +9
1 +4	3 +7	7 +0	2 +3	5 +1	6 +6	4 +1	8 +2	2 +4	6 +0
5 +3	4 +2	9 +7	0 +6	7 +8	0 +0	5 +9	3 +3	8 +1	2 +7

A common noun is the general type of person, place, thing, or idea.

A proper noun is the name of a particular person, place, thing, or idea.

Capitalize a common noun only if it is the first word of a sentence or title. Always capitalize a proper noun.

Common nouns= school, museum, astronaut, president

Proper nouns==Springdale School, John Glenn, Thomas Jefferson, December

Fill in the chart with either a proper or common noun to match the opposite noun

common	proper
teacher	
state	France
city	
	Tuxedo Park
person	
	Donald Trump

READING

Your other task for the day is to read a book. At this point you should be able to read for ½ hour to 1 hour each day. Look online for a variety of book lists. You can also check out my site www.plainandnotsoplain.com and see all of the books that we have enjoyed at this grade level.

Write the title of the book you are reading and how long you have read for.

_____

_____

week 2 copy your spelling words

bedtime

being

beverage

cedar

decoy

elegant

female

jelly

lemon

medicine

meteor

rectangle

recycle

secret

skeleton

Ordinal numbers

1st first 2nd second 3rd third 4th fourth

5th fifth 6th sixth 7th seventh 8th eighth

9th ninth 10th tenth 20th twentieth 21st twenty-first

Andy is 13th in line. Michael is 3rd in line. How many students are in between them?

At the store, there were 5 people in the first line, 6 people in the second line, and 4 people in the third line. Altogether, how many people were in the three lines?

Find the missing addend:

2 +6+x= 15   3 +z+5=15   r +5=11

Fill in the sequence:

12	15	18							

If I have 4 hundred dollar bills, 2-ten dollar bills, and 5 one dollar bills. How much do I have?

The digit 8 is in what place in 845?

4 +4	7 +5	0 +1	8 +7	3 +4	3 +2	8 +3	2 +1	5 +6	2 +9
0 +9	8 +9	7 +6	1 +3	6 +8	7 +3	1 +6	4 +7	0 +3	6 +4
9 +3	2 +6	3 +0	6 +1	3 +6	4 +0	5 +7	1 +1	5 +4	2 +8
4 +3	0 +9	0 +7	9 +4	7 +7	8 +6	0 +4	5 +8	7 +4	1 +7
9 +5	1 +5	9 +0	3 +8	1 +9	9 +1	8 +8	2 +2	4 +5	6 +2
7 +9	1 +2	6 +7	0 +8	9 +2	4 +8	8 +0	3 +9	1 +0	6 +3
2 +0	8 +4	3 +5	9 +8	5 +0	5 +5	3 +1	7 +2	8 +5	2 +5
5 +2	0 +5	6 +9	1 +8	9 +6	7 +1	4 +6	0 +2	6 +5	4 +9
1 +4	3 +7	7 +0	2 +3	5 +1	6 +6	4 +1	8 +2	2 +4	6 +0
5 +3	4 +2	9 +7	0 +6	7 +8	0 +0	5 +9	3 +3	8 +1	2 +7

Write these nouns on your paper. Capitalize the proper nouns.

1. actor 2. brazil 3. lake 4. jupiter 5. nathan   6 road

1_____

2_____

3_____

4_____

5_____

6_____

READING

Your other task for the day is to read a book. At this point you should be able to read for ½ hour to 1 hour each day. Look online for a variety of book lists. You can also check out my site www.plainandnotsoplain.com and see all of the books that we have enjoyed at this grade level.

Write the title of the book you are reading and how long you have read for.

_____

_____

```
H  M  G  M  P  I  M  T  B  I  Y  S  P  K  T
Q  B  E  V  E  R  A  G  E  J  R  W  G  P  S
R  E  C  Y  C  L  E  W  D  Y  A  R  C  Z  X
N  D  S  W  V  H  P  F  T  Y  D  H  Z  R  S
Z  C  L  R  B  E  X  M  I  N  E  B  D  O  T
G  N  I  E  B  L  E  E  M  Y  C  O  C  E  E
D  G  T  C  M  A  E  D  E  N  J  T  X  T  R
E  L  N  T  L  M  Z  I  F  O  B  E  R  E  C
C  E  A  A  F  E  Q  C  T  T  L  O  L  M  E
O  M  G  N  A  F  S  I  D  E  H  J  J  L  S
Y  O  E  G  B  G  E  N  L  L  A  A  V  A  Y
G  N  L  L  O  N  W  E  C  E  E  Q  B  Y  V
S  W  E  E  G  L  J  F  X  K  P  V  I  B  U
H  J  G  B  V  R  S  D  D  S  A  W  P  S  Q
G  I  J  D  O  Z  W  Y  D  G  T  X  R  W  Z
```

BEDTIME	BEING	BEVERAGE
CEDAR	DECOY	ELEGANT
FEMALE	JELLY	LEMON
MEDICINE	METEOR	RECTANGLE
RECYCLE	SECRET	SKELETON

A year is typically 365 days long. A leap year is 366. The extra day in a leap year is added to February.

month	order	days
January	first	31
February	second	28 or 29
march	third	31
April	fourth	30
May	fifth	31
June	sixth	30
July	seventh	31
August	eighth	31
September	ninth	30
October	tenth	31
November	eleventh	30
December	twelfth	31

When writing dates, we can use numbers to represent month, day, year. If Brooklyn was born on the sixth day of the twelfth month in the year 2006, then we could write her birthday:

12/06/2006

Jenny wrote her birth date as 7/8/94. What month was she born in?_____ In what year was she born?_____

Mrs. Maryon's driver's license was set to expire on 5/29/06. Write the date out with words and digits. For example: January 5, 2005

_____

In month/day/year form, write the date that Independence Day will next be celebrated?_____

Write your birth day in Month/day/year form:_____

4 +4	7 +5	0 +1	8 +7	3 +4	3 +2	8 +3	2 +1	5 +6	2 +9
0 +9	8 +9	7 +6	1 +3	6 +8	7 +3	1 +6	4 +7	0 +3	6 +4
9 +3	2 +6	3 +0	6 +1	3 +6	4 +0	5 +7	1 +1	5 +4	2 +8
4 +3	0 +9	0 +7	9 +4	7 +7	8 +6	0 +4	5 +8	7 +4	1 +7
9 +5	1 +5	9 +0	3 +8	1 +9	9 +1	8 +8	2 +2	4 +5	6 +2
7 +9	1 +2	6 +7	0 +8	9 +2	4 +8	8 +0	3 +9	1 +0	6 +3
2 +0	8 +4	3 +5	9 +8	5 +0	5 +5	3 +1	7 +2	8 +5	2 +5
5 +2	0 +5	6 +9	1 +8	9 +6	7 +1	4 +6	0 +2	6 +5	4 +9
1 +4	3 +7	7 +0	2 +3	5 +1	6 +6	4 +1	8 +2	2 +4	6 +0
5 +3	4 +2	9 +7	0 +6	7 +8	0 +0	5 +9	3 +3	8 +1	2 +7

An abbreviation is a short form of a word. Capitalize the abbreviation if the whole word is a proper noun.

New York NY   Doctor Clark   Dr. Clark

Most of the words in an address are proper nouns. Write these addresses on your paper. Capitalize all of the proper nouns. Use abbreviations when you can. Use the US Postal abbreviations for states

mr.joe keller
route 2, box 206
marshall, iowa 50152

_____

_____

_____

mrs.brooklyn Maryon
3276 brevard rd
brevard, Michigan 33866

_____

_____

_____

READING

Your other task for the day is to read a book. At this point you should be able to read for ½ hour to 1 hour each day. Look online for a variety of book lists. You can also check out my site www.plainandnotsoplain.com and see all of the books that we have enjoyed at this grade level.

Write the title of the book you are reading and how long you have read for.

_____

_____

Write a sentence for each of your words

Remember when we add, we combine two groups into one group.

4 +3=7

When we subtract, we separate one group into two groups. To take away two from six, we subtract.

6-2=4

When we subtract one number from another number, the answer is the difference. If we subtract two from six, the difference is four.

10-8=_____   7-5=_____   4-3=_____   8-8=_____

How many days are in the tenth month of the year?___

What digit is in the tenths place in 432?_____

Find the missing addend: 2 +m+3=14

Fill in the missing numbers

| 16 | 18 | 20 | | | | | | | |

| 25 | 30 | 35 | | | | | | | |

| 56 | 66 | 76 | | | | | | | |

| 68 | 70 | 72 | | | | | | | |

| 21 | 18 | 15 | | | | | | | |

| 1 | 3 | 5 | | | | | | | |

4 +4	7 +5	0 +1	8 +7	3 +4	3 +2	8 +3	2 +1	5 +6	2 +9
0 +9	8 +9	7 +6	1 +3	6 +8	7 +3	1 +6	4 +7	0 +3	6 +4
9 +3	2 +6	3 +0	6 +1	3 +6	4 +0	5 +7	1 +1	5 +4	2 +8
4 +3	0 +9	0 +7	9 +4	7 +7	8 +6	0 +4	5 +8	7 +4	1 +7
9 +5	1 +5	9 +0	3 +8	1 +9	9 +1	8 +8	2 +2	4 +5	6 +2
7 +9	1 +2	6 +7	0 +8	9 +2	4 +8	8 +0	3 +9	1 +0	6 +3
2 +0	8 +4	3 +5	9 +8	5 +0	5 +5	3 +1	7 +2	8 +5	2 +5
5 +2	0 +5	6 +9	1 +8	9 +6	7 +1	4 +6	0 +2	6 +5	4 +9
1 +4	3 +7	7 +0	2 +3	5 +1	6 +6	4 +1	8 +2	2 +4	6 +0
5 +3	4 +2	9 +7	0 +6	7 +8	0 +0	5 +9	3 +3	8 +1	2 +7

Names of part of the country are proper nouns. However, directions are common nouns.
I visited the West last summer.
Susan will drive west next week.

Write these sentences and capitalize the proper nouns.

1. When susan, graduated from high school, she took a trip to the south.

_____

_____

2 he started in kentucky and spent the first night in north carolina.

_____

_____

3. the next day alex headed southeast towards florida.

_____

_____

READING

Your other task for the day is to read a book. At this point you should be able to read for ½ hour to 1 hour each day. Look online for a variety of book lists. You can also check out my site www.plainandnotsoplain.com and see all of the books that we have enjoyed at this grade level.

Write the title of the book you are reading and how long you have read for.

_____

_____

QUIZ

To write the names of whole numbers through 999 (nine hundred ninety-nine) we need to know the following words and how to put them together:

0	zero	10	ten	20	twenty
1	one	11	eleven	30	thirty
2	two	12	twelve	40	forty
3	three	13	thirteen	50	fifty
4	four	14	fourteen	60	sixty
5	five	15	fifteen	70	seventy
6	six	16	sixteen	80	eighty
7	seven	17	seventeen	90	ninety
8	eight	18	eighteen	100	one hundred
9	nine	19	nineteen		

*The names of two-digit numbers that are greater than 20 and do not end with a number 0, are written with a hypen.

For example: Use words to write number 44.

Forty-four

To write a three digit number, do not use the word "and"

313= three hundred thirteen 705= seven hundred five

Use words to write each number:

0_____   81_____

99_____   909_____

444_____   515_____

Use digits to write five hundred twenty-four_____

4 +4	7 +5	0 +1	8 +7	3 +4	3 +2	8 +3	2 +1	5 +6	2 +9
0 +9	8 +9	7 +6	1 +3	6 +8	7 +3	1 +6	4 +7	0 +3	6 +4
9 +3	2 +6	3 +0	6 +1	3 +6	4 +0	5 +7	1 +1	5 +4	2 +8
4 +3	0 +9	0 +7	9 +4	7 +7	8 +6	0 +4	5 +8	7 +4	1 +7
9 +5	1 +5	9 +0	3 +8	1 +9	9 +1	8 +8	2 +2	4 +5	6 +2
7 +9	1 +2	6 +7	0 +8	9 +2	4 +8	8 +0	3 +9	1 +0	6 +3
2 +0	8 +4	3 +5	9 +8	5 +0	5 +5	3 +1	7 +2	8 +5	2 +5
5 +2	0 +5	6 +9	1 +8	9 +6	7 +1	4 +6	0 +2	6 +5	4 +9
1 +4	3 +7	7 +0	2 +3	5 +1	6 +6	4 +1	8 +2	2 +4	6 +0
5 +3	4 +2	9 +7	0 +6	7 +8	0 +0	5 +9	3 +3	8 +1	2 +7

The name of a language and a particular school course are proper nouns.
The name of a school subject is a common noun.
Proper nouns==German, Introduction to Algebra
common nouns==language, art, mathematics

Circle the correct way the words should be in each sentence.

1. Karl got an A in (English, english).

2. Next year, Alex is taking (math and history, Math and History.)

3. Jennifer signed up for (Math I, math I.)

4. I hope to visit the (south, South.)

5. Do you enjoy your (art, Art) class?

READING

Your other task for the day is to read a book. At this point you should be able to read for ½ hour to 1 hour each day. Look online for a variety of book lists. You can also check out my site www.plainandnotsoplain.com and see all of the books that we have enjoyed at this grade level.

Write the title of the book you are reading and how long you have read for.

_____

_____

week 3 spelling words—copy them

blindfold

cinnamon

dentist

giant

history

imagine

island

minus

pirate

principal

rifle

silence

skid

spinach

whine

Two digit addition: Add $32 + $7= (line up the numbers in vertical form first and then do the right side)

```
  $ 32
+ $  7
  $39
```

Your turn:
Add—rewrite them vertically

$53 +$6= $32+$42=

$27+$51= $32+$7=

Use digits to write each number:
Three hundred forty-three_____
Three hundred seven_____

Use words to write the number 592_____

Sam has $23 and Becky has $42. Together, they have how much money?

Kim was born on the fifth day of August in 1999. Write her birthday in month/day/year form.

Add 5+8+3+2+4+1=

7 -0	10 - 8	6 -3	14 - 5	3 - 1	16 - 9	7 - 1	18 - 9	11 - 3	13 - 7
13 - 8	7 - 4	10 - 7	0 -0	12 - 8	10 - 9	6 - 2	13 - 4	4 -0	10 - 5
5 -3	7 - 5	2 - 1	6 -6	8 - 4	7 -2	14 -7	8 - 1	11 - 6	3 - 3
1 - 1	11 - 9	10 - 4	9 -2	14 - 6	17 - 8	6 - 0	10 - 6	4 - 1	9 -5
7 -7	14 - 8	12 - 9	9 - 8	12 - 7	12 - 3	16 - 8	9 - 1	15 - 6	11 - 4
8 - 6	15 - 9	11 - 8	3 - 2	4 - 4	8 - 2	11 - 5	5 -0	17 - 9	6 - 1
5 -5	4 -3	8 -7	7 -3	7 -6	5 - 1	10 - 3	12 - 6	10 - 1	6 - 4
2 -2	13 - 6	15 - 8	2 -0	13 - 9	16 - 7	5 -2	12 - 4	3 -0	11 - 7
8 -0	9 -4	10 - 2	6 -5	8 -3	9 -0	5 -4	12 - 5	4 -2	9 - 3
9 -9	15 - 7	8 -8	14 - 9	9 -7	13 - 5	1 - 0	8 - 5	9 - 6	11 - 2

A noun can be a title. Books, songs, movies, and people are some of the things that can have titles. A title is a proper noun. Capitalize the first word and all main words in a title.

President John Adams   *Star Wars*   *A Tale of Two Cities*

Italicize or underline the title of a book, movie, magazine, opera, or play. Put quotation marks around the title of a song, poem, or short story.

Write these titles on your paper; capitalize the first word and all the main words.

the sound of music

_____

the world almanac

_____

dr. martin luther king, jr.

_____

READING

Your other task for the day is to read a book. At this point you should be able to read for ½ hour to 1 hour each day. Look online for a variety of book lists. You can also check out my site www.plainandnotsoplain.com and see all of the books that we have enjoyed at this grade level.

Write the title of the book you are reading and how long you have read for.

_____

_____

```
C   R   W   Q   X   T   R   E   X   M   Z   J   B   S   G
K   B   A   H   P   G   A   A   Y   O   H   S   P   G   I
D   P   O   B   G   A   Z   N   D   O   W   C   I   H   T
L   R   Y   H   S   X   M   J   O   Y   Y   A   V   A   R
O   I   R   K   G   H   Z   E   W   M   N   T   U   P   D
F   N   O   J   U   A   N   Z   L   T   A   B   M   A   H
D   C   T   O   R   I   F   L   E   P   E   N   I   M   W
N   I   S   Q   H   H   J   A   Q   Y   U   V   N   S   E
I   P   I   W   E   E   C   N   E   L   I   S   U   I   G
L   A   H   M   T   I   U   A   F   S   K   O   S   T   C
B   L   U   X   A   F   S   H   N   K   G   K   D   U   D
B   G   Z   Q   R   G   L   L   J   I   J   Z   R   K   B
O   G   E   I   I   P   I   U   A   D   P   X   I   U   I
M   N   Y   A   P   M   S   N   T   N   Y   S   V   Z   R
G   D   E   N   T   I   S   T   E   G   D   G   Y   O   B
```

BLINDFOLD	CINNAMON	DENTIST
GIANT	HISTORY	IMAGINE
ISLAND	MINUS	PIRATE
PRINCIPAL	RIFLE	SILENCE
SKID	SPINACH	WHINE

37

Regrouping addition. Add 39 +14=

     |
    39
   +14
    53

Do the ones column first and add 9 +4=13. You have to "regroup" and put the 1 on top
of the tens place and the three in the ones place. Then add the tens column to get 5

Rewrite in column form and add the following:

68 +24   46+26

42 +18   56+78

Use words to write 941

Use digits to write six hundred thirteen

What is the name for the answer when we add?

What is the name for the answer when we subtract?

Which month is two months after the twelfth month?

What digit is in the hundreds place in 832?

100 Subtraction facts

7 -0	10 -8	6 -3	14 -5	3 -1	16 -9	7 -1	18 -9	11 -3	13 -7
13 -8	7 -4	10 -7	0 -0	12 -8	10 -9	6 -2	13 -4	4 -0	10 -5
5 -3	7 -5	2 -1	6 -6	8 -4	7 -2	14 -7	8 -1	11 -6	3 -3
1 -1	11 -9	10 -4	9 -2	14 -6	17 -8	6 -0	10 -6	4 -1	9 -5
7 -7	14 -8	12 -9	9 -8	12 -7	12 -3	16 -8	9 -1	15 -6	11 -4
8 -6	15 -9	11 -8	3 -2	4 -4	8 -2	11 -5	5 -0	17 -9	6 -1
5 -5	4 -3	8 -7	7 -3	7 -6	5 -1	10 -3	12 -6	10 -1	6 -4
2 -2	13 -6	15 -8	2 -0	13 -9	16 -7	5 -2	12 -4	3 -0	11 -7
8 -0	9 -4	10 -2	6 -5	8 -3	9 -0	5 -4	12 -5	4 -2	9 -3
9 -9	15 -7	8 -8	14 -9	9 -7	13 -5	1 -0	8 -5	9 -6	11 -2

Copy these sentences and capitalize the proper nouns.

1. On wednesday, susan came home from florida.

_____

_____

2. "He wants you to report to the office on millstream drive tomorrow."

_____

_____

3. "Hello alex," jennifer said. "Welcome home from the south."

_____

_____

READING

Your other task for the day is to read a book. At this point you should be able to read for ½ hour to 1 hour each day. Look online for a variety of book lists. You can also check out my site www.plainandnotsoplain.com and see all of the books that we have enjoyed at this grade level.

Write the title of the book you are reading and how long you have read for.

_____

_____

Write a sentence for each of your words

The numbers we say when we count by 2 are even. Every other number ends with either 2,4,6,8, or 0.

2,4,6,8,10,12,14,16,18,20,22,24,26

Which of these numbers is an even number?

463   212   677

If a whole number is not an even number then it is an odd number. Odd numbers are all the rest numbers.

1,3,5,7,9,11,13,15,17,19,21

What number is odd:

323   678   870

Use the digits 2,7,and 6 to write two three-digit odd numbers.

The same number of boys and girls were in the classroom. Which of these numbers could be the total number of students in the classroom?

25   26   27

Circle the even numbers

43   76   88   90   77   11

Use digits to write five hundred forty-two

Use words to write 903

4 +4	7 +5	0 +1	8 +7	3 +4	3 +2	8 +3	2 +1	5 +6	2 +9
0 +9	8 +9	7 +6	1 +3	6 +8	7 +3	1 +6	4 +7	0 +3	6 +4
9 +3	2 +6	3 +0	6 +1	3 +6	4 +0	5 +7	1 +1	5 +4	2 +8
4 +3	0 +9	0 +7	9 +4	7 +7	8 +6	0 +4	5 +8	7 +4	1 +7
9 +5	1 +5	9 +0	3 +8	1 +9	9 +1	8 +8	2 +2	4 +5	6 +2
7 +9	1 +2	6 +7	0 +8	9 +2	4 +8	8 +0	3 +9	1 +0	6 +3
2 +0	8 +4	3 +5	9 +8	5 +0	5 +5	3 +1	7 +2	8 +5	2 +5
5 +2	0 +5	6 +9	1 +8	9 +6	7 +1	4 +6	0 +2	6 +5	4 +9
1 +4	3 +7	7 +0	2 +3	5 +1	6 +6	4 +1	8 +2	2 +4	6 +0
5 +3	4 +2	9 +7	0 +6	7 +8	0 +0	5 +9	3 +3	8 +1	2 +7

REVIEW

Copy the sentences correctly

1. Kim took math 101, not math 201, this year.

_____

_____

2. I'm going to take world history next year.

_____

_____

3. lisa and greg visited tuxedo park.

_____

_____

4. hannah's grandmother lives in michigan.

_____

_____

READING

Your other task for the day is to read a book. At this point you should be able to read for ½ hour to 1 hour each day. Look online for a variety of book lists. You can also check out my site www.plainandnotsoplain.com and see all of the books that we have enjoyed at this grade level.

Write the title of the book you are reading and how long you have read for.

_____

_____

QUIZ

Problem solving with words.

Sam had 8 balls. Then Tim gave him some more. Same now has 17 balls. How many balls did Tim give him? To solve this you will need to subtract what he had from what he has.

8 + _____ =17

The opposite of addition is subtraction --answer is 9

Your turn:

Jim had some pies. Then Frank gave his 5 more pies. Now he has 12 pies. How many pies did Jim have in the beginning?

Kim saw 4 horses at the fair. Then she saw 14 horses on the farm. How many did she see in all?

Tabitha read 6 pages before lunch. After lunch she read some more. If Tabitha read 13 pages in all, how many pages did she read after lunch?

Use digits to write the number six hundred forty-two

The books were put into two stacks so that an equal number of books were in each stack. Was the total number of books in each stack an odd or even number?

12	9	6			XXX	XXXX	XXX	XXX	XXX

93 +39=   29+47=   28+47=

4 +4	7 +5	0 +1	8 +7	3 +4	3 +2	8 +3	2 +1	5 +6	2 +9
0 +9	8 +9	7 +6	1 +3	6 +8	7 +3	1 +6	4 +7	0 +3	6 +4
9 +3	2 +6	3 +0	6 +1	3 +6	4 +0	5 +7	1 +1	5 +4	2 +8
4 +3	0 +9	0 +7	9 +4	7 +7	8 +6	0 +4	5 +8	7 +4	1 +7
9 +5	1 +5	9 +0	3 +8	1 +9	9 +1	8 +8	2 +2	4 +5	6 +2
7 +9	1 +2	6 +7	0 +8	9 +2	4 +8	8 +0	3 +9	1 +0	6 +3
2 +0	8 +4	3 +5	9 +8	5 +0	5 +5	3 +1	7 +2	8 +5	2 +5
5 +2	0 +5	6 +9	1 +8	9 +6	7 +1	4 +6	0 +2	6 +5	4 +9
1 +4	3 +7	7 +0	2 +3	5 +1	6 +6	4 +1	8 +2	2 +4	6 +0
5 +3	4 +2	9 +7	0 +6	7 +8	0 +0	5 +9	3 +3	8 +1	2 +7

Concrete noun is a word that names something you can see or touch. For example: money, clock, college, painting.

Abstract nouns is a word that names something you can think or talk about. You cannot see it or touch it. For example: expense, time, education, art.

Read each pair of nouns; circle the abstract noun in each pair.

1. teacher   learning
2. bravery   soldier
3. steel   strength
4. value   dollar
5. doctor   health
6. flag   freedom

READING

Your other task for the day is to read a book. At this point you should be able to read for ½ hour to 1 hour each day. Look online for a variety of book lists. You can also check out my site www.plainandnotsoplain.com and see all of the books that we have enjoyed at this grade level.

Write the title of the book you are reading and how long you have read for.

_____

_____

week 4 copy your spelling words

auto

bobbin

bony

closet

cobra

doctor

elbow

frozen

hotel

knot

object

poetry

solemn

solve

total

Find the missing number: b-5=7. We know that addition is the opposite of subtraction, so if we add 5 +7, we will get our answer of 12.

Your turn:

14-n=6   n-5= 2   9-n=2

7 +2+ n=   11   4+a+2=15

At first, thirty-five butterflies were flying about. Later, twenty-seven more butterflies began to fly about. In all, how many butterflies were flying about?

67+27=   65+21=   88+13=

How many cents are in nine nickels? Count by 5s

Write the largest three-digit number that has a 6 in the ones place and a 4 in the tens place.

4 +4	7 +5	0 +1	8 +7	3 +4	3 +2	8 +3	2 +1	5 +6	2 +9
0 +9	8 +9	7 +6	1 +3	6 +8	7 +3	1 +6	4 +7	0 +3	6 +4
9 +3	2 +6	3 +0	6 +1	3 +6	4 +0	5 +7	1 +1	5 +4	2 +8
4 +3	0 +9	0 +7	9 +4	7 +7	8 +6	0 +4	5 +8	7 +4	1 +7
9 +5	1 +5	9 +0	3 +8	1 +9	9 +1	8 +8	2 +2	4 +5	6 +2
7 +9	1 +2	6 +7	0 +8	9 +2	4 +8	8 +0	3 +9	1 +0	6 +3
2 +0	8 +4	3 +5	9 +8	5 +0	5 +5	3 +1	7 +2	8 +5	2 +5
5 +2	0 +5	6 +9	1 +8	9 +6	7 +1	4 +6	0 +2	6 +5	4 +9
1 +4	3 +7	7 +0	2 +3	5 +1	6 +6	4 +1	8 +2	2 +4	6 +0
5 +3	4 +2	9 +7	0 +6	7 +8	0 +0	5 +9	3 +3	8 +1	2 +7

A singular noun is the name of one person, place, thing, or idea.
A plural noun is the name of more than one person, place, thing, or idea.

Most plural nouns end in –s, -es.
singular—leash, peach
plural-leashes, peaches

Write the plural of each singular noun. Add –s or –es

address   _____

car   _____

school   _____

tax   _____

mountain _____

READING

Your other task for the day is to read a book. At this point you should be able to read for ½ hour to 1 hour each day. Look online for a variety of book lists. You can also check out my site www.plainandnotsoplain.com and see all of the books that we have enjoyed at this grade level.

Write the title of the book you are reading and how long you have read for.

_____

_____

```
P  J  U  R  E  N  U  P  J  O  K  L  U  W  H
E  I  D  W  K  V  Z  D  M  T  A  G  E  E  F
C  E  D  O  F  Y  B  S  Y  T  D  P  V  N  V
X  W  C  Z  C  J  O  N  O  C  O  H  C  N  B
U  W  O  K  E  T  O  T  M  E  G  T  M  P  R
L  C  I  B  U  B  O  Z  T  J  U  E  V  G  W
K  G  J  A  L  K  D  R  V  B  L  S  T  A  E
J  B  C  C  E  E  Y  H  N  O  B  O  O  F  N
J  C  L  C  Z  P  I  V  S  Q  N  L  M  U  H
I  X  R  W  F  J  D  D  S  K  C  C  M  L  E
N  E  Z  O  R  F  T  C  O  B  R  A  D  T  J
S  X  B  D  H  O  T  E  L  X  A  T  U  F  N
A  C  E  W  I  Y  S  S  V  N  I  B  B  O  B
L  I  Z  R  R  I  V  K  E  Z  F  R  P  S  M
Y  Y  G  K  U  A  Q  B  W  O  F  L  C  M  K
```

AUTO	BOBBIN	BONY
CLOSET	COBRA	DOCTOR
ELBOW	FROZEN	HOTEL
KNOT	OBJECT	POETRY
SOLEMN	SOLVE	TOTAL

53

Adding three digit numbers and regrouping.

```
  | \
 '456
+374
 830
```

Do the ones column first, then regroup, then do the tens column, then regroup. Finally do the hundreds column and write down the answer.

Your turn:

```
  408          $498          125
+243         + $194        +675
```

Five of the twelve children at the party were girls. How many boys were at the party?

Use words to write the number 913

Use digits to write the number seven hundred forty-three

Add $475 + $232=   743+367=

4 +4	7 +5	0 +1	8 +7	3 +4	3 +2	8 +3	2 +1	5 +6	2 +9
0 +9	8 +9	7 +6	1 +3	6 +8	7 +3	1 +6	4 +7	0 +3	6 +4
9 +3	2 +6	3 +0	6 +1	3 +6	4 +0	5 +7	1 +1	5 +4	2 +8
4 +3	0 +9	0 +7	9 +4	7 +7	8 +6	0 +4	5 +8	7 +4	1 +7
9 +5	1 +5	9 +0	3 +8	1 +9	9 +1	8 +8	2 +2	4 +5	6 +2
7 +9	1 +2	6 +7	0 +8	9 +2	4 +8	8 +0	3 +9	1 +0	6 +3
2 +0	8 +4	3 +5	9 +8	5 +0	5 +5	3 +1	7 +2	8 +5	2 +5
5 +2	0 +5	6 +9	1 +8	9 +6	7 +1	4 +6	0 +2	6 +5	4 +9
1 +4	3 +7	7 +0	2 +3	5 +1	6 +6	4 +1	8 +2	2 +4	6 +0
5 +3	4 +2	9 +7	0 +6	7 +8	0 +0	5 +9	3 +3	8 +1	2 +7

Write whether each word is singular or plural

bosses_____-

nations_____

doctor_____

Alex_____-

cousin_____

crowds_____

READING

Your other task for the day is to read a book. At this point you should be able to read for ½ hour to 1 hour each day. Look online for a variety of book lists. You can also check out my site www.plainandnotsoplain.com and see all of the books that we have enjoyed at this grade level.

Write the title of the book you are reading and how long you have read for.

_____

_____

Write a sentence for each of your words

Subtraction

$$432$$
$$\underline{-121}$$
$$3\ 11$$

Start in the ones column and subtract and move to the tens and then the hundreds.

Your turn: write vertically

$485-$242=$ $56-$33

24 +q=65   *remember addition is opposite of subtraction

Y+45=99

Use the digits 1,2,3 once each and write an even number less than 200.

What is the total number of days in the first two months of a common year?

346+298=   421+389=   506+210=

4 +4	7 +5	0 +1	8 +7	3 +4	3 +2	8 +3	2 +1	5 +6	2 +9
0 +9	8 +9	7 +6	1 +3	6 +8	7 +3	1 +6	4 +7	0 +3	6 +4
9 +3	2 +6	3 +0	6 +1	3 +6	4 +0	5 +7	1 +1	5 +4	2 +8
4 +3	0 +9	0 +7	9 +4	7 +7	8 +6	0 +4	5 +8	7 +4	1 +7
9 +5	1 +5	9 +0	3 +8	1 +9	9 +1	8 +8	2 +2	4 +5	6 +2
7 +9	1 +2	6 +7	0 +8	9 +2	4 +8	8 +0	3 +9	1 +0	6 +3
2 +0	8 +4	3 +5	9 +8	5 +0	5 +5	3 +1	7 +2	8 +5	2 +5
5 +2	0 +5	6 +9	1 +8	9 +6	7 +1	4 +6	0 +2	6 +5	4 +9
1 +4	3 +7	7 +0	2 +3	5 +1	6 +6	4 +1	8 +2	2 +4	6 +0
5 +3	4 +2	9 +7	0 +6	7 +8	0 +0	5 +9	3 +3	8 +1	2 +7

Nouns that end in –y and have a consonant before the y become plural by changing the y to an "I" and adding –es.

Nouns that end in –y and have a vowel before the y become plural by simply adding –s.

country   countries   turkey   turkeys

Write the plural of the singular nouns

monkey_____

country_____

body_____

army_____

bay_____

day_____

READING

Your other task for the day is to read a book. At this point you should be able to read for ½ hour to 1 hour each day. Look online for a variety of book lists. You can also check out my site www.plainandnotsoplain.com and see all of the books that we have enjoyed at this grade level.

Write the title of the book you are reading and how long you have read for.

_____

_____

QUIZ

Subtraction with regrouping

Find the difference of 56-29

$$
\begin{array}{r}
\overset{4}{\cancel{5}}6 \\
-\ 29 \\
\hline
27
\end{array}
$$

We need to start in the ones column and understand that we can't take 9 from 6. So we have to borrow from the neighbor (5). We borrow 1 which is really 10—because going from one place value to another is by tens. Then we add it to our number and subtract. Then move to the next column and subtract.

Your turn: rewrite vertically and solve

$53-$29= $42-$24= $60-$27=

40-13=   63-36=   24-18=

Use the digits 3,6,7 once and write an even number less than 400.

The smallest two-digit odd number is 11. What is the smallest two-digit even number?

Subtract 245 from 375.

4 +4	7 +5	0 +1	8 +7	3 +4	3 +2	8 +3	2 +1	5 +6	2 +9
0 +9	8 +9	7 +6	1 +3	6 +8	7 +3	1 +6	4 +7	0 +3	6 +4
9 +3	2 +6	3 +0	6 +1	3 +6	4 +0	5 +7	1 +1	5 +4	2 +8
4 +3	0 +9	0 +7	9 +4	7 +7	8 +6	0 +4	5 +8	7 +4	1 +7
9 +5	1 +5	9 +0	3 +8	1 +9	9 +1	8 +8	2 +2	4 +5	6 +2
7 +9	1 +2	6 +7	0 +8	9 +2	4 +8	8 +0	3 +9	1 +0	6 +3
2 +0	8 +4	3 +5	9 +8	5 +0	5 +5	3 +1	7 +2	8 +5	2 +5
5 +2	0 +5	6 +9	1 +8	9 +6	7 +1	4 +6	0 +2	6 +5	4 +9
1 +4	3 +7	7 +0	2 +3	5 +1	6 +6	4 +1	8 +2	2 +4	6 +0
5 +3	4 +2	9 +7	0 +6	7 +8	0 +0	5 +9	3 +3	8 +1	2 +7

We make the plural of most nouns that end in –f or –fe by adding –s
roof- roofs   chief-chiefs

Some nouns that end in –f or –fe change the f to a v and add –s or –es
leaf-leaves   calf-calves   wolf-wolves

To form the plural of some nouns ending with a consonant and –o, we add –es. We add only –s to others.
hero-heroes   tomato-tomatoes   photo-photos

To form the plural of nouns ending with a vowel and –o, we add –s.
radio-radios   rodeo-rodeos

A few nouns become plural by changing letters within the word.
man-men   mouse-mice   tooth-teeth   foot-feet

Sometimes the singular and plural nouns are the same.
one deer-or a herd of deer
one trout-a school of trout

Find the spelling mistakes and rewrite them.

1. Two deers surprised the mans in the woods.

_____

_____

2. They ate two loafs of bread and 10 potatos.

_____

_____

READING

Your other task for the day is to read a book. At this point you should be able to read for ½ hour to 1 hour each day. Look online for a variety of book lists. You can also check out my site www.plainandnotsoplain.com and see all of the books that we have enjoyed at this grade level.

Write the title of the book you are reading and how long you have read for.

_____

_____

week 5 copy your spelling words

amuse

bubble

budding

budge

computer

customer

duty

humor

hungry

husky

Jupiter

number

sundown

summer

total

Expanded form

The number 365 means "3 hundreds and 6 tens and 5 ones" We can write this as   300+60+5   This is called expanded form.

Write 274 in expanded form: 200+70+4

Your turn:

Write 407 in expanded form ** there are no tens so don't write that

Write 86 in expanded form

Write 325 in expanded form

Write 507 in expanded form

Solve:

36-p=21   47-b=24   m-22=16

$576 +$128=   186+285=

4 +4	7 +5	0 +1	8 +7	3 +4	3 +2	8 +3	2 +1	5 +6	2 +9
0 +9	8 +9	7 +6	1 +3	6 +8	7 +3	1 +6	4 +7	0 +3	6 +4
9 +3	2 +6	3 +0	6 +1	3 +6	4 +0	5 +7	1 +1	5 +4	2 +8
4 +3	0 +9	0 +7	9 +4	7 +7	8 +6	0 +4	5 +8	7 +4	1 +7
9 +5	1 +5	9 +0	3 +8	1 +9	9 +1	8 +8	2 +2	4 +5	6 +2
7 +9	1 +2	6 +7	0 +8	9 +2	4 +8	8 +0	3 +9	1 +0	6 +3
2 +0	8 +4	3 +5	9 +8	5 +0	5 +5	3 +1	7 +2	8 +5	2 +5
5 +2	0 +5	6 +9	1 +8	9 +6	7 +1	4 +6	0 +2	6 +5	4 +9
1 +4	3 +7	7 +0	2 +3	5 +1	6 +6	4 +1	8 +2	2 +4	6 +0
5 +3	4 +2	9 +7	0 +6	7 +8	0 +0	5 +9	3 +3	8 +1	2 +7

Review

Write the plural of each noun

radio_____

tomato_____

key_____

spy_____

dish_____

deer_____

tooth_____

READING

Your other task for the day is to read a book. At this point you should be able to read for ½ hour to 1 hour each day. Look online for a variety of book lists. You can also check out my site www.plainandnotsoplain.com and see all of the books that we have enjoyed at this grade level.

Write the title of the book you are reading and how long you have read for.

_____

_____

```
N  S  S  O  S  H  S  H  G  E  S  U  M  A  B
D  V  T  L  O  H  U  D  N  R  O  M  U  H  I
H  B  E  W  T  R  A  S  Q  I  C  G  G  U  Y
H  U  N  G  R  Y  U  J  K  U  T  N  R  U  N
H  B  L  C  W  B  L  X  S  Y  W  W  E  S  K
M  B  T  F  O  Q  T  T  K  O  U  T  T  U  D
D  L  A  J  L  M  O  T  D  E  U  N  I  A  T
D  E  U  B  L  M  P  N  N  Q  P  H  P  L  D
G  C  L  G  E  V  U  X  I  K  T  U  Y  D
I  N  V  R  S  M  W  T  A  P  H  J  L  F
F  C  I  R  B  B  B  G  E  E  Y  B  S  D  G
Z  K  B  D  E  S  U  M  M  E  R  T  R  X  P
S  R  U  R  D  E  T  C  G  H  Q  H  U  W  Z
B  U  D  G  E  U  B  W  B  H  T  Z  L  D  R
U  M  H  W  X  O  B  F  W  I  E  R  F  K  E
```

AMUSE	BUBBLE	BUDDING
BUDGE	COMPUTER	CUSTOMER
DUTY	HUMOR	HUNGRY
HUSKY	JUPITER	NUMBER
SUNDOWN	SUMMER	USUAL

Regrouping with more than two numbers

Add 227 + 88+6 Just line them up vertically and add. Regroup if necessary

```
 12
227
 88
+ 6
321
```

Line up the following vertically and add:

47+29+46+95=   534+76+9=

213+42+3=   103+398+12+9=

Four hundred seven tulips were in front. Three hundred sixty-two tulips were in back. How many tulips were there in all?

Write 813 in expanded form.

7 -0	10 - 8	6 -3	14 - 5	3 - 1	16 - 9	7 - 1	18 - 9	11 - 3	13 - 7
13 - 8	7 - 4	10 - 7	0 -0	12 - 8	10 - 9	6 - 2	13 - 4	4 -0	10 - 5
5 -3	7 - 5	2 - 1	6 -6	8 - 4	7 -2	14 -7	8 -1	11 - 6	3 - 3
1 - 1	11 -9	10 -4	9 -2	14 - 6	17 - 8	6 -0	10 -6	4 -1	9 -5
7 -7	14 - 8	12 -9	9 -8	12 -7	12 - 3	16 -8	9 -1	15 - 6	11 -4
8 - 6	15 -9	11 -8	3 - 2	4 - 4	8 -2	11 -5	5 -0	17 -9	6 -1
5 -5	4 -3	8 -7	7 -3	7 -6	5 -1	10 -3	12 -6	10 -1	6 -4
2 -2	13 -6	15 - 8	2 -0	13 -9	16 -7	5 -2	12 -4	3 -0	11 -7
8 -0	9 -4	10 - 2	6 -5	8 -3	9 -0	5 -4	12 -5	4 -2	9 - 3
9 -9	15 -7	8 -8	14 -9	9 -7	13 -5	1 -0	8 -5	9 -6	11 -2

A possessive noun is one that shows ownership or a relationship. A possessive noun ends in –s and has an apostrophe ('). An apostrophe is a punctuation mark that indicates that a noun is possessive.

Ownership: That jacket belongs to Jennifer. That is Jennifer's jacket.
Relationship: Nicole is the sister of Devon. Nicole is Devon's sister.

Write whether each bold word is plural or possessive.

1. **Alex's** insurance policy came in the mail._____

2. The policy had several **pages.**_____

3. They came to see their **friend's** car._____

4. They went to inspect the **car's** tires._____

5. A few of her **friends** came over to play._____

READING

Your other task for the day is to read a book. At this point you should be able to read for ½ hour to 1 hour each day. Look online for a variety of book lists. You can also check out my site www.plainandnotsoplain.com and see all of the books that we have enjoyed at this grade level.

Write the title of the book you are reading and how long you have read for.

_____

_____

Write a sentence for each of your words

Time

How many hours equal a whole day?

How many minutes equal an hour?

Draw the hands on the clock to say the following times:

4:10   1:40   3:45

Add $468+$293= $187+$687=

44-27=   62-43=   23-18=

7 -0	10 - 8	6 -3	14 - 5	3 -1	16 - 9	7 -1	18 - 9	11 - 3	13 - 7
13 - 8	7 - 4	10 - 7	0 -0	12 - 8	10 - 9	6 - 2	13 - 4	4 -0	10 - 5
5 -3	7 - 5	2 - 1	6 -6	8 - 4	7 -2	14 - 7	8 - 1	11 - 6	3 - 3
1 - 1	11 - 9	10 - 4	9 -2	14 - 6	17 - 8	6 -0	10 - 6	4 - 1	9 -5
7 -7	14 - 8	12 - 9	9 - 8	12 -7	12 - 3	16 -8	9 - 1	15 - 6	11 -4
8 - 6	15 - 9	11 - 8	3 - 2	4 - 4	8 - 2	11 - 5	5 -0	17 - 9	6 - 1
5 -5	4 -3	8 -7	7 -3	7 -6	5 - 1	10 - 3	12 - 6	10 - 1	6 - 4
2 -2	13 - 6	15 - 8	2 -0	13 - 9	16 - 7	5 -2	12 - 4	3 -0	11 - 7
8 -0	9 -4	10 - 2	6 -5	8 -3	9 -0	5 -4	12 - 5	4 -2	9 - 3
9 -9	15 - 7	8 -8	14 - 9	9 -7	13 - 5	1 - 0	8 - 5	9 - 6	11 - 2

A possessive noun can be singular or plural.
1. Make a singular noun possessive by adding an apostrophe and –s ('s)
Greg   --Greg's laptop
2. Make a plural noun possessive by adding only an apostrophe (').
ladies -ladies' purses
3. When a plural noun does not end in –s, make it possessive by adding an apostrophe and –s ('s).
women-women's shoes

Write the possessive nouns in these sentences on your paper. Next to each one write whether it is singular or plural.
For example: Kim's bicycle has a flat tire.   Kim's -singular

1. The teachers' meeting was canceled.

_____

2. The cat slept on the sofa's cushion.

_____

3. The mice's tracks led under the baseboard.

_____

4. Last week the children's room was painted.

_____

5. Sam had to replace the camera's batteries.

_____

READING

Your other task for the day is to read a book. At this point you should be able to read for ½ hour to 1 hour each day. Look online for a variety of book lists. You can also check out my site www.plainandnotsoplain.com and see all of the books that we have enjoyed at this grade level.

Write the title of the book you are reading and how long you have read for.

_____

_____

QUIZ

The radio costs about $70. The radio costs exactly $68.47

The first sentence uses the rounded number. Rounded numbers usually end with zero. We often round numbers in place of exact numbers because they are easy to understand and work with.

To round an exact number to the nearest ten, we choose the closest number that ends in zero.

Draw a number line to help you understand how to round 67

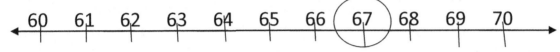

67 is between 60 and 70. Since 67 is closer to 70, we say it is about 70.

*A key is to look at the halfway mark, if your ending number is 5 or more, you go up to the next even number, if it is less you go down.

Round 82 to the nearest ten. Rounding to the nearest ten means rounding to a number you would count by tens (10,20,30,40,50,etc)

Look at the "2" Is it 5 or more? Then you go down to 80 instead of up to 90.

When you round dollars and cents to the nearest dollar, we look at the cents. You look at if it is 50 cents or more, then you round up. If not you round down to the nearest dollar.

$6.49 rounded to nearest dollar is $6

$12.95 rounded to nearest dollar is $13

Your turn:

Round each number to the nearest ten. Draw a number line if you need to.

78   43   61   45

Round each money amount to the nearest dollar:

$14.29 $8.95 $21.45 $29.89

7 -0	10 - 8	6 -3	14 - 5	3 - 1	16 - 9	7 - 1	18 - 9	11 - 3	13 - 7
13 - 8	7 - 4	10 - 7	0 -0	12 - 8	10 - 9	6 - 2	13 - 4	4 -0	10 - 5
5 -3	7 - 5	2 - 1	6 -6	8 - 4	7 -2	14 -7	8 - 1	11 - 6	3 - 3
1 - 1	11 - 9	10 - 4	9 -2	14 - 6	17 - 8	6 - 0	10 - 6	4 - 1	9 -5
7 - 7	14 - 8	12 - 9	9 - 8	12 - 7	12 - 3	16 - 8	9 - 1	15 - 6	11 - 4
8 - 6	15 - 9	11 - 8	3 - 2	4 - 4	8 - 2	11 - 5	5 -0	17 - 9	6 - 1
5 -5	4 -3	8 -7	7 -3	7 -6	5 - 1	10 - 3	12 - 6	10 - 1	6 - 4
2 -2	13 - 6	15 - 8	2 -0	13 - 9	16 - 7	5 -2	12 - 4	3 -0	11 - 7
8 -0	9 -4	10 - 2	6 -5	8 -3	9 -0	5 -4	12 - 5	4 -2	9 - 3
9 -9	15 - 7	8 -8	14 - 9	9 -7	13 - 5	1 - 0	8 - 5	9 - 6	11 - 2

Write the singular possessive form and the plural possessive form for these words on your paper.

Example: book book's   books'

chapter_____

person_____

fox_____

man_____

foot_____

county_____

navy_____

READING

Your other task for the day is to read a book. At this point you should be able to read for ½ hour to 1 hour each day. Look online for a variety of book lists. You can also check out my site www.plainandnotsoplain.com and see all of the books that we have enjoyed at this grade level.

Write the title of the book you are reading and how long you have read for.

_____

_____

week 6 spelling words copy them

already

balcony

country

deny

early

envy

February

greedy

hydrant

hymn

library

reply

satisfy

skyline

syllable

Perimeter. The distance around an object is its perimeter. All you do is add up all the sides.

If the rectangles sides are 4 inch by 2 inch, the perimeter is 12 inch. Add up all the sides to get your answer.

Measure this rectangle in centimeters

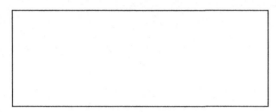

What is the length_____ Width_____ perimeter_____

Tammy put forty jacks in a pile. After Sarah added up all her jacks there were seventy-two jacks in the pile. How many jacks did Sarah put in?

Write seven hundred fifty-three in expanded form

493+278= $524+$109=

45-29=   15+24+36+99=

What comes next:

28	35	42			

7 -0	10 -8	6 -3	14 -5	3 -1	16 -9	7 -1	18 -9	11 -3	13 -7
13 -8	7 -4	10 -7	0 -0	12 -8	10 -9	6 -2	13 -4	4 -0	10 -5
5 -3	7 -5	2 -1	6 -6	8 -4	7 -2	14 -7	8 -1	11 -6	3 -3
1 -1	11 -9	10 -4	9 -2	14 -6	17 -8	6 -0	10 -6	4 -1	9 -5
7 -7	14 -8	12 -9	9 -8	12 -7	12 -3	16 -8	9 -1	15 -6	11 -4
8 -6	15 -9	11 -8	3 -2	4 -4	8 -2	11 -5	5 -0	17 -9	6 -1
5 -5	4 -3	8 -7	7 -3	7 -6	5 -1	10 -3	12 -6	10 -1	6 -4
2 -2	13 -6	15 -8	2 -0	13 -9	16 -7	5 -2	12 -4	3 -0	11 -7
8 -0	9 -4	10 -2	6 -5	8 -3	9 -0	5 -4	12 -5	4 -2	9 -3
9 -9	15 -7	8 -8	14 -9	9 -7	13 -5	1 -0	8 -5	9 -6	11 -2

NOUN REVIEW

Circle the nouns in these sentences. Write whether they are abstract or concrete.

1. The party was over._____

2. It had been a big surprise for their teacher. _____

3. Alex and Jennifer cleaned up their friend's mess._____

4. A group of students gathered in the classroom._____

Write all the proper nouns properly after each sentence.

5. In august, sam and paul will return to school.

_____

6. Her brother, works at mr. wilson's store.

_____

7. This year sam is taking french, math, and science.

_____

Write the plural form of each of these singular nouns

wolf_____quiz_____

READING

Your other task for the day is to read a book. At this point you should be able to read for ½ hour to 1 hour each day. Look online for a variety of book lists. You can also check out my site www.plainandnotsoplain.com and see all of the books that we have enjoyed at this grade level.

Write the title of the book you are reading and how long you have read for.

_____

_____

```
B  V  N  K  T  J  H  J  U  S  T  Q  Y  O  W
E  K  J  F  Z  H  C  C  T  N  A  R  D  Y  H
H  Y  M  N  K  Y  X  E  J  Z  T  C  E  R  K
U  E  Z  E  Y  D  L  L  D  N  F  N  J  A  C
X  J  H  L  E  D  R  R  U  K  I  O  R  R  K
X  B  T  B  X  N  A  O  A  L  R  V  F  B  L
H  B  A  A  V  X  C  E  Y  E  U  Y  U  I  Y
L  D  Z  L  H  X  W  K  R  P  R  E  P  L  Y
N  A  C  L  C  C  S  F  Y  L  N  I  K  J  X
D  P  M  Y  Z  O  R  M  G  V  A  E  D  R  O
E  X  B  S  A  Q  N  C  Y  M  S  X  M  N  A
N  S  L  X  L  K  X  Y  X  C  Y  N  X  W  L
Y  F  S  I  T  A  S  V  Y  D  E  E  R  G  R
A  L  U  S  M  F  E  B  R  U  A  R  Y  U  R
W  Z  G  Y  I  J  E  A  I  B  G  M  B  U  D
```

ALREADY	BALCONY	COUNTRY
DENY	EARLY	ENVY
FEBRUARY	GREEDY	HYDRANT
HYMN	LIBRARY	REPLY
SATISFY	SKYLINE	SYLLABLE

Part of a whole number can be named with a fraction. A fraction is written with two numbers. The bottom number of a fraction is called the denominator. The denominator tells how many equal parts are in the whole   The top number is called the numerator. The numerator tells how many of the parts are being counted.

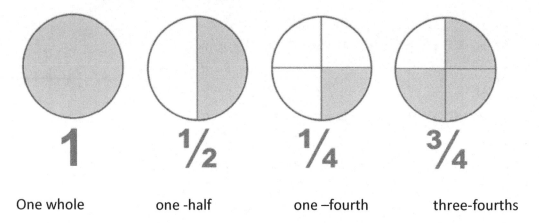

One whole   one -half   one –fourth   three-fourths

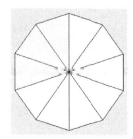   What part of the shape is shaded

What part of the shape is shaded

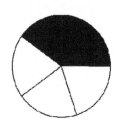

A quarter is what fraction of a dollar ? *think how many quarters make up a dollar and how many one of those quarters would be.

A nickel is what fraction of a dollar

Add $2.75+ $2.75= $3.65+$4.28=

4 +4	7 +5	0 +1	8 +7	3 +4	3 +2	8 +3	2 +1	5 +6	2 +9
0 +9	8 +9	7 +6	1 +3	6 +8	7 +3	1 +6	4 +7	0 +3	6 +4
9 +3	2 +6	3 +0	6 +1	3 +6	4 +0	5 +7	1 +1	5 +4	2 +8
4 +3	0 +9	0 +7	9 +4	7 +7	8 +6	0 +4	5 +8	7 +4	1 +7
9 +5	1 +5	9 +0	3 +8	1 +9	9 +1	8 +8	2 +2	4 +5	6 +2
7 +9	1 +2	6 +7	0 +8	9 +2	4 +8	8 +0	3 +9	1 +0	6 +3
2 +0	8 +4	3 +5	9 +8	5 +0	5 +5	3 +1	7 +2	8 +5	2 +5
5 +2	0 +5	6 +9	1 +8	9 +6	7 +1	4 +6	0 +2	6 +5	4 +9
1 +4	3 +7	7 +0	2 +3	5 +1	6 +6	4 +1	8 +2	2 +4	6 +0
5 +3	4 +2	9 +7	0 +6	7 +8	0 +0	5 +9	3 +3	8 +1	2 +7

Mike went to _____.
   a) Wade high School
   b) Wade High School
   c) wade high school
   d) wade High School

"Did you get your _____ worth?" she asked.
   a) moneys
   b) money's
   c) monies
   d) moneys'

We baked four_____ of bread.
   a) loafs
   b) loaves'
   c) loaves
   d) loaf's

I like to read _____ stories.
   a) Charles Dickens'
   b) Charles Dickens
   c) Charles Dickens's
   d) Charles Dickenses

The _____ live four miles west of town.
   a) Maryons
   b) Maryons's
   c) Maryon's
   d) Maryonses

READING

Your other task for the day is to read a book. At this point you should be able to read for ½ hour to 1 hour each day. Look online for a variety of book lists. You can also check out my site www.plainandnotsoplain.com and see all of the books that we have enjoyed at this grade level.

Write the title of the book you are reading and how long you have read for.

_____

_____

Write a sentence for each of your words

A line goes on and on. When we draw a line, we include an arrowhead on each end to show that the line continues in both directions..

Part of a line is a line segment, or just segment. When we draw a segment, we do not include arrowheads. WE can use dots on the ends or leave it plain.

A ray is sometimes called a half line. Think of a ray of sunshine, it comes off the circle, so it has an endpoint and then it goes on forever.

Lines that go in the same direction and do not touch are called parallel lines

Lines that touch are called intersecting lines

Lines that form "square corners" are called perpendicular

Angles are formed when the lines intersect

Right angles make perfectly square corners. They usually will have a small box in the corner to show that they are right. If it is smaller than a right, it is acute angle. If it is larger than a right, it is called an obtuse angle.

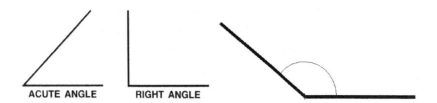

ACUTE ANGLE   RIGHT ANGLE

7 - 0	10 - 8	6 - 3	14 - 5	3 - 1	16 - 9	7 - 1	18 - 9	11 - 3	13 - 7
13 - 8	7 - 4	10 - 7	0 - 0	12 - 8	10 - 9	6 - 2	13 - 4	4 - 0	10 - 5
5 - 3	7 - 5	2 - 1	6 - 6	8 - 4	7 - 2	14 - 7	8 - 1	11 - 6	3 - 3
1 - 1	11 - 9	10 - 4	9 - 2	14 - 6	17 - 8	6 - 0	10 - 6	4 - 1	9 - 5
7 - 7	14 - 8	12 - 9	9 - 8	12 - 7	12 - 3	16 - 8	9 - 1	15 - 6	11 - 4
8 - 6	15 - 9	11 - 8	3 - 2	4 - 4	8 - 2	11 - 5	5 - 0	17 - 9	6 - 1
5 - 5	4 - 3	8 - 7	7 - 3	7 - 6	5 - 1	10 - 3	12 - 6	10 - 1	6 - 4
2 - 2	13 - 6	15 - 8	7 - 0	13 - 9	16 - 7	5 - 2	12 - 4	3 - 0	11 - 7
8 - 0	9 - 4	10 - 2	6 - 5	8 - 3	9 - 0	5 - 4	12 - 5	4 - 2	9 - 3
9 - 9	15 - 7	8 - 8	14 - 9	9 - 7	13 - 5	1 - 0	8 - 5	9 - 6	11 - 2

A pronoun is a word that replaces a noun. Without pronouns, you would have to repeat the same nouns over and over again.

Ex: Sam said that Sam was going to call Sam's brother.

Sam said that he was going to call his brother.

Every pronoun has an antecedent. The antecedent is the noun that the pronoun replaces. The pronouns must agree in number and gender.

Write each antecedent that refers to the bold pronoun.

1. Jack and I went to the game, and then **we** went to the dance.

_____

2. Jack drove **his** father's van.

_____

3. Alice's history book is in **her** locker.

_____

4. Mr. and Mrs. Maryon drove **their** daughter to school.

_____

READING

Your other task for the day is to read a book. At this point you should be able to read for ½ hour to 1 hour each day. Look online for a variety of book lists. You can also check out my site www.plainandnotsoplain.com and see all of the books that we have enjoyed at this grade level.

Write the title of the book you are reading and how long you have read for.

_____

_____

QUIZ

Draw a set of parallel segments

Draw perpendicular lines

Draw a right angle   Draw an acute angle   Draw an obtuse angle

Draw two segments that intersect but are not perpendicular   Draw a ray

Are the rails of a train track perpendicular or parallel

A triangle has how many angles

Twenty-eight children were in the first line. Forty-two children were in the second line. Altogether, how many children were in both lines?

Round 92 to the nearest ten

Round $19.67 to the nearest dollar

7 -0	10 -8	6 -3	14 -5	3 -1	16 -9	7 -1	18 -9	11 -3	13 -7
13 -8	7 -4	10 -7	0 -0	12 -8	10 -9	6 -2	13 -4	4 -0	10 -5
5 -3	7 -5	2 -1	6 -6	8 -4	7 -2	14 -7	8 -1	11 -6	3 -3
1 -1	11 -9	10 -4	9 -2	14 -6	17 -8	6 -0	10 -6	4 -1	9 -5
7 -7	14 -8	12 -9	9 -8	12 -7	12 -3	16 -8	9 -1	15 -6	11 -4
8 -6	15 -9	11 -8	3 -2	4 -4	8 -2	11 -5	5 -0	17 -9	6 -1
5 -5	4 -3	8 -7	7 -3	7 -6	5 -1	10 -3	12 -6	10 -1	6 -4
7 -2	13 -6	15 -8	2 -0	13 -9	16 -7	5 -2	12 -4	3 -0	11 -7
8 -0	9 -4	10 -2	6 -5	8 -3	9 -0	5 -4	12 -5	4 -2	9 -3
9 -9	15 -7	8 -8	14 -9	9 -7	13 -5	1 -0	8 -5	9 -6	11 -2

Personal pronouns refer to people or things. They distinguish among the speaker, the person spoken to, and the person or thing spoken about.

A first-person pronoun refers to the speaker.
I am late.

A second-person pronouns refers to the person spoken to.
You are late.

A third-person pronoun refers to the person or thing spoken about.
He is late.

Personal pronouns express number. They can be singular or plural.
ex: singular==I am late.
plural==We are late.

We use personal pronouns in different ways
- as the subject of a sentence
- as the object of a sentence
- as a possessive that shows ownership

Subject pronouns are I, he, she, it, we, you, they
Object pronouns are me, him, her, it, us, you, them

Possessive pronouns are: my, mine, your, yours, his, hers, its, ours, theirs
Replace the words in bold with a pronoun.

1. I have a **hammer and a saw.** _____

2. **The gloves** are lost._____

3. **An airplane** is flying overhead._____

4. **Anita's** house is in the country._____

5. That is **Lauren and Ashley's** room._____
READING
Your other task for the day is to read a book. At this point you should be able to read for ½ hour to 1 hour each day. Look online for a variety of book lists. You can also check out my site www.plainandnotsoplain.com and see all of the books that we have enjoyed at this grade level. Write the title of the book you are reading and how long you have read for.

_____

_____

week 7 copy your spelling words

afraid

aide

bay

break

chain

delay

failure

great

maize

payment

prey

refrain

remain

stain

waist

Kim placed two – 1 foot rulers end to end. What was the total length of the two rulers in inches

There were 47 apples in the big tree. There was a total of 82 apples in the big and the little tree. How many apples were in the little tree

Round 77 to the nearest ten

Round $29.39 to the nearest dollar

Draw me 7:10 on the clock   8:40   12:55

How many dimes equal one dollar

One dime is what fraction of a dollar

Draw a rectangle that is 5 centimeters long and 2 centimeters wide. What is the perimeter

465+35+27+5=

7 −0	10 − 8	6 −3	14 − 5	3 − 1	16 − 9	7 − 1	18 − 9	11 − 3	13 − 7
13 − 8	7 − 4	10 − 7	0 −0	12 − 8	10 − 9	6 − 2	13 − 4	4 −0	10 − 5
5 −3	7 − 5	2 − 1	6 −6	8 − 4	7 −2	14 − 7	8 − 1	11 − 6	3 − 3
1 − 1	11 − 9	10 − 4	9 −2	14 − 6	17 − 8	6 − 0	10 − 6	4 − 1	9 −5
7 − 7	14 − 8	12 − 9	9 − 8	12 − 7	12 − 3	16 − 8	9 − 1	15 − 6	11 − 4
8 − 6	15 − 9	11 − 8	3 − 2	4 − 4	8 − 2	11 − 5	5 − 0	17 − 9	6 − 1
5 −5	4 −3	8 −7	7 −3	7 −6	5 − 1	10 − 3	12 − 6	10 − 1	6 − 4
2 −2	13 − 6	15 − 8	2 −0	13 − 9	16 − 7	5 −2	12 − 4	3 −0	11 − 7
8 −0	9 −4	10 − 2	6 −5	8 −3	9 −0	5 −4	12 − 5	4 −2	9 − 3
9 −9	15 − 7	8 −8	14 − 9	9 −7	13 − 5	1 − 0	8 − 5	9 − 6	11 − 2

Relative pronouns are who, whom, whose, which, that, and what.
Circle the relative pronouns in each sentence.

1. The car that Sam bought is black.

2. Kim wanted a car that had four doors.

3. Bob has a friend who is a mechanic.

4. Mike also had a friend whose father owned a garage.

5. The man who owned the garage sold Sam new tires.

Circle the pronouns in the list below.

him	he	car	whoever
Andy	I	Mrs. Maryon	its
friend	what	that	

Circle the correct pronoun

1. There are the shoes (who, that) I want.

2. The puppy (who, that) I found at the shelter is nice.

3. There is the girl (whom, what) I met at the library.

4. I like a house (who, that) has a big yard.

5. Did you see the lady (which, who) was wearing the red hat?

READING

Your other task for the day is to read a book. At this point you should be able to read for ½ hour to 1 hour each day. Look online for a variety of book lists. You can also check out my site www.plainandnotsoplain.com and see all of the books that we have enjoyed at this grade level.

Write the title of the book you are reading and how long you have read for.

_____

_____

```
W  F  A  I  L  U  R  E  R  Y  N  O  L  V  S
C  Z  I  P  W  X  U  I  D  I  I  K  P  E  T
X  Y  U  I  T  K  Z  G  A  Z  A  I  G  T  N
I  P  R  T  M  O  A  M  M  Q  H  N  V  I  E
Q  D  K  M  B  J  E  E  D  L  C  P  X  M  M
C  T  X  A  W  R  E  G  R  N  Y  K  J  P  Y
F  Y  T  Z  D  W  R  V  B  B  L  S  N  D  A
Z  Y  I  J  I  E  N  B  I  W  J  K  S  P  P
L  D  E  L  A  Y  E  R  P  Z  D  M  M  Q  L
M  J  O  T  R  E  F  R  A  I  N  A  X  B  Y
W  B  M  P  F  Y  U  J  S  T  A  I  N  D  T
M  U  I  R  A  C  O  Q  M  B  A  Z  O  N  E
A  P  O  B  O  A  D  Q  Q  H  E  E  H  D  K
V  L  X  J  N  E  C  E  W  X  S  M  O  Q  A
F  E  D  I  A  B  E  A  B  W  A  I  S  T
```

AFRAID	AIDE	BAY
BREAK	CHAIN	DELAY
FAILURE	GREAT	MAIZE
PAYMENT	PREY	REFRAIN
REMAIN	STAIN	WAIST

Subtraction story problems

Jim had some marbles. Then he lost 15 marbles. Now he has 22 marbles left. How many marbles did Jim have in the beginning? Subtraction is the opposite of subtraction. Take 22 and add it to 15. This gives you how many he had in the beginning.

Cara had 42 balls. She lost some. She has 29 balls left. How many balls did Cara lose?

Mike had 42 balls. Then he lost some. Now he has 26 balls. How many balls did Mike lose?

Ruth had 75 cents. Then she spent 27 cents. How many cents did she have now?

Round 78 to nearest ten.

Round $7.80 to nearest dollar.

52-14=   62-38=   55-17=

900+90+9=   52-22=

432+42+17=   763-172=

7 -0	10 - 8	6 -3	14 - 5	3 - 1	16 - 9	7 - 1	18 - 9	11 - 3	13 - 7
13 - 8	7 - 4	10 - 7	0 -0	12 - 8	10 - 9	6 - 2	13 - 4	4 -0	10 - 5
5 -3	7 - 5	2 - 1	6 -6	8 - 4	7 -2	14 - 7	8 - 1	11 - 6	3 - 3
1 - 1	11 - 9	10 - 4	9 -2	14 - 6	17 - 8	6 -0	10 - 6	4 - 1	9 -5
7 -7	14 - 8	12 - 9	9 - 8	12 - 7	12 - 3	16 - 8	9 - 1	15 - 6	11 - 4
8 - 6	15 - 9	11 - 8	3 - 2	4 - 4	8 - 2	11 - 5	5 -0	17 - 9	6 - 1
5 -5	4 -3	8 -7	7 -3	7 -6	5 - 1	10 - 3	12 - 6	10 - 1	6 - 4
2 -2	13 - 6	15 - 8	2 -0	13 - 9	16 - 7	5 -2	12 - 4	3 -0	11 - 7
8 -0	9 -4	10 - 2	6 -5	8 -3	9 -0	5 -4	12 - 5	4 -2	9 - 3
9 -9	15 - 7	8 -8	14 - 9	9 -7	13 - 5	1 - 0	8 -5	9 - 6	11 - 2

The interrogative pronouns are who, whom, which, what, and whose. They are called interrogative because they ask questions.

Circle the correct form

(Which, What) of these fish is larger?

(Whom,, Whose) did Kevin ask to the dance?

(Who, What) will win the World Series?

(Who, Whose) mother teachers at our school?

(Which, What) do you want for dinner?

READING

Your other task for the day is to read a book. At this point you should be able to read for ½ hour to 1 hour each day. Look online for a variety of book lists. You can also check out my site www.plainandnotsoplain.com and see all of the books that we have enjoyed at this grade level.

Write the title of the book you are reading and how long you have read for.

_____

_____

Write a sentence for each of your words

We can understand fractions better if we learn to draw them. Draw a rectangle and shade two thirds of it.   Make sure the lines are equal parts.

Draw a circle and shade one fourth of it.

Draw a square and shade half of it

Draw a circle and shade three fourths of it

Use the digits 4,5,6 and write an even number less than 500

What is the perimeter of a triangle whose sides are : 10 cm, 6cm, and 8 cm

Round 19 to nearest ten

Round $10.90 to nearest dollar

7 -0	10 - 8	6 -3	14 - 5	3 - 1	16 - 9	7 - 1	18 - 9	11 - 3	13 - 7
13 - 8	7 - 4	10 - 7	0 -0	12 - 8	10 - 9	6 - 2	13 - 4	4 -0	10 - 5
5 -3	7 - 5	2 - 1	6 -6	8 - 4	7 -2	14 -7	8 - 1	11 - 6	3 -3
1 - 1	11 - 9	10 - 4	9 -2	14 - 6	17 - 8	6 -0	10 - 6	4 - 1	9 -5
7 -7	14 - 8	12 - 9	9 - 8	12 - 7	12 - 3	16 - 8	9 - 1	15 - 6	11 - 4
8 - 6	15 - 9	11 - 8	3 - 2	4 - 4	8 - 2	11 - 5	5 -0	17 - 9	6 - 1
5 -5	4 -3	8 -7	7 -3	7 -6	5 - 1	10 - 3	12 - 6	10 - 1	6 - 4
2 -2	13 - 6	15 - 8	2 -0	13 - 9	16 - 7	5 -2	12 - 4	3 -0	11 - 7
8 -0	9 -4	10 - 2	6 -5	8 -3	9 -0	5 -4	12 - 5	4 -2	9 - 3
9 -9	15 - 7	8 -8	14 - 9	9 -7	13 - 5	1 - 0	8 - 5	9 - 6	11 - 2

Demonstrative pronouns point out particular persons or things. The demonstrative pronouns are this, these, that, and those.

Circle the demonstrative pronouns

1. Is that the movie you saw?

2. Those are new socks.

3. These are the pictures from my vacation.

4. Are these your favorite colors?

5. Is this the book you wanted?

6. Did Don buy that?

7. This is my favorite CD.

Circle the correct pronoun.

(This, These) is my house.

Are (that, those) the people who just moved in?

Tom bought two new CDs. "(These, That) are really great!" he said to Jim.

A car went speeding down the street. "Did you see (this, that)? asked Amanda.

READING

Your other task for the day is to read a book. At this point you should be able to read for ½ hour to 1 hour each day. Look online for a variety of book lists. You can also check out my site www.plainandnotsoplain.com and see all of the books that we have enjoyed at this grade level.

Write the title of the book you are reading and how long you have read for.

_____

_____

QUIZ

Multiplication

Change this addition problem to a multiplication problem

6+6+6+6+6

5 x 6   or 6
            X5

Your turn:

Change each addition to a multiplication problem:

3 +3+3+3+3   9+9+9

7+7+7+7+7+7+7+7   5+5+5+5+5+5+5

List the even numbers between 31 and 39

Round 63 to the nearest ten

Round $6.30 to nearest dollar

Draw a circle and shade ¾ of it

$5.88+$2.39=   71-39=   483+378=

7 -0	10 -8	6 -3	14 -5	3 -1	16 -9	7 -1	18 -9	11 -3	13 -7
13 -8	7 -4	10 -7	0 -0	12 -8	10 -9	6 -2	13 -4	4 -0	10 -5
5 -3	7 -5	2 -1	6 -6	8 -4	7 -2	14 -7	8 -1	11 -6	3 -3
1 -1	11 -9	10 -4	9 -2	14 -6	17 -8	6 -0	10 -6	4 -1	9 -5
7 -7	14 -8	12 -9	9 -8	12 -7	12 -3	16 -8	9 -1	15 -6	11 -4
8 -6	15 -9	11 -8	3 -2	4 -4	8 -2	11 -5	5 -0	17 -9	6 -1
5 -5	4 -3	8 -7	7 -3	7 -6	5 -1	10 -3	12 -6	10 -1	6 -4
2 -2	13 -6	15 -8	2 -0	13 -9	16 -7	5 -2	12 -4	3 -0	11 -7
8 -0	9 -4	10 -2	6 -5	8 -3	9 -0	5 -4	12 -5	4 -2	9 -3
9 -9	15 -7	8 -8	14 -9	9 -7	13 -5	1 -0	8 -5	9 -6	11 -2

Indefinite pronouns replace nouns that are understood by the listener or reader.

Here are some: Singular indefinite pronouns

another	each other	much	one
anybody	either	neither	one another
anyone	everybody	nobody	somebody
anything	everyone	no one	someone
each	everything	nothing	something

Plural indefinite pronouns

both   few   many   others   several

Circle the indefinite pronouns

1. Everyone brought food to the picnic.

2. Jack did not know anyone at the park.

3. Several of the boys were late.

4. Try to be nice to one another.

5. Everything is ready for the party.

READING

Your other task for the day is to read a book. At this point you should be able to read for ½ hour to 1 hour each day. Look online for a variety of book lists. You can also check out my site www.plainandnotsoplain.com and see all of the books that we have enjoyed at this grade level.

Write the title of the book you are reading and how long you have read for.

_____

_____

week 8 copy your spelling words

agree

between

breathe

disease

eagle

easel

greenery

greetings

meek

people

preach

season

wheat

wheel

yeast

The amount of time between two different clock times is called elapsed time. We can count forward or backward on a clock to solve elapsed time problems.

If it is the afternoon, what time will it be in 3 hours and 20 minutes.

If it is the morning, what time would it be 2 hours and 25 minutes earlier?

400-300=   663-363=

How many pennies equal one dollar

Eleven pennies are what fraction of a dollar

Draw a dot on your paper to represent a point, and from that point draw two perpendicular rays

765-328=   765+599=

7 -0	10 -8	6 -3	14 -5	3 -1	16 -9	7 -1	18 -9	11 -3	13 -7
13 -8	7 -4	10 -7	0 -0	12 -8	10 -9	6 -2	13 -4	4 -0	10 -5
5 -3	7 -5	2 -1	6 -6	8 -4	7 -2	14 -7	8 -1	11 -6	3 -3
1 -1	11 -9	10 -4	9 -2	14 -6	17 -8	6 -0	10 -6	4 -1	9 -5
7 -7	14 -8	12 -9	9 -8	12 -7	12 -3	16 -8	9 -1	15 -6	11 -4
8 -6	15 -9	11 -8	3 -2	4 -4	8 -2	11 -5	5 -0	17 -9	6 -1
5 -5	4 -3	8 -7	7 -3	7 -6	5 -1	10 -3	12 -6	10 -1	6 -4
2 -2	13 -6	15 -8	2 -0	13 -9	16 -7	5 -2	12 -4	3 -0	11 -7
8 -0	9 -4	10 -2	6 -5	8 -3	9 -0	5 -4	12 -5	4 -2	9 -3
9 -9	15 -7	8 -8	14 -9	9 -7	13 -5	1 -0	8 -5	9 -6	11 -2

Contractions

We also use an apostrophe (') in a contraction. A contraction is a word made from two words by leaving out one or more letters. An apostrophe takes the place of the missing letter (s). Contractions can come from a pronoun and a verb

I'd= I would or I had
I'll= I will
I'm-I am
I've-I have
you'll-you will
you're-you are
he's=he is
it's = it is, it has
who's=who is
we're=we are
we've=we have
they're-they are
that's-that is
what's=what is

Circle the contractions in this paragraph below. Rewrite each contraction as two words.

By the time Maya Angelou was 25, she'd been a cook, a dancer, and a streetcar conductor. Since then she's become a director, an actor, and a playwright. However, that's not what has made her famous. She's one of America's most popular writers. If you've read her first book, *I Know Why the Caged Bird Sings,* you know why she's so well liked. It's an autobiography that tells of her life up to age 16. I'm sure you'd like her poetry, too.

READING

Your other task for the day is to read a book. At this point you should be able to read for ½ hour to 1 hour each day. Look online for a variety of book lists. You can also check out my site www.plainandnotsoplain.com and see all of the books that we have enjoyed at this grade level.

Write the title of the book you are reading and how long you have read for.

_____

_____

```
D  I  H  K  E  P  Z  S  E  R  B  H  I  T  V
J  G  P  N  V  A  R  M  E  Z  E  M  X  L  B
N  P  R  E  A  C  H  S  Z  A  C  A  H  L  O
J  G  E  S  J  W  U  W  L  Y  S  Y  S  G  X
P  J  W  A  S  Z  H  H  K  R  E  O  Z  E  N
J  Y  E  J  G  B  M  E  E  K  C  U  N  A  L
Z  P  D  F  G  L  L  E  A  E  S  F  C  G  O
D  E  O  P  E  R  E  L  R  T  O  M  V  R  V
M  O  M  Y  B  T  E  B  R  E  A  T  H  E  D
I  P  G  R  E  E  N  E  R  Y  Q  O  Q  E  I
L  L  E  R  S  A  T  B  T  L  G  J  T  U  S
C  E  B  X  B  J  S  W  S  I  Z  Z  I  A  E
E  Y  N  G  V  B  L  T  E  Y  N  E  D  A  A
B  X  G  L  H  B  B  F  Q  E  Z  G  D  R  S
P  M  N  B  U  Z  P  R  B  P  N  O  S  Q  E
```

AGREE	BETWEEN	BREATHE
DISEASE	EAGLE	EASEL
GREENERY	GREETINGS	MEEK
PEOPLE	PREACH	SEASON
WHEAT	WHEEL	YEAST

117

We know how to count by 1,2, and 5's easily. This will help us with our multiplication facts. When we have 3 x2, we can say count by 3, two times. Or 5x6 count by 5s, six times.

Solve: 2 x2=   5x3=   1 x9=

4x2=   5x8=   1x5=

10x10=   10x8=   12x1=

Greg ate seventy-two pieces of cake. Sarah ate forty-two pieces of cake. How many pieces of cake did they eat in all?

Kim needs $35 to buy a baseball glove. She has saved $18. How much more money does she need?

Draw a rectangle that is 4 cm and 3 cm wide. What is the perimeter of it?

Round 28 to nearest ten

Round $12.29 to nearest dollar

It is 10:15 am. What time will it be ten minutes from now?

386 +388=   73-29=

Which of the following shows 3 ones and 4 hundreds

304   403   4003   3400

100 Addition facts

4 +4	7 +5	0 +1	8 +7	3 +4	3 +2	8 +3	2 +1	5 +6	2 +9
0 +9	8 +9	7 +6	1 +3	6 +8	7 +3	1 +6	4 +7	0 +3	6 +4
9 +3	2 +6	3 +0	6 +1	3 +6	4 +0	5 +7	1 +1	5 +4	2 +8
4 +3	0 +9	0 +7	9 +4	7 +7	8 +6	0 +4	5 +8	7 +4	1 +7
9 +5	1 +5	9 +0	3 +8	1 +9	9 +1	8 +8	2 +2	4 +5	6 +2
7 +9	1 +2	6 +7	0 +8	9 +2	4 +8	8 +0	3 +9	1 +0	6 +3
2 +0	8 +4	3 +5	9 +8	5 +0	5 +5	3 +1	7 +2	8 +5	2 +5
5 +2	0 +5	6 +9	1 +8	9 +6	7 +1	4 +6	0 +2	6 +5	4 +9
1 +4	3 +7	7 +0	2 +3	5 +1	6 +6	4 +1	8 +2	2 +4	6 +0
5 +3	4 +2	9 +7	0 +6	7 +8	0 +0	5 +9	3 +3	8 +1	2 +7

Chris is a person_____likes to be active.
   a) whom
   b) which
   c) who
   d) whose

Biking is an exercise_____he enjoys.
   a) that
   b) whom
   c) who
   d) whatever

He wears a helmet to protect_____.
   a) hisself
   b) ourselves
   c) oneself
   d) himself

On your paper write contractions as two words.

Jentzen decided he'd take the puppy for a walk. _____

Madelyn said she'd go to the mall, and we'd meet her there._____

_____

I'll let you know when I'm ready to
leave._____

READING

Your other task for the day is to read a book. At this point you should be able to read for ½ hour to 1 hour each day. Look online for a variety of book lists. You can also check out my site www.plainandnotsoplain.com and see all of the books that we have enjoyed at this grade level. Write the title of the book you are reading and how long you have read for.

_____

_____

Write a sentence for each of your words

We will begin memorizing the basic multiplication facts

Zero times any number equals zero

9 x 0=0   12x0=0

One times any number equals that number:

1 x8=8   6 x1=6   5 x1=5

Two times any number doubles that number

2 x5=10   2 x6=12   2x8=16

Five times any number equals a number that ends in zero or in five

5 x1=5   5x4=20   5x8=40

Ninety-two birds squawked nosily in the tree. Then some flew away. Twenty-four birds remained. How many birds flew away?

Use the digits 4,5,6 to write a three-digit odd number less than 640.

It is 3:25 pm. What time will it be in 6 hours

Draw a rectangle 3 cm and 1 cm wide. What is the perimeter

83-19=   72-38 $5.87+$2.79=

525-521=   870-470=

1+9+2+7+4+2+10+1+2=

Multiplication Facts 0s, 1s,2s,5s,

0 x8	3 x 2	5 x 1	4 x 5	2 x 0	1 x 8	7 x 2	1 x1
5 x2	4 x0	2 x8	1 x 3	7 x 5	7 x 0	8 x 5	0 x5
8 x1	6 x5	9 x0	2 x6	0 x1	4 x2	1 x6	9 x2
6 x0	3 x5	5 x7	4 x1	2 x2	8 x0	5 x9	1 x2
5 x5	1 x7	0 x0	8 x2	5 x8	5 x6	3 x0	9 x1
5 x3	0 x4	6 x1	9 x 5	5 x0	7 x1	2 x5	0 x9
2 x1	6 x2	0 x7	2 x3	1 x4	2 x9	1 x0	5 x4
0 x2	1 x9	3 x1	2 x7	0 x7	1 x5	2 x4	0 x6

READING

Your other task for the day is to read a book. At this point you should be able to read for ½ hour to 1 hour each day. Look online for a variety of book lists. You can also check out my site www.plainandnotsoplain.com and see all of the books that we have enjoyed at this grade level. Write the title of the book you are reading and how long you have read for.

_____

_____

An adjective is a word that describes or tells about a noun or pronoun. One way to make your writer clearer and more interesting is by using adjectives.

It may tell what kind, which one, how many, or how much. You can use more than one adjective to describe a noun or pronoun

Write each noun that the adjectives describe. The adjectives are in bold.

What a **fantastic summer** vacation they had at the lake!_____

We did not have e**nough** time to do everything._____

The **next** day, Collin hooked **three** trout._____

At night, a **large black** bear came into **our** camp._____

Write these sentences and add one or more adjectives to describe each noun.

Students brought books to class.

_____

People brought food.

_____

I saw mountains and rivers.

_____

QUIZ

Subtracting three digit numbers with regrouping—do this with your teacher

```
 2 5
 3̶6̶5̶
-187
 178
```
If you cannot subtract, borrow from the neighbor.
Remember you are borrowing 1 (tens really) so
place that in front of your number

Your turn—rewrite vertically

240-65   459-176   157-98

$4.30-$1.12= $355-$287=

It is 9:20 am, what time will it be in 15 minutes

Write 843 in expanded form.

Write 343 in words

There are 100 cents in a dollar. How many cents are in a half dollar

4+3+8+7+5+1+1+2+10

Multiplication Facts 0s, 1s,2s,5s,

0 x8	3 x 2	5 x 1	4 x 5	2 x 0	1 x 8	7 x 2	1 x1
5 x2	4 x0	2 x8	1 x 3	7 x 5	7 x 0	8 x 5	0 x5
8 x1	6 x5	9 x0	2 x6	0 x1	4 x2	1 x6	9 x2
6 x0	3 x5	5 x7	4 x1	2 x2	8 x0	5 x9	1 x2
5 x5	1 x7	0 x0	8 x2	5 x8	5 x6	3 x0	9 x1
5 x3	0 x4	6 x1	9 x 5	5 x0	7 x1	2 x5	0 x9
2 x1	6 x2	0 x7	2 x3	1 x4	2 x9	1 x0	5 x4
0 x2	1 x9	3 x1	2 x7	0 x7	1 x5	2 x4	0 x6

READING

Your other task for the day is to read a book. At this point you should be able to read for ½ hour to 1 hour each day. Look online for a variety of book lists. You can also check out my site www.plainandnotsoplain.com and see all of the books that we have enjoyed at this grade level. Write the title of the book you are reading and how long you have read for.

_____

_____

Circle the adjectives in the following sentences. Draw an arrow to the noun or pronoun that the adjective describes.

1. The lake was beautiful on that morning.

2. The water was clear and cool.

3. Greg saw a large fish jump out of the sparkling water.

4. Collin used a trusty old rod.

5. By late afternoon, they had caught many fish.

Rewrite these sentences with more exciting adjectives.

The cat has **nice** fur.

_____

The gardens were **pretty** today.

_____

That was a **bad** excuse.

_____

week 9 copy your spelling words

account

aloud

amount

boundary

couch

county

doubt

foul

fountain

hound

mountain

noun

ounce

pound

south

Subtraction word problems

Forty-two apples is how many more than 13 apples? When you see the words "how many more" or "how many less" your key is to subtract. 42-13 =29 apples

Your turn:

Seventeen apples is how many fewer than 64 apples

Nineteen is how much less than 42

Forty-three is how much greater than twenty-seven

Mary has 42 peanuts. Sam has 22 peanuts. How many fewer peanuts does Sam have?

One hundred fifty is how much greater than twenty-three? Write a subtraction pattern and solve it

It is 8:05pm. What time will it be in three hours from now?

Write 412 in expanded form

Write 432 in words

How many quarters equal one dollar

Multiplication Facts 0s, 1s,2s,5s,

0 x8	3 x 2	5 x 1	4 x 5	2 x 0	1 x 8	7 x 2	1 x1
5 x2	4 x0	2 x8	1 x 3	7 x 5	7 x 0	8 x 5	0 x5
8 x1	6 x5	9 x0	2 x6	0 x1	4 x2	1 x6	9 x2
6 x0	3 x5	5 x7	4 x1	2 x2	8 x0	5 x9	1 x2
5 x5	1 x7	0 x0	8 x2	5 x8	5 x6	3 x0	9 x1
5 x3	0 x4	6 x1	9 x 5	5 x0	7 x1	2 x5	0 x9
2 x1	6 x2	0 x7	2 x3	1 x4	2 x9	1 x0	5 x4
0 x2	1 x9	3 x1	2 x7	0 x7	1 x5	2 x4	0 x6

READING

Your other task for the day is to read a book. At this point you should be able to read for ½ hour to 1 hour each day. Look online for a variety of book lists. You can also check out my site www.plainandnotsoplain.com and see all of the books that we have enjoyed at this grade level. Write the title of the book you are reading and how long you have read for.

_____

_____

The articles: "a, an, the" are always adjectives. They come before nouns in a sentence.
Use "a" before a word that begins with a consonant
Use "an" before a word that begins with a vowel

an orange   an apple   a bike   a car

Vowels are a,e,i,o,u

Circle the correct article.

Kim packed (a, an) apple for lunch.

They waited for (a, an) hour.

The teacher spoke in (a, an) soft voice.

They had (a, an) Math lesson.

I read (a, an) book about elephants.

```
H  L  J  F  Y  J  D  M  A  M  Y  O  L  I  Z
C  Z  Z  Z  N  Z  P  M  M  B  O  W  T  S  N
S  O  D  C  C  O  L  N  O  T  P  F  C  I  B
A  Y  U  O  J  N  U  U  U  R  Q  A  T  G
P  C  Q  C  U  A  P  N  N  Q  N  T  W  F  V
O  P  C  I  H  B  D  P  T  O  N  T  A  A  K
J  U  D  O  P  Z  T  B  O  U  N  D  A  R  Y
Z  E  N  S  U  D  O  H  O  U  N  D  B  I  P
E  H  U  C  N  N  X  F  M  J  F  F  M  V  N
G  I  J  U  E  S  T  B  W  F  S  O  W  Y  W
Q  V  O  B  G  O  Z  T  X  L  E  F  U  A  M
I  P  W  Q  K  U  B  J  M  X  A  C  A  L  J
M  I  L  V  S  T  W  X  X  J  V  B  P  O  V
F  D  N  B  O  H  L  W  Z  U  W  Q  E  U  F
S  L  C  O  U  N  T  Y  G  I  V  Q  M  D  F
```

ACCOUNT	ALOUD	AMOUNT
BOUNDARY	COUCH	COUNTY
DOUBT	FOUL	FOUNTAIN
HOUND	MOUNTAIN	NOUN
OUNCE	POUND	SOUTH

We are going to practice the 3s for multiplication today

If you don't know how to count by 3's lets practice

3,6,9,12,15,18,21,24,27,30

3 x 2=   3x5=   3x7=   3x6=   3x3=

We will be doing lots of practice with these. Keep memorizing them!

There are two hundred fourteen pages in a book. Kim has read eighty-six pages. How many more pages are left to read?

Use the digits 7,8,9 to make an even number greater than 800

Write 729 in expanded form

Round 66 to nearest ten

Round $6.67 to nearest dollar

62-x=38 what is x

Is the value of three nickels and two dimes an even number of cents or an an odd number of cents

$3.60-$1.37=   875-218=

Multiplication facts 0s,1s,2s,3s,5s

0 x8	3 x 2	5 x 1	4 x 5	2 x 0	1 x 8	7 x 2	1 x1
5 x2	4 x0	2 x8	1 x 3	7 x 5	3 x3	8 x 5	0 x5
8 x1	6 x5	9 x0	2 x6	0 x1	4 x2	1 x6	9 x2
3 x7	3 x5	2 x3	4 x1	2 x2	8 x0	5 x9	1 x2
5 x5	1 x7	0 x0	8 x2	5 x8	5 x6	3 x0	9 x1
5 x3	0 x4	6 x1	9 x 5	5 x0	4 x3	2 x5	0 x9
6 x0	7 x3	2 x3	5 x7	3 x6	9 x3	7 x 0	5 x3
3 x3	9 x3	0 x7	3 x2	4 x3	7 x1	3 x5	8 x3
2 x1	6 x2	0 x7	9 x3	1 x4	2 x9	1 x0	5 x4
0 x2	1 x9	3 x1	2 x7	3 x1	1 x5	2 x4	0 x6

Review

Kim is (a,an) talented writer.

She has written (a, an) book.

The article is about (a, the) Rocky Mountains.

She enjoys studying (a, the) land.

He thinks music makes (a, an) interesting topic.

Look up the topic in (a, the) index.

They saw(a, an) funny film.

Jill is (an,a) honest woman.

Bailey likes (an, the) blue coat in the window.

Look at all (a, the) stars.

We went to Chicago to see (a, an) play.

They did (a, the) activity in class.

Being invited was (a, an) honor.

READING

Your other task for the day is to read a book. At this point you should be able to read for ½ hour to 1 hour each day. Look online for a variety of book lists. You can also check out my site www.plainandnotsoplain.com and see all of the books that we have enjoyed at this grade level. Write the title of the book you are reading and how long you have read for.

_____

_____

Write a sentence for each of your words

hundred millions	ten millions	millions	comma	hundred thousands	ten thousands	thousands	comma	hundreds	tens	ones
7	9	4	,	4	3	2	,	6	9	4

794,432,694 is read : seven hundred ninety-four million, four hundred thirty-two thousand, six hundred ninety-four

Use commas to help separate the numbers. Start from the right and go towards the left and count over three places.

Place commas in proper place:

123456432   65899

When we write it in words, we place a comma (,) where the words millions, thousands would go. This shows how to separate each section.

Write 12345678 in words. *first place commas

_____

Write 75, 634 in expanded form.

70,000+5000+600+30+4

You write 43,278 in expanded form

Write 14,413 in words

Write 3, 500,000 in words

Write 2040 in expanded form

Write 5280 in expanded form

What digit in 7,243,490 is in the ten thousands place

Arrange these in chronological order, from earliest to latest

1969,1903, 1957, 1927

Multiplication facts 0s,1s,2s,3s,5s

0 x8	3 x 2	5 x 1	4 x 5	2 x 0	1 x 8	7 x 2	1 x1
5 x2	4 x0	2 x8	1 x 3	7 x 5	3 x3	8 x 5	0 x5
8 x1	6 x5	9 x0	2 x6	0 x1	4 x2	1 x6	9 x2
3 x7	3 x5	2 x3	4 x1	2 x2	8 x0	5 x9	1 x2
5 x5	1 x7	0 x0	8 x2	5 x8	5 x6	3 x0	9 x1
5 x3	0 x4	6 x1	9 x 5	5 x0	4 x3	2 x5	0 x9
6 x0	7 x3	2 x3	5 x7	3 x6	9 x3	7 x 0	5 x3
3 x3	9 x3	0 x7	3 x2	4 x3	7 x1	3 x5	8 x3
2 x1	6 x2	0 x7	9 x3	1 x4	2 x9	1 x0	5 x4
0 x2	1 x9	3 x1	2 x7	3 x1	1 x5	2 x4	0 x6

Proper adjectives are proper nouns that we use as adjectives. It always begins with a capital letter.

Proper noun: He is an American.
Proper adjective: He is an American citizen.
Proper noun: I visited France.
Proper adjective: I love French food.

Draw an arrow from the proper adjective to the noun or pronoun it describes. Not all capitalized words are proper adjectives.

1. Bailey had Spanish class during first period.

2. He almost forgot his French book.

3. This year in social studies, we learned about American Indian cultures.

4. Mike had never tasted Thai food.

Complete each sentence with a proper adjective.

5. We ordered _____dressing for our salad.

6. Mr Maryon likes _____cheese.

7. Is _____-cooking easier than it looks?

8. Both his grandparents are_____.

9. We studied _____history last year.

10. Ashlyn enjoys _____cooking

READING
Your other task for the day is to read a book. At this point you should be able to read for ½ hour to 1 hour each day. Look online for a variety of book lists. You can also check out my site www.plainandnotsoplain.com and see all of the books that we have enjoyed at this grade level. Write the title of the book you are reading and how long you have read for.

_____

_____

QUIZ

Use digits to write eight hundred ninety-five thousand, two hundred seventy.

* We know at the word "thousand" to place a comma

Answer is:

Use digits to write one hundred thirty-five million. *we know after the word "million" to place a comma. In this number, there is nothing so we put zeros.

Answer is:

Use digits to write seven thousand, twenty-five. *If we don't have the place value amount, we just write zeros.

Answer is:

Use digits to write:

Twelve thousand, seventy-five

Twelve million, five hundred thousand

Two hundred eighty million

Four hundred sixty-five is how much greater than twenty-four?

Write the number 25,463 in expanded form

If it is 4:10 pm, what time will it be in four and a half hours

Change this addition problem to a multiplication problem 8+8+8+8+8+8

Round 76 to the nearest tens

Round $12.51 to the nearest dollar

535-268= $471-$345=

Multiplication facts 0s,1s,2s,3s,5s

0 x8	3 x 2	5 x 1	4 x 5	2 x 0	1 x 8	7 x 2	1 x1
5 x2	4 x0	2 x8	1 x 3	7 x 5	3 x3	8 x 5	0 x5
8 x1	6 x5	9 x0	2 x6	0 x1	4 x2	1 x6	9 x2
3 x7	3 x5	2 x3	4 x1	2 x2	8 x0	5 x9	1 x2
5 x5	1 x7	0 x0	8 x2	5 x8	5 x6	3 x0	9 x1
5 x3	0 x4	6 x1	9 x 5	5 x0	4 x3	2 x5	0 x9
6 x0	7 x3	2 x3	5 x7	3 x6	9 x3	7 x 0	5 x3
3 x3	9 x3	0 x7	3 x2	4 x3	7 x1	3 x5	8 x3
2 x1	6 x2	0 x7	9 x3	1 x4	2 x9	1 x0	5 x4
0 x2	1 x9	3 x1	2 x7	3 x1	1 x5	2 x4	0 x6

We often use common nouns as adjectives. To decide whether a word is a noun or adjective, look at how the writer used it in the sentence.

Noun: Kim plays the piano.
Adjective: Kim enjoys her piano lessons.

Noun: Bill plays baseball.
Adjective: Bill plays on the baseball team.

Write whether the bold faced words are used as adjective or nouns.

1. I'm looking for a **summer** job.

2. My sister found a great job for the **summer.**

3. Kailey will be working as a **park** leader.

4. She will probably work at the **park** near our house.

5. In fact, three different **college** coaches have called her.

6. Susan has not decided which **college** she will go to yet.

Circle the common nouns used as adjectives. Draw a line to the noun it describes

7. Stephen grabbed his lunch bag and ran out the door.

8. He was going to be late for the newspaper meeting.

9. As the sports reporter, he went to all the games.

READING
Your other task for the day is to read a book. At this point you should be able to read for ½ hour to 1 hour each day. Look online for a variety of book lists. You can also check out my site www.plainandnotsoplain.com and see all of the books that we have enjoyed at this grade level. Write the title of the book you are reading and how long you have read for.

_____

_____

week 10 copy your spelling words

brook

bush

could

cushion

during

notebook

pudding

should

sugar

understood

wolf

woman

wool

would

yours

A mixed number is a whole number combined with a fraction. The mixed number 3 ½ is read "three and one half."

How many circles are shaded? 1 ½

Mixed Fraction

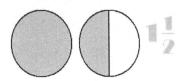

Use words to write 21 ½ ? We use the word "and" when naming mixed numbers. Twenty-one and one half.

Write fifteen dollars and twenty-five cents using a dollar sign? $15.25

Use words to write $30.76===thirty dollars and seventy-six cents

Your turn:

Use words to write 1? ¾

Write with a dollar sign : 8 cents

Write the value of two quarters, two dimes, and one penny.

Use words to write $12.25

$6.05-$2.53= $5.32+$8.99=

Use digits to write two hundred fifty million

Round 77 to the nearest ten

Round $7.82 to the nearest dollar

Multiplication facts 0s,1s,2s,3s,5s

0 x8	3 x 2	5 x 1	4 x 5	2 x 0	1 x 8	7 x 2	1 x1
5 x2	4 x0	2 x8	1 x 3	7 x 5	3 x3	8 x 5	0 x5
8 x1	6 x5	9 x0	2 x6	0 x1	4 x2	1 x6	9 x2
3 x7	3 x5	2 x3	4 x1	2 x2	8 x0	5 x9	1 x2
5 x5	1 x7	0 x0	8 x2	5 x8	5 x6	3 x0	9 x1
5 x3	0 x4	6 x1	9 x 5	5 x0	4 x3	2 x5	0 x9
6 x0	7 x3	2 x3	5 x7	3 x6	9 x3	7 x 0	5 x3
3 x3	9 x3	0 x7	3 x2	4 x3	7 x1	3 x5	8 x3
2 x1	6 x2	0 x7	9 x3	1 x4	2 x9	1 x0	5 x4
0 x2	1 x9	3 x1	2 x7	3 x1	1 x5	2 x4	0 x6

Possessive pronouns can also be possessive adjectives. They describe nouns.
His house is next door. (Which house is next door?)
Is that their yard?(Whose yard is that?)
That is my sister's bike. (my describes sister)

Write the noun the possessive adjective describes.

1. He left **his** hat on the bus.

2. **Our** family has always shopped in their store.

3. **Your** dog has a guilty look on its face.

4. WE are having **her** birthday party next Sunday.

5. **His** bike is missing.

READING

Your other task for the day is to read a book. At this point you should be able to read for ½ hour to 1 hour each day. Look online for a variety of book lists. You can also check out my site www.plainandnotsoplain.com and see all of the books that we have enjoyed at this grade level. Write the title of the book you are reading and how long you have read for.

_____

_____

```
E  W  T  R  J  S  U  G  D  N  W  O  O  L  I
Q  V  Q  F  H  B  N  D  K  Y  V  W  J  C  D
Z  J  O  C  K  I  D  O  N  O  S  P  H  U  H
B  B  I  P  R  L  E  L  T  U  U  M  O  S  F
P  T  R  U  K  U  R  V  B  R  G  W  R  H  J
C  U  D  Y  M  S  S  E  M  S  A  L  G  I  W
A  P  D  A  G  P  T  M  D  U  R  N  P  O  Q
K  G  M  D  S  A  O  G  A  U  T  O  N  N  D
I  B  N  P  I  H  O  W  I  K  E  T  O  L  V
C  E  R  E  V  N  D  P  W  F  O  E  Y  R  D
O  V  C  O  U  A  G  N  L  K  M  B  R  L  W
D  P  O  N  O  D  W  O  M  A  N  O  U  K  P
W  O  U  L  D  K  W  B  U  S  H  O  L  X  O
G  J  L  K  A  A  X  X  X  Y  H  K  B  P  T
N  I  D  V  R  G  I  A  N  S  Q  N  A  L  J
```

BROOK	BUSH	COULD
CUSHION	DURING	NOTEBOOK
PUDDING	SHOULD	SUGAR
UNDERSTOOD	WOLF	WOMAN
WOOL	WOULD	YOURS

149

We have learned that 100 pennies equals one dollar. Each penny is 1/100 of a dollar. Since 20 nickels equals a dollar, each nickel is 1/20 of a dollar. So we may describe part of a dollar by using a fraction or by using a dollar sign and a decimal point.

Three pennies are what fraction of a dollar? 3/100

Write the value of three pennies using a dollars sign and decimal point $0.03

Which coin equals one fourth of a dollar? A quarter

Write ¼ of a dollar using a dollar sign and a decimal point $0.25

Three dimes are what fraction of a dollar? 3/10

Your turn:

Write the value of three quarters using a dollar sign and a decimal point.

Write three quarters as a fraction of a dollar

Fifty pennies are what fraction of a dollar

Evan is 49 inches tall. His dad is 70 inches tall. Evan is how many inches shorter than his dad?

Lauren went to the pawn shop with $36.49. She bought a movie and left the store with $11.80. How much money did she spend?

Which letter has no right angles?   T H E N

Use digits to write eighty-two thousand, five hundred

Round 176 to nearest ten

Round $17.60 to nearest dollar

Multiplication facts 0s,1s,2s,3s,5s

0 x8	3 x 2	5 x 1	4 x 5	2 x 0	1 x 8	7 x 2	1 x1
5 x2	4 x0	2 x8	1 x 3	7 x 5	3 x3	8 x 5	0 x5
8 x1	6 x5	9 x0	2 x6	0 x1	4 x2	1 x6	9 x2
3 x7	3 x5	2 x3	4 x1	2 x2	8 x0	5 x9	1 x2
5 x5	1 x7	0 x0	8 x2	5 x8	5 x6	3 x0	9 x1
5 x3	0 x4	6 x1	9 x 5	5 x0	4 x3	2 x5	0 x9
6 x0	7 x3	2 x3	5 x7	3 x6	9 x3	7 x 0	5 x3
3 x3	9 x3	0 x7	3 x2	4 x3	7 x1	3 x5	8 x3
2 x1	6 x2	0 x7	9 x3	1 x4	2 x9	1 x0	5 x4
0 x2	1 x9	3 x1	2 x7	3 x1	1 x5	2 x4	0 x6

A number can be an adjective. Numbers describe by telling how many.

Twelve people came to the party.

Find the number words that are used as adjectives in the sentences. Draw a line to the word they describe.

1. Twenty-four people are coming to my party.

2. Two students dropped out of class.

3. After a few weeks, the teacher gave a test.

4. Several members of the class got a perfect grade.

5. Most students enjoyed the teacher.

READING

Your other task for the day is to read a book. At this point you should be able to read for ½ hour to 1 hour each day. Look online for a variety of book lists. You can also check out my site www.plainandnotsoplain.com and see all of the books that we have enjoyed at this grade level. Write the title of the book you are reading and how long you have read for.

_____

_____

Write a sentence for each of your words

Three quarters are what fraction of a dollar

Write the value of three quarters using a dollar sign and a decimal point

$4.99 +$2.88=   523- x= 145

28+46+64+32+344

Write 2503 in expanded form

Five hundred seventy-five thousand, five hundred forty-two in digits

Round 624 to nearest ten

Round $6.24 to nearest dollar

It is morning 7:25. What time will it be 5 hours and 15 minutes from now

Use words to write 2 1/3

Multiplication facts 0s,1s,2s,3s,5s

0 x8	3 x 2	5 x 1	4 x 5	2 x 0	1 x 8	7 x 2	1 x1
5 x2	4 x0	2 x8	1 x 3	7 x 5	3 x3	8 x 5	0 x5
8 x1	6 x5	9 x0	2 x6	0 x1	4 x2	1 x6	9 x2
3 x7	3 x5	2 x3	4 x1	2 x2	8 x0	5 x9	1 x2
5 x5	1 x7	0 x0	8 x2	5 x8	5 x6	3 x0	9 x1
5 x3	0 x4	6 x1	9 x 5	5 x0	4 x3	2 x5	0 x9
6 x0	7 x3	2 x3	5 x7	3 x6	9 x3	7 x 0	5 x3
3 x3	9 x3	0 x7	3 x2	4 x3	7 x1	3 x5	8 x3
2 x1	6 x2	0 x7	9 x3	1 x4	2 x9	1 x0	5 x4
0 x2	1 x9	3 x1	2 x7	3 x1	1 x5	2 x4	0 x6

Adjectives describe people or things. We also use adjectives to compare two or more people or things. Adjectives have three forms: positive form, the comparative form, and the superlative form.

positive form
describe one thing

comparative form
compare two things

superlative
compare more than two

strong
careful
good

stronger
more careful
better

strongest
most careful
best

1. Who is (taller, tallest) –Kim or Sue?

2. Mrs. Maryon knits the (softer, softest) blankets.

3. Mike is the (funnier, funniest) of all my friends.

4. Apple juice is the (tasty, tastiest).

5. I think apples are (sweeter, sweetest) than oranges.

Write the forms of the adjectives

POSITIVE	COMPARATIVE	SUPERLATIVE
young		
old		
kind		
slow		
high		

READING

Your other task for the day is to read a book. At this point you should be able to read for ½ hour to 1 hour each day. Look online for a variety of book lists. You can also check out my site www.plainandnotsoplain.com and see all of the books that we have enjoyed at this grade level. Write the title of the book you are reading and how long you have read for.

_____

_____

QUIZ

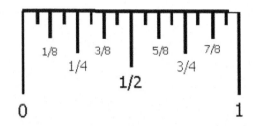

Notice the measurements on the above marker. We are going to measure to ¼ inch ½ inch and ¾ inch

Measure this line to the closest quarter inch

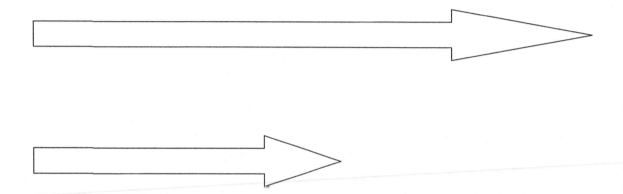

Ann is twelve years old. Ann's mother is thirty-five years old. Ann's mother is how many years older than Ann?

Four hundred sixty-eight thousand, five hundred two boxes were in the warehouse. Use digits to write that number of boxes.

Write the 3905 in expanded form.

893-677=   642+740=

Multiplication facts 0s,1s,2s,3s,5s

0 x8	3 x2	5 x 1	4 x 5	2 x 0	1 x 8	7 x 2	1 x1
5 x2	4 x0	2 x8	1 x 3	7 x 5	3 x3	8 x 5	0 x5
8 x1	6 x5	9 x0	2 x6	0 x1	4 x2	1 x6	9 x2
3 x7	3 x5	2 x3	4 x1	2 x2	8 x0	5 x9	1 x2
5 x5	1 x7	0 x0	8 x2	5 x8	5 x6	3 x0	9 x1
5 x3	0 x4	6 x1	9 x 5	5 x0	4 x3	2 x5	0 x9
6 x0	7 x3	2 x3	5 x7	3 x6	9 x3	7 x 0	5 x3
3 x3	9 x3	0 x7	3 x2	4 x3	7 x1	3 x5	8 x3
2 x1	6 x2	0 x7	9 x3	1 x4	2 x9	1 x0	5 x4
0 x2	1 x9	3 x1	2 x7	3 x1	1 x5	2 x4	0 x6

Some adjectives use the words more or most to compare. Longer adjectives use more or less to compare. and most or least.

popular   more popular   most popular

powerful   more/less powerful   most/least powerful

These are the irregular ones that don't follow any of the rules

good   better   best
bad   worse   worst

That is the (redder, reddest) sunset I have ever seen.

Which of those two buildings is (taller, tallest)?

That movie was the (goodest, best) I have ever seen.

Sia is (gracefuller, more graceful) than I could ever be.

bad		
	prettier	
	less difficult	
	worse	
popular		
generous		
	less comfortable	
		nicest

READING
Your other task for the day is to read a book. At this point you should be able to read for ½ hour to 1 hour each day. Look online for a variety of book lists. You can also check out my site www.plainandnotsoplain.com and see all of the books that we have enjoyed at this grade level. Write the title of the book you are reading and how long you have read for.

_____

_____

week 11 copy your spelling words

balloon

bruise

canoe

cartoon

choose

cougar

drew

group

lieutenant

loose

movable

route

shoot

through

troupe

321-199=   899+301=

Measurements

1 gallon of milk—for visual

4 quarts = one gallon   Think four quart jars for one gallon

2 pints—think two smaller glass jars = 1 quart

2 cups into 1 pint jar

How many ½ gallons in one gallon?

How many quarts in one gallon?

How many quarters equals a dollar?

Write the number 7,500,000 in expanded form

What digit is in the thousands place   27,384,509

536+n=621   416-g=323

What is the perimeter of a triangle with sides 4 cm, 2cm, and 3 cm

What is the sides of a square whose perimeter is 8 inches

432+890=   876-399=

Multiplication facts 0s,1s,2s,3s,5s

0 x8	3 x 2	5 x 1	4 x 5	2 x 0	1 x 8	7 x 2	1 x1
5 x2	4 x0	2 x8	1 x 3	7 x 5	3 x3	8 x 5	0 x5
8 x1	6 x5	9 x0	2 x6	0 x1	4 x2	1 x6	9 x2
3 x7	3 x5	2 x3	4 x1	2 x2	8 x0	5 x9	1 x2
5 x5	1 x7	0 x0	8 x2	5 x8	5 x6	3 x0	9 x1
5 x3	0 x4	6 x1	9 x 5	5 x0	4 x3	2 x5	0 x9
6 x0	7 x3	2 x3	5 x7	3 x6	9 x3	7 x 0	5 x3
3 x3	9 x3	0 x7	3 x2	4 x3	7 x1	3 x5	8 x3
2 x1	6 x2	0 x7	9 x3	1 x4	2 x9	1 x0	5 x4
0 x2	1 x9	3 x1	2 x7	3 x1	1 x5	2 x4	0 x6

REVIEW

Sarah was _____ to help than Russ.
   a) eagerest
   b) eager
   c) eagerer
   d) more eager

The day was clear and _____.
   a) bright
   b) brightly
   c) most bright
   d) brightest

She felt bad before the movie and _____ after.
   a) badder
   b) worst
   c) worse
   d) more worse

I am _____ than my brother.
   a) tall
   b) more tall
   c) tallest
   d) taller

READING
Your other task for the day is to read a book. At this point you should be able to read for ½ hour to 1 hour each day. Look online for a variety of book lists. You can also check out my site www.plainandnotsoplain.com and see all of the books that we have enjoyed at this grade level. Write the title of the book you are reading and how long you have read for.

_____

_____

```
B  N  Z  X  P  X  J  W  T  R  D  I  C  S  L
P  N  P  U  Z  J  H  N  D  Y  R  Y  H  F  V
G  K  A  B  R  U  I  S  E  Z  E  J  O  E  A
M  T  A  Y  M  Q  V  E  S  B  W  T  O  H  C
I  P  H  H  Z  O  N  E  D  G  R  H  S  Y  V
M  G  D  R  Z  O  V  U  R  Z  P  O  E  P  T
B  A  L  L  O  O  N  A  B  B  S  L  U  N  J
R  R  H  T  P  U  G  K  B  J  I  H  A  T  H
N  Z  R  G  Q  U  G  D  O  L  M  N  O  E  E
M  A  M  A  O  U  L  H  X  T  E  F  F  O  W
C  P  L  C  D  F  A  S  D  T  R  T  Q  W  T
M  Q  I  N  D  N  K  X  U  I  X  O  D  Z  G
Q  R  J  L  O  O  S  E  Z  F  M  R  U  K  D
U  H  R  T  K  R  I  P  H  G  R  O  U  P  H
D  U  L  L  G  L  R  G  C  F  C  A  N  O  E
```

BALLOON	BRUISE	CANOE
CARTOON	CHOOSE	COUGAR
DREW	GROUP	LIEUTENANT
LOOSE	MOVABLE	ROUTE
SHOOT	THROUGH	TROUPE

Now we are going to add the 4s for multiplication. Work on memorizing these facts

405
-126

In the above problem, we are going to have to regroup twice before we can do the ones place subtraction. We can't borrow from the "0" so we have to go to the "4" and then since we can't jump place values, we need to add it to the zero first and then we can borrow from the 0 to do the ones place.

```
 3   9
 4⁄0 ⁄5
-1 2 6
 2 7 9
```

Your turn: rewrite vertically

300-123=   803-179=

201-102=   703-198=

Use digits to write one million, fifty thousand

4x7=   6x4=   3x4=   2x4=

9x4=   8x4=   1x4=   4x5=

4 x0	3 x 2	5 x 1	4 x 5	2 x 0	1 x 8	7 x 2	1 x1
5 x2	4 x0	2 x8	1 x 4	7 x 5	3 x3	8 x 5	0 x5
8 x1	6 x5	9 x0	2 x4	0 x1	4 x2	1 x6	9 x2
3 x7	3 x5	4 x3	4 x1	2 x2	8 x0	5 x9	1 x2
5 x4	1 x7	0 x0	8 x2	5 x8	5 x6	3 x0	9 x1
5 x3	0 x4	6 x4	9 x 5	5 x0	4 x4	4 x8	0 x9
6 x0	7 x3	2 x3	4 x5	3 x6	9 x3	7 x 4	5 x3
3 x3	9 x3	0 x7	3 x2	4 x3	7 x4	3 x5	8 x3
4 x7	6 x2	4 x4	9 x3	1 x4	4 x9	1 x0	5 x4
0 x2	1 x9	3 x1	4 x7	3 x1	1 x5	2 x4	8 x4
1 x4	2 x1	4 x4	2 x7	0 x7	5 x7	2 x5	4 x9

A verb is a word that expresses action or state of being. An action verb is a word that expresses the action in a sentence. The verb tells what the subject does, did, or will do. The subject is the part of the sentence that tells who or what the sentence is about.

Find the verb by asking who or what is doing something or what are they doing.

Circle the verbs.

Mr Smith parked his car.

Several of his friends shouted and waved to him.

She likes all the people at the office.

Kelly called her boss.

Kelly reminded her about the meeting.

Some people sort mail.

The computer prints the checks.

READING
Your other task for the day is to read a book. At this point you should be able to read for ½ hour to 1 hour each day. Look online for a variety of book lists. You can also check out my site www.plainandnotsoplain.com and see all of the books that we have enjoyed at this grade level. Write the title of the book you are reading and how long you have read for.

_____

_____

Write a sentence for each of your words

The multiples of 10 are the numbers we say when we count by 10: 10,20,30,40…

Likewise the multiples of 100: 100,200,300,400…..

When multiplying by multiples of 10 and 100, we focus our attention on the first digit of the multiple.

3 x 200

We just multiple the 3 x2, which is 6 and then add two zeros== 600

5 x 40

We just multiple the 5 x 4, which is 20 and then add that zero==200

Round 472 to nearest hundred---look at the hundreds place and determine which hundreds its in between 400 and 500. Since 450 is the halfway point, 472 is above that so it rounds to 500.

If we were to round 472 to nearest ten. It is in between 470 and 480. Since 475 is the halfway point and it is less, we round down to 470

Round 5280 to nearest hundred. Since this would be 5200 or 5300, we know that 5250 is the halfway point and since it is more, we would round up to 5300.

Your turn:

Round to nearest hundred: 813   685   2573

50x7=   500x3=   6x400   6x40

2x200   2x20   4x100   5x50

4 x0	3 x 2	5 x 1	4 x 5	2 x 0	1 x 8	7 x 2	1 x1
5 x2	4 x0	2 x8	1 x 4	7 x 5	3 x3	8 x 5	0 x5
8 x1	6 x5	9 x0	2 x4	0 x1	4 x2	1 x6	9 x2
3 x7	3 x5	4 x3	4 x1	2 x2	8 x0	5 x9	1 x2
5 x4	1 x7	0 x0	8 x2	5 x8	5 x6	3 x0	9 x1
5 x3	0 x4	6 x4	9 x 5	5 x0	4 x4	4 x8	0 x9
6 x0	7 x3	2 x3	4 x5	3 x6	9 x3	7 x 4	5 x3
3 x3	9 x3	0 x7	3 x2	4 x3	7 x4	3 x5	8 x3
4 x7	6 x2	4 x4	9 x3	1 x4	4 x9	1 x0	5 x4
0 x2	1 x9	3 x1	4 x7	3 x1	1 x5	2 x4	8 x4
1 x4	2 x1	4 x4	2 x7	0 x7	5 x7	2 x5	4 x9

A verb phrase contains a main verb and one or more helping verbs. A main verb is the last verb in a verb phrasae.

Mr. Paul **has poured** his drink.

Paul **will come** to our home.

Underline the verb phrase.

Mrs. Anter had spoken to Mr. Franklin.

Later, she had remembered their friends.

She will recognize the problem eventually.

They will help each other out.

Mrs. Maryon has announced a new policy.

Circle the verbs:

Many different people work at the fire department.

The public appreciates their efforts.

Letter carriers load the mail into sacks.

Millions of pieces of mail travel from place to place.

Mom enjoys her work.

Dad helps her tonight.

READING

Your other task for the day is to read a book. At this point you should be able to read for ½ hour to 1 hour each day. Look online for a variety of book lists. You can also check out my site www.plainandnotsoplain.com and see all of the books that we have enjoyed at this grade level.

Write the title of the book you are reading and how long you have read for.

_____

_____

QUIZ

To add or subtract money amounts with a dollar sign and a decimal, we line up the decimal.

$3.45-$0.75= $5.35-$2=

$3.75+$4+ 15 cents

$1.46+ 87 cents   98 cents plus 89 cents

One hundred pennies are separated into two piles. In one pile there are thirty-five pennies. How many pennies are in the other pile?

Round 572 to nearest hundred

Round 572 to nearest ten

Are the rails of a railroad track parallel or perpendicular?

4 x0	3 x 2	5 x 1	4 x 5	2 x 0	1 x 8	7 x 2	1 x1
5 x2	4 x0	2 x8	1 x 4	7 x 5	3 x3	8 x 5	0 x5
8 x1	6 x5	9 x0	2 x4	0 x1	4 x2	1 x6	9 x2
3 x7	3 x5	4 x3	4 x1	2 x2	8 x0	5 x9	1 x2
5 x4	1 x7	0 x0	8 x2	5 x8	5 x6	3 x0	9 x1
5 x3	0 x4	6 x4	9 x 5	5 x0	4 x4	4 x8	0 x9
6 x0	7 x3	2 x3	4 x5	3 x6	9 x3	7 x 4	5 x3
3 x3	9 x3	0 x7	3 x2	4 x3	7 x4	3 x5	8 x3
4 x7	6 x2	4 x4	9 x3	1 x4	4 x9	1 x0	5 x4
0 x2	1 x9	3 x1	4 x7	3 x1	1 x5	2 x4	8 x4
1 x4	2 x1	4 x4	2 x7	0 x7	5 x7	2 x5	4 x9

The verb in a sentence expresses tense. A verb tense tells the time when an action takes place.

Present tense   play
past tense   played
future tense   will play

Write whether the verbs are present, past, or future tense.

1. I will play at the school tomorrow._____

2. He baked a cake on Saturday._____

3. She plays ball on the team._____

4. We will goto the park._____

5. I hated to leave my family._____

6. Please follow me._____

READING
Your other task for the day is to read a book. At this point you should be able to read for ½ hour to 1 hour each day. Look online for a variety of book lists. You can also check out my site www.plainandnotsoplain.com and see all of the books that we have enjoyed at this grade level. Write the title of the book you are reading and how long you have read for.

_____

_____

week 12 copy your words

appointment

avoid

choice

destroy

employer

enjoy

join

loyalty

moisture

poison

rejoice

royal

soybean

voice

voyage

It is 8:05am, what time was it two hours ago

If there are 21 children in each classroom, then how many children are in 3 classrooms?

We could add 21, three different times to get our answer, or learn the quick multiplication way

2 1
X 3

You multiply 3 x1 first. Then put your answer down. Then do 3x2.

21
X3
63

Your turn: rewrite them vertically

42 x3   31 x2   43x3

30x2   30x4   24x0

73x2   51x6   40x7

4 x0	3 x 2	5 x 1	4 x 5	2 x 0	1 x 8	7 x 2	1 x1
5 x2	4 x0	2 x8	1 x 4	7 x 5	3 x3	8 x 5	0 x5
8 x1	6 x5	9 x0	2 x4	0 x1	4 x2	1 x6	9 x2
3 x7	3 x5	4 x3	4 x1	2 x2	8 x0	5 x9	1 x2
5 x4	1 x7	0 x0	8 x2	5 x8	5 x6	3 x0	9 x1
5 x3	0 x4	6 x4	9 x 5	5 x0	4 x4	4 x8	0 x9
6 x0	7 x3	2 x3	4 x5	3 x6	9 x3	7 x 4	5 x3
3 x3	9 x3	0 x7	3 x2	4 x3	7 x4	3 x5	8 x3
4 x7	6 x2	4 x4	9 x3	1 x4	4 x9	1 x0	5 x4
0 x2	1 x9	3 x1	4 x7	3 x1	1 x5	2 x4	8 x4
1 x4	2 x1	4 x4	2 x7	0 x7	5 x7	2 x5	4 x9

Present perfect tense—shows an action started in the past and continuing to the present.
Amy has tackled this book.

Past perfect tense—shows one action completed before another action began.
Amy had tackled that topic before.

Future perfect—shows an action that will be completed before a certain time in the future.
Amy will have tackled that book in the next few days.

Underline the verb phrase

1. The team has scored many touchdowns.

2. The coach has ordered shirts for the players.

3. The team have earned the victory.

Underline the main verb and/or the helping verb

4. The quarterback has worked hard all day.

5. He has thrown several good passes.

6. The team has a good record so far.

7 They have one win and no losses.

8. The circus has arrived in town.

9. The clowns had thrown confetti into the crowd.

READING
Your other task for the day is to read a book. At this point you should be able to read for ½ hour to 1 hour each day. Look online for a variety of book lists. You can also check out my site www.plainandnotsoplain.com and see all of the books that we have enjoyed at this grade level. Write the title of the book you are reading and how long you have read for.

_____

_____

```
A  X  T  F  B  B  M  N  H  R  I  K  B  M  G
R  X  Y  A  P  E  Q  P  E  V  S  A  U  W  U
O  F  V  V  M  F  S  Y  F  N  O  P  U  U  U
Y  I  O  O  D  H  O  A  Y  E  Y  P  T  A  F
A  U  Y  I  P  L  P  V  C  V  B  O  N  Y  L
L  X  A  D  P  C  H  O  I  C  E  I  Y  V  R
D  A  G  M  S  X  A  I  D  C  A  N  C  J  E
L  Y  E  U  U  I  T  C  E  H  N  T  O  K  J
O  R  J  T  P  U  P  E  S  V  T  M  G  Z  O
Y  G  A  O  P  N  J  S  T  A  Q  E  R  L  I
A  T  J  B  I  O  K  T  R  Q  E  N  K  L  C
L  D  D  X  A  N  I  M  O  I  S  T  U  R  E
T  A  Z  B  F  T  I  S  Y  U  H  S  S  G  F
Y  J  L  M  M  I  R  O  O  E  N  J  O  Y  L
F  U  Y  W  T  H  K  M  B  N  Z  A  S  X  Y
```

APPOINTMENT	AVOID	CHOICE
DESTROY	EMPLOYER	ENJOY
JOIN	LOYALTY	MOISTURE
POISON	REJOICE	ROYAL
SOYBEAN	VOICE	VOYAGE

When you have parentheses in an arithmetic problem, we work inside the parentheses first.

2 x (3+4)

First add 3 +4=7, then 7 x2=14

Your turn:

3 x (4+5)

(3+3) x 2

8- (4+2)

9-(6-3)

3 x (10+20)

A whole hour is 60 minutes, how many minutes is half of an hour

How much change should you get back if you give the clerk $5 for a box of candy that costs $3.85

Write 234,540 in words

4 x0	3 x 2	5 x 1	4 x 5	2 x 0	1 x 8	7 x 2	1 x1
5 x2	4 x0	2 x8	1 x 4	7 x 5	3 x3	8 x 5	0 x5
8 x1	6 x5	9 x0	2 x4	0 x1	4 x2	1 x6	9 x2
3 x7	3 x5	4 x3	4 x1	2 x2	8 x0	5 x9	1 x2
5 x4	1 x7	0 x0	8 x2	5 x8	5 x6	3 x0	9 x1
5 x3	0 x4	6 x4	9 x 5	5 x0	4 x4	4 x8	0 x9
6 x0	7 x3	2 x3	4 x5	3 x6	9 x3	7 x 4	5 x3
3 x3	9 x3	0 x7	3 x2	4 x3	7 x4	3 x5	8 x3
4 x7	6 x2	4 x4	9 x3	1 x4	4 x9	1 x0	5 x4
0 x2	1 x9	3 x1	4 x7	3 x1	1 x5	2 x4	8 x4
1 x4	2 x1	4 x4	2 x7	0 x7	5 x7	2 x5	4 x9

Circle the correct form

1. Mrs. Maryon (be, was) the coach two years ago.

2. The children have already (eat, eaten) their lunch already.

3. They (do, done) their chores every night.

4. Mike has (cut, cuts) his finger.

5. I have (bend, bent) my bicycle wheel on the curb.

6. Steven has (know, known) Mike for many years.

7. Eliza has (write, written) her cousin in Washington.

8. Callie has (seen, see) that movie twice.

9. They had (know, known) each other for years.

10. Helen has (write, written) a poem for her mom.

READING
Your other task for the day is to read a book. At this point you should be able to read for ½ hour to 1 hour each day. Look online for a variety of book lists. You can also check out my site www.plainandnotsoplain.com and see all of the books that we have enjoyed at this grade level. Write the title of the book you are reading and how long you have read for.

_____

_____

Write a sentence for each of your words

Remember that multiplication problems have three numbers. The multiplied numbers are factors and the answer is product.
Factor x factor = product

If we know the two factors, we can multiply to get the product 4 x3=?   12
If we only know one factor and the product, you can use the missing factor by using division to find the number. Division "undoes" multiplication. Look at how to use the table to solve this
4 x ?=12

Times Table - 12x12

	1	2	3	4	5	6	7	8	9	10	11	12
1	1	2	3	4	5	6	7	8	9	10	11	12
2	2	4	6	8	10	12	14	16	18	20	22	24
3	3	6	9	12	15	18	21	24	27	30	33	36
4	4	8	12	16	20	24	28	32	36	40	44	48
5	5	10	15	20	25	30	35	40	45	50	55	60
6	6	12	18	24	30	36	42	48	54	60	66	72
7	7	14	21	28	35	42	49	56	63	70	77	84
8	8	16	24	32	40	48	56	64	72	80	88	96
9	9	18	27	36	45	54	63	72	81	90	99	108
10	10	20	30	40	50	60	70	80	90	100	110	120
11	11	22	33	44	55	66	77	88	99	110	121	132
12	12	24	36	48	60	72	84	96	108	120	132	144

Solve 32 ÷ 4= ,use the chart above to solve

18÷2=   21÷7=   30÷5=

48÷6=   40÷5=   12÷6=

Round 786 to nearest hundred

Round 786 to nearest ten

Draw and shade rectangles that show 2   1/3

Multiplication facts 0s, 1s, 2s, 3s, 4s, 5s 6s

4 x0	3 x 2	6 x 1	4 x 5	2 x 0	1 x 8	7 x 2	1 x1
5 x2	4 x0	2 x6	1 x 4	7 x 5	3 x6	8 x 5	0 x5
8 x1	6 x5	9 x0	2 x4	0 x1	4 x2	1 x6	9 x2
3 x7	3 x5	6 x3	4 x6	2 x2	8 x0	5 x9	1 x2
5 x4	1 x7	0 x0	8 x2	5 x8	5 x6	3 x0	9 x1
5 x3	0 x4	6 x4	9 x 5	5 x0	4 x4	4 x8	0 x9
6 x0	7 x3	2 x3	6 x5	3 x6	9 x3	7 x 4	5 x3
3 x3	9 x3	0 x7	3 x2	4 x3	7 x4	3 x5	8 x3
4 x7	6 x2	4 x4	9 x3	1 x6	4 x9	6 x6	5 x4
0 x2	6 x7	3 x1	4 x7	3 x1	1 x5	2 x4	8 x4
6 x9	2 x1	4 x4	6 x7	0 x7	5 x7	2 x5	6 x9

Choose the correct form

1. Ron has been (playing, played) the piano for several years.

2. He has (playing, played) in the school band for three years.

3. This year the band is (going, gone) to Florida for a national contest.

4. So far they have (raising, raised) more than one thousand dollars.

Write the singular and plural form of the following nouns

lots of…..	but only one….
lamps	lamp
stages	
inches	
cherries	
deer	
men	

READING

Your other task for the day is to read a book. At this point you should be able to read for ½ hour to 1 hour each day. Look online for a variety of book lists. You can also check out my site www.plainandnotsoplain.com and see all of the books that we have enjoyed at this grade level. Write the title of the book you are reading and how long you have read for.

_____

_____

QUIZ

There is more than one way to write a division problem. Here are three ways and they all say 20 divided by 5

$20 \div 5 =$ 	$\dfrac{20}{5}$ 	$5\overline{)20}$

In this math, we will do the first one typically

$36 \div 6 =$ 	$42 \div 6 =$ 	$12 \div 6 =$

$18 \div 6 =$ 	$30 \div 6 =$ 	$42 \div 6 =$

Use the digits 1,5,6,8 to write an even number greater than 8420

Write the value of five dimes using a dollar sign and decimal point

Round 3296 to nearest hundred

Use words to write 15,000,000

$95 - (3 \times 20)$ 	$\$2.53 + 45$ cents $+ 3$ cents

Is $12.90 closer to $12 or $13

Multiplication facts 0s, 1s, 2s, 3s, 4s, 5s 6s

4 x0	3 x 2	6 x 1	4 x 5	2 x 0	1 x 8	7 x 2	1 x1
5 x2	4 x0	2 x6	1 x 4	7 x 5	3 x6	8 x 5	0 x5
8 x1	6 x5	9 x0	2 x4	0 x1	4 x2	1 x6	9 x2
3 x7	3 x5	6 x3	4 x6	2 x2	8 x0	5 x9	1 x2
5 x4	1 x7	0 x0	8 x2	5 x8	5 x6	3 x0	9 x1
5 x3	0 x4	6 x4	9 x 5	5 x0	4 x4	4 x8	0 x9
6 x0	7 x3	2 x3	6 x5	3 x6	9 x3	7 x 4	5 x3
3 x3	9 x3	0 x7	3 x2	4 x3	7 x4	3 x5	8 x3
4 x7	6 x2	4 x4	9 x3	1 x6	4 x9	6 x6	5 x4
0 x2	6 x7	3 x1	4 x7	3 x1	1 x5	2 x4	8 x4
6 x9	2 x1	4 x4	6 x7	0 x7	5 x7	2 x5	6 x9

Pronoun review

1. The wet children left _____ drippy umbrellas hanging on the porch rail.
   a. his
   b. their
   c. her
   d. they
2. Soon, each umbrella had a good-sized puddle beneath_____.
   a. her
   b. they
   c. it
   d. him
3. Inside, _____ mother handed them fluffy towels.
   a. us
   b. your
   c. she
   d. their
4. "Gee, _____ is the worst rain storm all spring," the children remarked.
   a. these
   b. them
   c. they
   d. this
5. The fort,_____ was high on a hill, would be too muddy and slippery.
   a. whom
   b. whose
   c. who
   d. which
6. The children went to_____computer and checked a local weather site.
   a. their
   b. your
   c. they
   d. what

READING

Your other task for the day is to read a book. At this point you should be able to read for ½ hour to 1 hour each day. Look online for a variety of book lists. You can also check out my site www.plainandnotsoplain.com and see all of the books that we have enjoyed at this grade level. Write the title of the book you are reading and how long you have read for.

_____

_____

week 13 copy your words

beige

believe

conceited

eight

field

fiend

freight

friend

height

leisure

neighbor

receive

sleigh

thief

weigh

Two digit regroup multiplication

Often when we multiply the ones, the result is a two digit number. When this happens, we do not write both digits below the line. Instead, write the second digit above the tens column.

Seven times two is 14. We write the four and carry the one

$$
\begin{array}{r}
\overset{1}{1\,2} \\
\times\ 7 \\
\hline
8\,4
\end{array}
$$

Then we multiply the tens digit and add the digit that we carried above this column. Seven times one is seven, plus one is eight.

Your turn: write vertically

8 x 64   16 x4

24 x3   35x8

14 x3   42x8

100 + (4x50)   36÷6=

Multiplication facts 0s, 1s, 2s, 3s, 4s, 5s 6s

4 x0	3 x 2	6 x 1	4 x 5	2 x 0	1 x 8	7 x 2	1 x1
5 x2	4 x0	2 x6	1 x 4	7 x 5	3 x6	8 x 5	0 x5
8 x1	6 x5	9 x0	2 x4	0 x1	4 x2	1 x6	9 x2
3 x7	3 x5	6 x3	4 x6	2 x2	8 x0	5 x9	1 x2
5 x4	1 x7	0 x0	8 x2	5 x8	5 x6	3 x0	9 x1
5 x3	0 x4	6 x4	9 x 5	5 x0	4 x4	4 x8	0 x9
6 x0	7 x3	2 x3	6 x5	3 x6	9 x3	7 x 4	5 x3
3 x3	9 x3	0 x7	3 x2	4 x3	7 x4	3 x5	8 x3
4 x7	6 x2	4 x4	9 x3	1 x6	4 x9	6 x6	5 x4
0 x2	6 x7	3 x1	4 x7	3 x1	1 x5	2 x4	8 x4
6 x9	2 x1	4 x4	6 x7	0 x7	5 x7	2 x5	6 x9

Verb review

1. Jenny and I decided to _____ members of the camera club.
   a. become
   b. becoming
   c. became
2. We_____meetings twice a week—on Tuesday and Saturday.
   a. has
   b. have
   c. having
3. Our advisor_____once a photojournalist in Chicago.
   a. were
   b. will
   c. was
4. Each member may also_____--a digital camera to use.
   a. borrowed
   b. borrowing
   c. borrow
5. We are _____--to capture a scene to make it interesting.
   a. learned
   b. learn
   c. learning
6. We hope you can_____to the party where we will celebrate together.
   a. coming
   b. came
   c. come
7. The evening will _____with a short skit about photography.
   a. begun
   b. began
   c. begin

READING

Your other task for the day is to read a book. At this point you should be able to read for ½ hour to 1 hour each day. Look online for a variety of book lists. You can also check out my site www.plainandnotsoplain.com and see all of the books that we have enjoyed at this grade level. Write the title of the book you are reading and how long you have read for.

_____

_____

```
G  Z  Z  H  E  I  G  H  T  V  W  C  H  J  T
C  Y  Y  T  E  M  M  Y  N  H  E  G  K  H  Z
E  R  E  C  E  I  V  E  D  F  I  E  L  D  P
K  R  I  T  Y  A  F  E  H  E  B  E  U  D  G
F  R  I  E  N  D  T  J  W  D  Q  M  F  D  R
N  Y  E  W  D  I  B  S  K  A  L  M  B  H  E
Y  E  X  I  E  Z  H  M  B  Y  O  I  W  V  I
O  V  I  C  A  G  L  E  I  S  U  R  E  L  J
C  C  N  G  I  X  D  X  R  E  J  I  R  Y  Q
Q  O  E  H  P  Y  B  F  G  L  C  B  A  D
C  O  L  M  U  B  N  O  E  E  E  I  S  Q  F
V  S  Z  X  A  M  O  G  B  I  I  R  N  I  I
J  Q  N  U  U  G  R  T  G  G  N  D  G  E
A  C  S  P  Z  F  Z  Y  D  U  H  E  L  Q  N
V  F  R  E  I  G  H  T  O  V  T  B  E  X  D
```

BEIGE	BELIEVE	CONCEITED
EIGHT	FIELD	FIEND
FREIGHT	FRIEND	HEIGHT
LEISURE	NEIGHBOR	RECEIVE
SLEIGH	THIEF	WEIGH

We have added and subtracted decimal numbers by lining up the decimal points and adding or subtracting the digits in each column. We line up the decimal points to ensure that we are adding and subtracting digits with the same place value.

hundreds	tens	ones	decimal	tenths 1/10	hundredths 1/100
4	3	2	.	5	6

432.56

Notice the places to the right of the decimal end in "ths"

Name the place value of the 3 in each number

23.4=ones   2.34=tenths   32.4=tens   4.23=hundredths

Add 3.75+12.5+2.47

```
  3.75
12.5    -it helps to add a zero to hold a place here
+2.47
```

```
  3.75
12.50
+2.47
18.72
```

Subtract 4.25
        -2.5____treat this empty space with a zero

```
 4.25
-2.50
```

Your turn:

4.35 + 2.6   4.35-2.6

12.1+3.25   0.75-0.7

4 x0	3 x 2	6 x 1	4 x 5	2 x 0	1 x 8	7 x 2	1 x1
5 x2	4 x0	2 x6	1 x 4	7 x 5	3 x6	8 x 5	0 x5
8 x1	6 x5	9 x0	2 x4	0 x1	4 x2	1 x6	9 x2
3 x7	3 x5	6 x3	4 x6	2 x2	8 x0	5 x9	1 x2
5 x4	1 x7	0 x0	8 x2	5 x8	5 x6	3 x0	9 x1
5 x3	0 x4	6 x4	9 x 5	5 x0	4 x4	4 x8	0 x9
6 x0	7 x3	2 x3	6 x5	3 x6	9 x3	7 x 4	5 x3
3 x3	9 x3	0 x7	3 x2	4 x3	7 x4	3 x5	8 x3
4 x7	6 x2	4 x4	9 x3	1 x6	4 x9	6 x6	5 x4
0 x2	6 x7	3 x1	4 x7	3 x1	1 x5	2 x4	8 x4
6 x9	2 x1	4 x4	6 x7	0 x7	5 x7	2 x5	6 x9

Linking verbs

1. Last spring, my brother and I _____ helping Uncle Sam, who is a rancher.
   a. are
   b. was
   c. were
   d. have been
2. The first day we go there-it _____ a Friday—we will see the horses.
   a. has been
   b. was
   c. may be
   d. was being
3. That was the first time I _____ so close to such a big newborn animal.
   a. being
   b. were
   c. have been
   d. had been
4. Just before the birth, the mother horse_____ quietly pacing in her stall.
   a. had been
   b. has been
   c. were
   d. would be
5. The newborn's wobbly legs _____ longer than its body, yet the baby stood right up.
   a. are
   b. was
   c. were
   d. have been
6. We had such a great time on the ranch, Uncle Sam predicted that we _____ back soon.
   a. was
   b. would be
   c. were
   d. have been

READING

Your other task for the day is to read a book. At this point you should be able to read for ½ hour to 1 hour each day. Look online for a variety of book lists. You can also check out my site www.plainandnotsoplain.com and see all of the books that we have enjoyed at this grade level. Write the title of the book you are reading and how long you have read for.

_____

_____

Write a sentence for each of your words

Adding numbers with more than three digits

We do the same as we have done before with adding, start with the ones column and move to the left. Carry, when needed.

$$\begin{array}{r} \overset{\text{\small\textbackslash\ \ \textbackslash\ \textbackslash}}{43,287} \\ +68,595 \\ \hline 111,882 \end{array}$$

Add 456+1327+52+3624   Put vertically, you should get 5459

4356+5644   46,027+39,682

To check a division problem, we can multiply to check

21 ÷3=7   or we can say 7x3=21

Divide and check by multiplication:

49÷7   42÷6=   14÷7=   28÷7=

35÷7=   35÷5=   21÷3=   21÷7=

4 x0	3 x 2	6 x 7	4 x 5	2 x 0	1 x 8	7 x 2	1 x1
5 x2	4 x0	2 x6	5 x 7	7 x 5	3 x6	8 x 5	0 x5
8 x1	6 x5	9 x0	2 x4	0 x1	4 x2	1 x6	9 x2
3 x7	3 x5	6 x3	4 x6	2 x2	8 x0	5 x9	1 x2
5 x4	1 x7	7 x7	8 x2	5 x8	5 x6	3 x0	9 x1
5 x3	7 x4	6 x4	9 x 5	5 x0	4 x4	4 x8	7 x9
6 x0	7 x3	2 x3	6 x5	3 x6	9 x3	7 x 4	5 x3
3 x3	9 x3	0 x7	3 x2	4 x3	7 x4	3 x5	8 x3
4 x7	6 x2	4 x4	9 x3	1 x6	4 x9	6 x6	5 x4
8 x7	6 x7	3 x1	4 x7	3 x1	7 x5	2 x4	8 x4
6 x9	2 x1	4 x4	6 x7	4 x7	5 x7	2 x5	6 x9

Subject-verb agreement

A verb must agree in number (singular or plural) with its subject.

Jack (hope, hopes) to win the race.

They (love, loves) history class.

I (want, wants) a new box of colored pencils.

He (watch, watches) his neighbor's dog.

The robin (fly, flies) to the feeder.

All of the noise (has, have) stopped.

Anyone (is, are) welcome at the play.

None of us(are, is) going.

None of you(need, needs) braces.

Most of the teachers (eats, eat) lunch in the faculty room.

Everyone (is, are) coming to the football game.

Few of them (was, were) prepared for the exam.

Both of you (need, needs) to finish getting dressed now.

Several of the students (choose, chooses) hot food for lunch.

READING

Your other task for the day is to read a book. At this point you should be able to read for ½ hour to 1 hour each day. Look online for a variety of book lists. You can also check out my site www.plainandnotsoplain.com and see all of the books that we have enjoyed at this grade level. Write the title of the book you are reading and how long you have read for.

_____

_____

QUIZ

Subtracting using more than three digits. Same concepts just work from column to column. Rewrite them vertically.

36,125-9,415

$5000- $2345=

4783-2497   4000-257 $20.00-$12.25

What are next three numbers:

.....6000,7000,8000,_____,_____,_____

49 x6 rewrite vertically   70 x 8

4 x0	3 x 2	6 x 7	4 x 5	2 x 0	1 x 8	7 x 2	1 x1
5 x2	4 x0	2 x6	5 x 7	7 x 5	3 x6	8 x 5	0 x5
8 x1	6 x5	9 x0	2 x4	0 x1	4 x2	1 x6	9 x2
3 x7	3 x5	6 x3	4 x6	2 x2	8 x0	5 x9	1 x2
5 x4	1 x7	7 x7	8 x2	5 x8	5 x6	3 x0	9 x1
5 x3	7 x4	6 x4	9 x 5	5 x0	4 x4	4 x8	7 x9
6 x0	7 x3	2 x3	6 x5	3 x6	9 x3	7 x 4	5 x3
3 x3	9 x3	0 x7	3 x2	4 x3	7 x4	3 x5	8 x3
4 x7	6 x2	4 x4	9 x3	1 x6	4 x9	6 x6	5 x4
8 x7	6 x7	3 x1	4 x7	3 x1	7 x5	2 x4	8 x4
6 x9	2 x1	4 x4	6 x7	4 x7	5 x7	2 x5	6 x9

The audience (like,likes) the performance.

The group (was, were) planning a party.

I hope the team(score, scores).

Your club (meet, meets) on Friday.

The troop (hold,holds) an annual party.

The troop (meet, meets) after lunch.

The jury (was, were) undecided.

The committee (record, records) the facts.

Jay (teach, teaches) people to play tennis.

He (participated, participate) in the tournament.

None of the workers (is, are) finished.

Anyone (is, are) invited.

None of us (has, have) prepared.

All of the students (go, goes) to the pep rally.

READING

Your other task for the day is to read a book. At this point you should be able to read for ½ hour to 1 hour each day. Look online for a variety of book lists. You can also check out my site www.plainandnotsoplain.com and see all of the books that we have enjoyed at this grade level. Write the title of the book you are reading and how long you have read for.

_____

_____

week 14 copy your spelling words

alphabetize

arise

concise

enterprise

justice

memorize

office

police

price

prize

service

surmise

surprise

twice

wise

Division with remainder

WE can divide 12 objects into equal groups of 4.

WE get 3 groups.

However, we cannot divide 13 objects into equal groups of 4.

We get 3 groups with one leftover. This is called the remainder

```
      3 r 1
    _____
 4 |  13
     -12
       1
```

```
           5 r 1
         _____
Divide  3 |  16        We have to know how many times 3 can go into 16 =5
           -15
             1
```

You try: 20÷6

15÷2   26÷5

Which months have exactly 30 days

Round 4728 to nearest hundred

Round 4728 to nearest ten

Multiplication facts 0-7

4 x0	3 x 2	6 x 7	4 x 5	2 x 0	1 x 8	7 x 2	1 x1
5 x2	4 x0	2 x6	5 x 7	7 x 5	3 x6	8 x 5	0 x5
8 x1	6 x5	9 x0	2 x4	0 x1	4 x2	1 x6	9 x2
3 x7	3 x5	6 x3	4 x6	2 x2	8 x0	5 x9	1 x2
5 x4	1 x7	7 x7	8 x2	5 x8	5 x6	3 x0	9 x1
5 x3	7 x4	6 x4	9 x 5	5 x0	4 x4	4 x8	7 x9
6 x0	7 x3	2 x3	6 x5	3 x6	9 x3	7 x 4	5 x3
3 x3	9 x3	0 x7	3 x2	4 x3	7 x4	3 x5	8 x3
4 x7	6 x2	4 x4	9 x3	1 x6	4 x9	6 x6	5 x4
8 x7	6 x7	3 x1	4 x7	3 x1	7 x5	2 x4	8 x4
6 x9	2 x1	4 x4	6 x7	4 x7	5 x7	2 x5	6 x9

Every day Ken will (exercise, exercises) at the gym.

They could (exercise, exercises) on a regular basis.

Julie (might, mights) exercise today.

He would (goes, go) every day if he had the time.

Karen (must, musts) leave early.

I could (win, wins) if I tried.

(May, Mays) I take your picture?

The train (will, wills) leave at noon.

Did Paul_____home yet?
   a) go
   b) went
   c) goes
   d) going
The herd_____over the hill.
   a) runned
   b) running
   c) run
   d) runs
Yesterday there _____jugglers and clowns at the party.
   a) is
   b) was
   c) am
   d) be

READING
Your other task for the day is to read a book. At this point you should be able to read for ½ hour to 1 hour each day. Look online for a variety of book lists. You can also check out my site www.plainandnotsoplain.com and see all of the books that we have enjoyed at this grade level. Write the title of the book you are reading and how long you have read for.

_____

_____

```
X  M  T  B  K  K  J  S  D  H  U  R  M  C  N
D  C  A  L  P  H  A  B  E  T  I  Z  E  O  W
N  E  W  M  U  R  D  Q  C  B  M  S  M  N  I
W  R  N  O  V  N  B  P  R  G  I  O  O  C  S
Y  W  S  Q  U  A  E  M  X  R  P  R  R  I  E
F  F  M  A  R  I  S  E  P  D  X  T  I  S  C
W  P  R  I  C  E  H  R  Q  Y  O  X  Z  E  F
T  U  L  Z  D  J  U  S  T  I  C  E  E  U  X
G  K  A  T  L  S  U  R  M  I  S  E  S  B  E
S  B  S  E  N  T  E  R  P  R  I  S  E  C  X
L  O  Y  E  O  Y  O  P  K  R  E  C  I  B  P
T  O  X  E  R  S  B  Y  V  Q  I  W  G  H  R
J  Z  K  M  N  L  K  O  D  L  T  N  N  B  I
L  O  F  F  I  C  E  S  O  S  F  R  R  G  Z
S  E  R  V  I  C  E  P  N  P  A  R  N  G  E
```

ALPHABETIZE	ARISE	CONCISE
ENTERPRISE	JUSTICE	MEMORIZE
OFFICE	POLICE	PRICE
PRIZE	SERVICE	SURMISE
SURPRISE	TWICE	WISE

213

A year is the length of time it takes the Earth to travel around the sun. A day is the length of time it takes the Earth to spin around once on its axis. It takes the Earth exactly 365 ¼ days to travel around the sun. To make the number of days in every year a whole number, we have three years in a row that have 365 days each. These years are called common years. Then we have one year that has 366 days. This is called a leap year.

A year is divided into 12 months. The month of February has 28 days in a common year and 29 in a leap year. Four months have 30 days each. The rest have 31. If we can remember this poem, it will help us to remember how many days are in each month:

Thirty days hath September
April, June, and November
February has twenty-eight alone,
All the rest have thirty-one
Except in leap year,when February's days are 29

A decade is ten years. A century is one hundred years.

How many days does December have?

How many years were there from 1630 to 1776?

Rounding a number to the nearest thousand. We find the multiples of 1000 to which the number is closest. 1000,2000,3000.....etc
Round 7836 to nearest thousand.
Its in between 7000 and 8000 and halfway would be 7500. Since it is more, then it rounds to 8000.

Round 34,186 to nearest thousands. Since it is in between 34,000 and 35,000 and halfway is 34,500 it is less. So it rounds to 34,000

Your turn:
Round 5486 to nearest thousand

How many days in a leap year

A century is how many decades

Round 21,694 to nearest thousand

4 x0	3 x 2	6 x 7	4 x 5	2 x 0	1 x 8	7 x 2	1 x1
5 x2	4 x0	2 x6	5 x 7	7 x 5	3 x6	8 x 5	0 x5
8 x1	6 x5	9 x0	2 x4	0 x1	4 x2	1 x6	9 x2
3 x7	3 x5	6 x3	4 x6	2 x2	8 x0	5 x9	1 x2
5 x4	1 x7	7 x7	8 x2	5 x8	5 x6	3 x0	9 x1
5 x3	7 x4	6 x4	9 x 5	5 x0	4 x4	4 x8	7 x9
6 x0	7 x3	2 x3	6 x5	3 x6	9 x3	7 x 4	5 x3
3 x3	9 x3	0 x7	3 x2	4 x3	7 x4	3 x5	8 x3
4 x7	6 x2	4 x4	9 x3	1 x6	4 x9	6 x6	5 x4
8 x7	6 x7	3 x1	4 x7	3 x1	7 x5	2 x4	8 x4
6 x9	2 x1	4 x4	6 x7	4 x7	5 x7	2 x5	6 x9

Will Carol _____at the meeting tomorrow?

    a) be

    b) been

    c) being

    d) is

She_____almost always on time.

    a) be

    b) been

    c) is

    d) being

They_____old friends of Sarah's.

    a) is

    b) be

    c) was

    d) are

Everyone_____happy about the news.

    a) were

    b) be

    c) was

    d) been

Kelly _____-glad about the new car.

    a) seem

    b) seems

    c) seeming

    d) do seem

READING

Your other task for the day is to read a book. At this point you should be able to read for ½ hour to 1 hour each day. Look online for a variety of book lists. You can also check out my site www.plainandnotsoplain.com and see all of the books that we have enjoyed at this grade level. Write the title of the book you are reading and how long you have read for.

_____

_____

Write a sentence for each of your words

There were 7 students in each row. If there were 56 students in all, how many rows were there?

There were 7 nails in each board. If there were 42 boards, how many nails were there?

How many years is 5 decades?

Round 5236 to nearest thousand

Round 6929 to nearest thousand

When I opened my piggy bank, I found 17 pennies, 4 nickels, 5 dimes, and 2 quarters. What is the value of the money I found?

784,250 +9,284= $51,236+$36,357=

41,212-29,899=   2942-1879

39x8   54x8

43÷7   64÷8

What is the perimeter of a square with sides measuring 8 inches

Multiplication facts 0-8

4 x0	3 x 2	6 x 7	8 x2	4 x 5	2 x 0	1 x 8	7 x 2	1 x1
5 x2	4 x0	3 x8	2 x6	5 x 7	7 x 5	3 x6	8 x 5	0 x5
8 x1	6 x5	9 x0	8 x4	2 x4	0 x1	4 x2	1 x6	9 x2
3 x7	3 x5	6 x3	1 x7	4 x6	2 x2	8 x0	5 x9	1 x2
5 x4	8 x3	7 x7	8 x5	8 x2	5 x8	5 x6	3 x0	9 x1
5 x3	7 x4	6 x4	9 x3	9 x 5	5 x0	4 x4	4 x8	7 x9
6 x0	7 x3	2 x3	7 x8	6 x5	3 x6	6 x8	7 x 4	5 x3
3 x3	9 x3	0 x7	6 x6	3 x2	4 x3	7 x4	3 x5	8 x3
4 x7	6 x2	4 x4	9 x8	9 x3	1 x6	4 x9	8 x8	5 x4
8 x7	6 x7	3 x1	5 x7	4 x7	3 x1	7 x5	2 x4	8 x4
6 x9	2 x1	4 x4	8 x3	6 x7	4 x7	7 x8	2 x5	6 x9

Homophones. For each pair of homophones, write a single sentence that contains both words.

hear, here

_____

guessed, guest

_____

new, knew

_____

right, write

_____

there, their

_____

wood, would

_____

chews, choose

_____

weather, whether

_____

READING
Your other task for the day is to read a book. At this point you should be able to read for ½ hour to 1 hour each day. Look online for a variety of book lists. You can also check out my site www.plainandnotsoplain.com and see all of the books that we have enjoyed at this grade level. Write the title of the book you are reading and how long you have read for.

_____

_____

QUIZ

Multiples

If we multiply 4 by the numbers 1,2,3,4,5,6...we get

4,8,12,16,20,24,30....

These numbers are multiples of 4. Or we could count by 4s

The following are multiples of 6:

6,12,18,24,30,36.....

Your turn: List the first four multiples of 5

What is the third multiple of 8

What are the first five multiples of ten

Draw a rectangle that is 4 cm long and 3 cm wide

It is 3:50 in the afternoon. What time was it 30 minutes ago?

How long is this in centimeters

How long in inches to nearest ¼ inch

4 x0	3 x 2	6 x 7	8 x2	4 x 5	2 x 0	1 x 8	7 x 2	1 x1
5 x2	4 x0	3 x8	2 x6	5 x 7	7 x 5	3 x6	8 x 5	0 x5
8 x1	6 x5	9 x0	8 x4	2 x4	0 x1	4 x2	1 x6	9 x2
3 x7	3 x5	6 x3	1 x7	4 x6	2 x2	8 x0	5 x9	1 x2
5 x4	8 x3	7 x7	8 x5	8 x2	5 x8	5 x6	3 x0	9 x1
5 x3	7 x4	6 x4	9 x3	9 x 5	5 x0	4 x4	4 x8	7 x9
6 x0	7 x3	2 x3	7 x8	6 x5	3 x6	6 x8	7 x 4	5 x3
3 x3	9 x3	0 x7	6 x6	3 x2	4 x3	7 x4	3 x5	8 x3
4 x7	6 x2	4 x4	9 x8	9 x3	1 x6	4 x9	8 x8	5 x4
8 x7	6 x7	3 x1	5 x7	4 x7	3 x1	7 x5	2 x4	8 x4
6 x9	2 x1	4 x4	8 x3	6 x7	4 x7	7 x8	2 x5	6 x9

What is an adverb? An adverb is a word that answers questions about a verb, an adjective, or another adverb.

They usually end in –ly. They answer the question, how, when, where, and to what extent.

Circle the adverb in the sentence below. They answer the questions when or how often.

Please begin immediately!

I will go first.

They jumped up instantly.

Lois hit a home run today.

I saw the movie before.

The weather has been nice lately.

Circle the adverbs that answers questions where or in what direction.

The team advanced the ball forward.

The storm was near.

Turn right at the corner.

Hang your coats here.

READING

Your other task for the day is to read a book. At this point you should be able to read for ½ hour to 1 hour each day. Look online for a variety of book lists. You can also check out my site www.plainandnotsoplain.com and see all of the books that we have enjoyed at this grade level.

Write the title of the book you are reading and how long you have read for.

_____

_____

week 15 copy your words

coffee

cough

different

elephant

elf

enough

graph

half

laughter

oneself

photo

rough

sniffle

telephone

tough

$5.00-$2.25 $5.00-$1.63

560-200   35+49+110

When we multiply a three digit number, we multiply the ones first, then the tens and then the hundreds.

If we have to carry, we do and then add it to the answer

```
  3 2
  6 5 4
X   7
  4578
```

Your turn

375 x 3 rewrite vertically

234 x 3   340 x 4   4.25 x 5

4 x0	3 x 2	6 x 7	8 x2	4 x 5	2 x 0	1 x 8	7 x 2	1 x1
5 x2	4 x0	3 x8	2 x6	5 x 7	7 x 5	3 x6	8 x 5	0 x5
8 x1	6 x5	9 x0	8 x4	2 x4	0 x1	4 x2	1 x6	9 x2
3 x7	3 x5	6 x3	1 x7	4 x6	2 x2	8 x0	5 x9	1 x2
5 x4	8 x3	7 x7	8 x5	8 x2	5 x8	5 x6	3 x0	9 x1
5 x3	7 x4	6 x4	9 x3	9 x 5	5 x0	4 x4	4 x8	7 x9
6 x0	7 x3	2 x3	7 x8	6 x5	3 x6	6 x8	7 x 4	5 x3
3 x3	9 x3	0 x7	6 x6	3 x2	4 x3	7 x4	3 x5	8 x3
4 x7	6 x2	4 x4	9 x8	9 x3	1 x6	4 x9	8 x8	5 x4
8 x7	6 x7	3 x1	5 x7	4 x7	3 x1	7 x5	2 x4	8 x4
6 x9	2 x1	4 x4	8 x3	6 x7	4 x7	7 x8	2 x5	6 x9

Adverbs answer questions about adjectives and other adverbs. The answer the questions: how much how little, how often, and to what degree.

Circle the adverb

His old truck is so noisy.

Your puppy is quite friendly.

That is an unusually large pumpkin.

He has an extremely bad headache.

Mike has a rather interesting idea for the project.

I am almost ready to go.

Do your homework carefully.

The band played unusually well.

He went far away.

READING

Your other task for the day is to read a book. At this point you should be able to read for ½ hour to 1 hour each day. Look online for a variety of book lists. You can also check out my site www.plainandnotsoplain.com and see all of the books that we have enjoyed at this grade level. Write the title of the book you are reading and how long you have read for.

_____

_____

```
R  E  E  E  P  C  J  S  Z  C  I  R  G  H  Q
D  C  O  F  F  E  E  K  W  O  V  Q  A  J  Z
W  R  T  B  N  E  L  E  P  H  A  N  T  G  Y
G  O  P  P  H  O  T  O  Z  O  T  E  K  R  T
M  U  X  J  P  C  K  O  T  N  Y  Q  R  A  E
V  G  Y  M  G  R  Z  W  A  E  I  T  Y  P  B
G  H  B  S  X  G  P  L  D  S  H  S  V  H  I
L  T  F  C  K  Y  X  C  I  E  H  A  B  G  J
I  A  D  M  K  Z  I  P  F  L  D  P  L  X  K
J  N  U  A  H  S  N  I  F  F  L  E  E  F  R
F  F  Q  G  L  G  L  Z  E  L  F  V  X  Z  G
C  M  U  K  H  N  W  R  R  A  P  E  R  H  S
X  O  M  T  L  T  E  L  E  P  H  O  N  E  U
C  G  K  O  T  E  E  E  N  O  U  G  H  L  Q
L  T  O  U  G  H  N  R  T  L  R  D  E  Y  Z
```

COFFEE	COUGH	DIFFERENT
ELEPHANT	ELF	ENOUGH
GRAPH	HALF	LAUGHTER
ONESELF	PHOTO	ROUGH
SNIFFLE	TELEPHONE	TOUGH

It takes 4 apples to make one pie. How many apples does it take to make 5 pies. Use a multiplication pattern to solve

59 x 6   397x4

29÷7   42÷5

585-294   82-39

59+68+81   607+891

Use digits to write fifteen million, two hundred ten thousand

4 x0	3 x 2	6 x 7	8 x2	4 x 5	2 x 0	1 x 8	7 x 2	1 x1
5 x2	4 x0	3 x8	2 x6	5 x 7	7 x 5	3 x6	8 x 5	0 x5
8 x1	6 x5	9 x0	8 x4	2 x4	0 x1	4 x2	1 x6	9 x2
3 x7	3 x5	6 x3	1 x7	4 x6	2 x2	8 x0	5 x9	1 x2
5 x4	8 x3	7 x7	8 x5	8 x2	5 x8	5 x6	3 x0	9 x1
5 x3	7 x4	6 x4	9 x3	9 x 5	5 x0	4 x4	4 x8	7 x9
6 x0	7 x3	2 x3	7 x8	6 x5	3 x6	6 x8	7 x 4	5 x3
3 x3	9 x3	0 x7	6 x6	3 x2	4 x3	7 x4	3 x5	8 x3
4 x7	6 x2	4 x4	9 x8	9 x3	1 x6	4 x9	8 x8	5 x4
8 x7	6 x7	3 x1	5 x7	4 x7	3 x1	7 x5	2 x4	8 x4
6 x9	2 x1	4 x4	8 x3	6 x7	4 x7	7 x8	2 x5	6 x9

Sometimes people are not sure whether a word is an adjective or an adverb.

An adjective describes a noun or pronoun. For ex: Julie is tall.
An adverbs answers a question about a verb, an adjective, or another adverb.
For ex: Julie walked outside.

Write whether the bold word is an adjective or adverb.

Bill is **late**._____

He is **here**._____

She works **hard**._____

Sam lives **here**._____

Today we ran._____

We looked **up**._____

He runs **fast**._____

He is a **fast** runner._____

Speak **clearly!**_____

Is this the **early** show?_____

READING
Your other task for the day is to read a book. At this point you should be able to read for ½ hour to 1 hour each day. Look online for a variety of book lists. You can also check out my site www.plainandnotsoplain.com and see all of the books that we have enjoyed at this grade level. Write the title of the book you are reading and how long you have read for.

_____

_____

Write a sentence for each of your words

Mike can sharpen 5 pencils in a minute. How long will it take him to sharpen 40 pencils?

Alex was paid $40 for 5 hours of work. How much money was he paid for each hour of work?

Round 286 to nearest hundred

Round 415 to nearest ten

Write a quarter to seven in the morning   a quarter after three in afternoon

350x 5=   204x7

4 x0	3 x 2	6 x 7	8 x2	4 x 5	2 x 0	1 x 8	7 x 2	1 x1
5 x2	4 x0	3 x8	2 x6	5 x 7	7 x 5	3 x6	8 x 5	0 x5
8 x1	6 x5	9 x0	8 x4	2 x4	0 x1	4 x2	1 x6	9 x2
3 x7	3 x5	6 x3	1 x7	4 x6	2 x2	8 x0	5 x9	1 x2
5 x4	8 x3	7 x7	8 x5	8 x2	5 x8	5 x6	3 x0	9 x1
5 x3	7 x4	6 x4	9 x3	9 x 5	5 x0	4 x4	4 x8	7 x9
6 x0	7 x3	2 x3	7 x8	6 x5	3 x6	6 x8	7 x 4	5 x3
3 x3	9 x3	0 x7	6 x6	3 x2	4 x3	7 x4	3 x5	8 x3
4 x7	6 x2	4 x4	9 x8	9 x3	1 x6	4 x9	8 x8	5 x4
8 x7	6 x7	3 x1	5 x7	4 x7	3 x1	7 x5	2 x4	8 x4
6 x9	2 x1	4 x4	8 x3	6 x7	4 x7	7 x8	2 x5	6 x9

REVIEW

Circle all the adverbs

1. A heavy snowfall arrived early in December.

2. At home Sam was not so pleased.

3. He went to work anyway.

4. She danced gracefully.

5. The class did_____-on the test.
    a) good
    b) well
    c) bad
    d) gooder

6. The truck was moving_____.
    a) fast
    b) fastly
    c) good
    d) gooder

7. Ron spoke_____-to the reporter.
    a) calm
    b) calmlier
    c) calmly
    d) more calm

READING
Your other task for the day is to read a book. At this point you should be able to read for ½ hour to 1 hour each day. Look online for a variety of book lists. You can also check out my site www.plainandnotsoplain.com and see all of the books that we have enjoyed at this grade level. Write the title of the book you are reading and how long you have read for.

_____

_____

QUIZ

Multiplying by 10

Remember how we multiplied by a multiple of tens, and hundreds? When we multiply by ten, we just add a zero. Because any number times one is the number. For example 32 x10 = 320

Your turn:

12x10	120x10	10x10

15x10	22x10	343x10

Brooklyn weighed 88 pounds. She put on her clothes, which weighed 2 pounds, and her shoes which weight 1 pound each. * Finally she put on a jacket that weighed 3 pounds and stepped on the scale. How much did the scale show that she weighed?

Which of these numbers is a multiple of ten?

2   5   25   50

Shade the rectangle 3/8

The pumpkin pie was sliced into 6 slices. After 1 piece was taken, what fraction of pie was left?

What is the perimeter of this rectangle?

8 cm

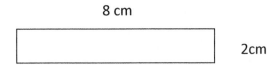

2cm

1000- (110x9)   3.675-1.76

39÷5   39÷7

100 Multiplication facts

9 x1	2 x2	5 x1	4 x3	0 x0	9 x9	3 x5	8 x5	2 x6	4 x7
5 x6	7 x5	3 x0	8 x8	1 x3	3 x4	5 x9	0 x2	7 x3	4 x 1
2 x3	8 x6	0 x5	6 x1	3 x8	1 x 1	9 x0	2 x8	6 x4	0 x7
7 x7	1 x4	6 x2	4 x5	2 x4	4 x 9	7 x0	1 x2	8 x4	6 x5
3 x2	4 x6	1 x9	5 x7	8 x2	0 x8	4 x2	9 x8	3 x6	5 x5
8 x9	3 x7	9 x7	1 x7	6 x0	0 x3	7 x2	1 x5	7 x8	4 x0
8 x3	5 x2	0 x4	9 x5	6 x7	2 x7	6 x3	5 x4	1 x0	9 x 2
7 x 6	1 x 8	9 x6	4 x 4	5 x3	8 x1	3 x3	4 x8	9 x3	2 x0
8 x0	3 x1	6 x8	0 x9	8 x7	2 x 9	9 x4	0 x1	7 x4	5 x8
0 x6	7 x1	2 x5	6 x9	3 x9	1 x6	5 x0	6 x6	2 x1	7 x9

Coordinating conjunction is a word that connects part of a sentence.
The most common ones are: and, but, or, for nor, so, yet, as well as

Circle the coordinating conjunctions.

Eight and eight makes sixteen.

All night the winds blew and the snow fell.

Matt is coming to the party as well as Tim.

The actor sang well, but he could not dance.

Fill in the blanks with conjunction

I will have milk_____-water with my dinner.

Paul hits well, _____-he cannot throw a curve ball.

Vince tried hard_____made the team.

Lori studies hard, _____-she has time for her friends.

READING
Your other task for the day is to read a book. At this point you should be able to read for ½ hour to 1 hour each day. Look online for a variety of book lists. You can also check out my site www.plainandnotsoplain.com and see all of the books that we have enjoyed at this grade level. Write the title of the book you are reading and how long you have read for.

_____

_____

week 16 copy your spelling words

argue

beautiful

beauty

cue

feud

few

hue

mew

newt

pew

queue

review

view

you

yule

To find the product of three numbers, we first multiply two of the numbers. Then we multiply the answer we get by the third number. To multiply four numbers, we must multiply once more.

3 x 4 x5

Do any of the numbers 5 x4 =20 , then 20 x 3= 60

Your turn:

4x5x10x10

2x3x4

3x4x10

887-291   432+89

476,438+259,710=   29÷5=

100 Multiplication facts

9 x1	2 x2	5 x1	4 x3	0 x0	9 x9	3 x5	8 x5	2 x6	4 x7
5 x6	7 x5	3 x0	8 x8	1 x3	3 x4	5 x9	0 x2	7 x3	4 x 1
2 x3	8 x6	0 x5	6 x1	3 x8	1 x 1	9 x0	2 x8	6 x4	0 x7
7 x7	1 x4	6 x2	4 x5	2 x4	4 x 9	7 x0	1 x2	8 x4	6 x5
3 x2	4 x6	1 x9	5 x7	8 x2	0 x8	4 x2	9 x8	3 x6	5 x5
8 x9	3 x7	9 x7	1 x7	6 x0	0 x3	7 x2	1 x5	7 x8	4 x0
8 x3	5 x2	0 x4	9 x5	6 x7	2 x7	6 x3	5 x4	1 x0	9 x 2
7 x 6	1 x 8	9 x6	4 x 4	5 x3	8 x1	3 x3	4 x8	9 x3	2 x0
8 x0	3 x1	6 x8	0 x9	8 x7	2 x 9	9 x4	0 x1	7 x4	5 x8
0 x6	7 x1	2 x5	6 x9	3 x9	1 x6	5 x0	6 x6	2 x1	7 x9

Words in a series are separated by commas. Place the comma after each item in the series except the last one.

I like apples, bananas, and pineapple.

Add commas to separate the series if needed. Circle the conjunction.

We planted bushes trees flowers around the house.

I ordered a salad and milk.

My brother sister father and mother ordered soup.

Write your own sentences

3 fruits you like

_____

3 places you like to visit

_____

3 friends you enjoy

_____

READING

Your other task for the day is to read a book. At this point you should be able to read for ½ hour to 1 hour each day. Look online for a variety of book lists. You can also check out my site www.plainandnotsoplain.com and see all of the books that we have enjoyed at this grade level. Write the title of the book you are reading and how long you have read for.

_____

_____

```
V  I  E  N  J  R  R  L  F  Y  B  Q  P  W  Y
A  S  O  G  O  T  T  T  T  B  L  I  M  D  Z
E  U  D  Q  J  P  W  B  J  I  U  D  W  U  P
V  C  H  M  C  F  E  L  M  L  G  I  C  J  J
P  I  U  E  D  Y  N  E  W  T  G  X  U  Y  O
E  D  E  D  C  Q  Y  F  D  I  R  N  Z  D  Z
W  M  U  W  I  T  O  Y  R  C  E  Z  I  K  U
X  E  X  A  D  K  U  B  O  W  V  A  U  U  E
F  W  X  R  C  L  G  G  B  M  I  Y  Q  I  G
U  H  L  O  G  U  A  N  G  B  E  A  U  T  Y
K  U  D  P  B  J  E  Q  E  H  W  W  E  L  X
B  E  A  U  T  I  F  U  L  B  S  B  U  R  E
Q  T  P  A  W  S  W  G  E  Z  I  O  E  F  P
E  E  N  J  X  A  R  G  U  E  E  Y  C  E  L
D  A  U  V  X  I  C  O  Z  K  U  V  Z  W  F
```

ARGUE	BEAUTIFUL	BEAUTY
CUE	FEUD	FEW
HUE	MEW	NEWT
PEW	QUEUE	REVIEW
VIEW	YOU	YULE

245

Polygons are closed, flat shapes formed by line segments.
Which of the following is a polygon?

A ⌐‾⌐   b ▱   c ▭   d ⬠

Figure A is not because it is not closed. B is not because it is not flat.
C is not because the sides are not straight. D is a polygon—closed and flat
and made of line segments.

Polygons are named according to number of sides they have. The lengths of the sides may or may not
be the same.

four sided polygons quadrilaterals			
five sided polygons are pentagons			
six sided polygons are hexagons			
eight sided polygons are octagons			

What kind of polygon is a square?

Three feet equals one yard. A car that is 15 feet long, is how many yards long?

Brook had 6 quarters, three dimes, and fourteen pennies. How much money did she have in all?

The cake was cut into 12 slices. Seven of the pieces were eaten. What fraction of the cake was left?

246

9 x1	2 x2	5 x1	4 x3	0 x0	9 x9	3 x5	8 x5	2 x6	4 x7
5 x6	7 x5	3 x0	8 x8	1 x3	3 x4	5 x9	0 x2	7 x3	4 x 1
2 x3	8 x6	0 x5	6 x1	3 x8	1 x 1	9 x0	2 x8	6 x4	0 x7
7 x7	1 x4	6 x2	4 x5	2 x4	4 x 9	7 x0	1 x2	8 x4	6 x5
3 x2	4 x6	1 x9	5 x7	8 x2	0 x8	4 x2	9 x8	3 x6	5 x5
8 x9	3 x7	9 x7	1 x7	6 x0	0 x3	7 x2	1 x5	7 x8	4 x0
8 x3	5 x2	0 x4	9 x5	6 x7	2 x7	6 x3	5 x4	1 x0	9 x 2
7 x 6	1 x 8	9 x6	4 x 4	5 x3	8 x1	3 x3	4 x8	9 x3	2 x0
8 x0	3 x1	6 x8	0 x9	8 x7	2 x 9	9 x4	0 x1	7 x4	5 x8
0 x6	7 x1	2 x5	6 x9	3 x9	1 x6	5 x0	6 x6	2 x1	7 x9

An interjection is a word or phrase that expresses a strong feeling. Always separate the interjection from the rest of the sentence with a punctuation mark.   Use a comma, a question mark, or an exclamation mark. Use an exclamation mark after strong interjection.

Hurry! I'll be late again.
Oh? I didn't know you were sick.
Hey, don't ask me again.

When ending punctuation comes after an interjection, capitalize the first word that follows.

If you use a comma, do not capitalize the next word of the sentence unless it is a proper noun.

Write these sentences and add punctuation after the interjection and at the end of each sentence. Capitalize the first words of the sentence.

quick I need help fast

_____

wow what a great party this is

_____

really I was surprised

_____

whew that was fun

_____

READING
Your other task for the day is to read a book. At this point you should be able to read for ½ hour to 1 hour each day. Look online for a variety of book lists. You can also check out my site www.plainandnotsoplain.com and see all of the books that we have enjoyed at this grade level. Write the title of the book you are reading and how long you have read for.

_____

Write a sentence for each of your words

Solve each problem

There are 1 dozen cans of peaches in each carton. How many cans are in 2 cartons? Remember there are 12 items in one dozen.

_____cans are in one dozen.

There are _____cartons.

There are _____cans of peaches in 2 cartons.

12 cans of pineapple are in each carton. How many cans are in 3 cartons?

There are _____cans of pineapple in 3 cartons.

There are 1 dozen cans of pears in each carton. How many cans are in 4 cartons?

There are _____cans of pears in 4 cartons.

Ten cans of orange sections come in each carton. How many cans are in 4 cartons?

There are____cans of orange sections in 4 cartons.

9 x1	2 x2	5 x1	4 x3	0 x0	9 x9	3 x5	8 x5	2 x6	4 x7
5 x6	7 x5	3 x0	8 x8	1 x3	3 x4	5 x9	0 x2	7 x3	4 x 1
2 x3	8 x6	0 x5	6 x1	3 x8	1 x 1	9 x0	2 x8	6 x4	0 x7
7 x7	1 x4	6 x2	4 x5	2 x4	4 x 9	7 x0	1 x2	8 x4	6 x5
3 x2	4 x6	1 x9	5 x7	8 x2	0 x8	4 x2	9 x8	3 x6	5 x5
8 x9	3 x7	9 x7	1 x7	6 x0	0 x3	7 x2	1 x5	7 x8	4 x0
8 x3	5 x2	0 x4	9 x5	6 x7	2 x7	6 x3	5 x4	1 x0	9 x 2
7 x 6	1 x 8	9 x6	4 x 4	5 x3	8 x1	3 x3	4 x8	9 x3	2 x0
8 x0	3 x1	6 x8	0 x9	8 x7	2 x 9	9 x4	0 x1	7 x4	5 x8
0 x6	7 x1	2 x5	6 x9	3 x9	1 x6	5 x0	6 x6	2 x1	7 x9

REVIEW

Circle the correct sentence.

   a) Paul bought a coat, he bought a scarf, He bought some gloves.
   b) Paul bought a coat. A scarf. Some gloves.
   c) Paul bought a coat, a scarf, and some gloves.
   d) Paul bought a coat, He bought a scarf, he bought some gloves

   e) It rained on Monday, it rained on Tuesday.
   f) It rained on Monday while it rained on Tuesday.
   g) It rained on Monday, nor it rain on Tuesday.
   h) It rained on Monday and Tuesday.

   i) Dan was absent, nor Rita was absent.
   j) Dan and Rita were absent.
   k) Dan but Rita was absent.
   l) Dan or Rita are absent.

READING

Your other task for the day is to read a book. At this point you should be able to read for ½ hour to 1 hour each day. Look online for a variety of book lists. You can also check out my site www.plainandnotsoplain.com and see all of the books that we have enjoyed at this grade level. Write the title of the book you are reading and how long you have read for.

_____

_____

QUIZ

Easy day---work on multiplication facts and getting them all correct.
Copy down any that you miss and say them over and over again.

READING

Your other task for the day is to read a book. At this point you should be able to read for ½ hour to 1 hour each day. Look online for a variety of book lists. You can also check out my site www.plainandnotsoplain.com and see all of the books that we have enjoyed at this grade level. Write the title of the book you are reading and how long you have read for.

_____

_____

9 x1	2 x2	5 x1	4 x3	0 x0	9 x9	3 x5	8 x5	2 x6	4 x7
5 x6	7 x5	3 x0	8 x8	1 x3	3 x4	5 x9	0 x2	7 x3	4 x 1
2 x3	8 x6	0 x5	6 x1	3 x8	1 x 1	9 x0	2 x8	6 x4	0 x7
7 x7	1 x4	6 x2	4 x5	2 x4	4 x 9	7 x0	1 x2	8 x4	6 x5
3 x2	4 x6	1 x9	5 x7	8 x2	0 x8	4 x2	9 x8	3 x6	5 x5
8 x9	3 x7	9 x7	1 x7	6 x0	0 x3	7 x2	1 x5	7 x8	4 x0
8 x3	5 x2	0 x4	9 x5	6 x7	2 x7	6 x3	5 x4	1 x0	9 x 2
7 x 6	1 x 8	9 x6	4 x 4	5 x3	8 x1	3 x3	4 x8	9 x3	2 x0
8 x0	3 x1	6 x8	0 x9	8 x7	2 x 9	9 x4	0 x1	7 x4	5 x8
0 x6	7 x1	2 x5	6 x9	3 x9	1 x6	5 x0	6 x6	2 x1	7 x9

A sentence is a group of words that expresses a complete thought. Every sentence begins with a capital letter and ends with an end punctuation mark.

A group of words may look like a sentence, but if it does not express a complete thought, it is not a sentence.

Read each group of words. Write S if it is a sentence, write NS if it is not a sentence.

Stop for the red light!

Before the storm was over.

In the house across the street.

That's nice he.

Where does he work?

She laughed at.

Jack went fishing.

week 17 copy your word list

anxious

ax

boxes

coax

example

except

excuse

exercise

Mexico

saxophone

sixteen

sixth

taxes

Texas

toxic

Easy day---work on multiplication facts and getting them all correct.
Copy down any that you miss and say them over and over again.

READING

Your other task for the day is to read a book. At this point you should be able to read for ½ hour to 1 hour each day. Look online for a variety of book lists. You can also check out my site www.plainandnotsoplain.com and see all of the books that we have enjoyed at this grade level. Write the title of the book you are reading and how long you have read for.

_____

_____

9 x1	2 x2	5 x1	4 x3	0 x0	9 x9	3 x5	8 x5	2 x6	4 x7
5 x6	7 x5	3 x0	8 x8	1 x3	3 x4	5 x9	0 x2	7 x3	4 x 1
2 x3	8 x6	0 x5	6 x1	3 x8	1 x 1	9 x0	2 x8	6 x4	0 x7
7 x7	1 x4	6 x2	4 x5	2 x4	4 x 9	7 x0	1 x2	8 x4	6 x5
3 x2	4 x6	1 x9	5 x7	8 x2	0 x8	4 x2	9 x8	3 x6	5 x5
8 x9	3 x7	9 x7	1 x7	6 x0	0 x3	7 x2	1 x5	7 x8	4 x0
8 x3	5 x2	0 x4	9 x5	6 x7	2 x7	6 x3	5 x4	1 x0	9 x 2
7 x 6	1 x 8	9 x6	4 x 4	5 x3	8 x1	3 x3	4 x8	9 x3	2 x0
8 x0	3 x1	6 x8	0 x9	8 x7	2 x 9	9 x4	0 x1	7 x4	5 x8
0 x6	7 x1	2 x5	6 x9	3 x9	1 x6	5 x0	6 x6	2 x1	7 x9

Turn each phrase into a complete sentence.

that she tried to read

_____

_____

when we left the park

_____

_____

if we are allowed to

_____

_____

as the light began to fade

_____

_____

```
O  S  U  K  X  Q  U  P  R  E  X  C  U  S  E
I  D  N  A  Y  G  M  S  E  F  O  W  D  Q  V
P  E  O  H  W  O  E  S  A  Y  E  W  S  O  S
Z  C  R  L  X  X  I  A  L  S  V  A  I  V  R
S  K  I  B  O  C  J  X  U  Z  Q  F  X  G  C
O  U  P  B  R  Q  C  O  M  P  L  E  T  E  F
E  X  C  E  P  T  I  P  Z  E  X  K  E  G  K
O  Y  X  S  K  X  W  H  L  Y  X  S  E  B  Z
V  E  N  N  N  H  W  O  Q  J  Y  I  N  Z  K
B  D  Z  A  T  B  C  N  S  S  X  B  C  H  P
H  W  A  X  Q  O  B  E  A  P  C  Y  R  O  K
G  F  I  D  I  I  X  X  X  I  O  K  F  F  Y
C  S  I  P  L  A  E  E  X  S  G  L  P  J  N
W  E  A  W  T  T  S  O  O  B  A  I  T  B  E
T  D  O  L  I  O  T  L  G  X  R  G  F  U  Y
```

ANXIOUS	AX	BOXES
COAX	COMPLETE	EXCEPT
EXCUSE	EXERCISE	MEXICO
SAXOPHONE	SIXTEEN	SIXTH
TAXES	TEXAS	TOXIC

Easy day---work on multiplication facts and getting them all correct.
Copy down any that you miss and say them over and over again.

READING

Your other task for the day is to read a book. At this point you should be able to read for ½ hour to 1 hour each day. Look online for a variety of book lists. You can also check out my site www.plainandnotsoplain.com and see all of the books that we have enjoyed at this grade level. Write the title of the book you are reading and how long you have read for.

_____

_____

100 Multiplication facts

9 x1	2 x2	5 x1	4 x3	0 x0	9 x9	3 x5	8 x5	2 x6	4 x7
5 x6	7 x5	3 x0	8 x8	1 x3	3 x4	5 x9	0 x2	7 x3	4 x 1
2 x3	8 x6	0 x5	6 x1	3 x8	1 x 1	9 x0	2 x8	6 x4	0 x7
7 x7	1 x4	6 x2	4 x5	2 x4	4 x 9	7 x0	1 x2	8 x4	6 x5
3 x2	4 x6	1 x9	5 x7	8 x2	0 x8	4 x2	9 x8	3 x6	5 x5
8 x9	3 x7	9 x7	1 x7	6 x0	0 x3	7 x2	1 x5	7 x8	4 x0
8 x3	5 x2	0 x4	9 x5	6 x7	2 x7	6 x3	5 x4	1 x0	9 x 2
7 x 6	1 x 8	9 x6	4 x 4	5 x3	8 x1	3 x3	4 x8	9 x3	2 x0
8 x0	3 x1	6 x8	0 x9	8 x7	2 x 9	9 x4	0 x1	7 x4	5 x8
0 x6	7 x1	2 x5	6 x9	3 x9	1 x6	5 x0	6 x6	2 x1	7 x9

Every sentence has two parts: the subject and the predicate.
The subject is the part of the sentence that tells what the sentence is about.
It may be one word or many words.

Amy opened the window.
The man who taught us how to fish became a shop owner.

The simple subject is the noun or pronoun that the sentence is about.

The **test** in history was easy.

The complete subject is "the test in history"

Underline the complete subject. Circle the simple subject. A complete
subject may be only one word.

1. Mr Ronald comes from Portland, Washington.
2. The entire class speaks in French every day.
3. The teacher asks the students questions in French.
4. They must answer her in French.
5. The students in this class learn quickly.
6. I am going to the store.
7. Three of our classmates went on the field trip.

Write a sentence for each of your words

Easy day---work on multiplication facts and getting them all correct.
Copy down any that you miss and say them over and over again.

READING

Your other task for the day is to read a book. At this point you should be able to read for ½ hour to 1 hour each day. Look online for a variety of book lists. You can also check out my site www.plainandnotsoplain.com and see all of the books that we have enjoyed at this grade level. Write the title of the book you are reading and how long you have read for.

_____

_____

9 x1	2 x2	5 x1	4 x3	0 x0	9 x9	3 x5	8 x5	2 x6	4 x7
5 x6	7 x5	3 x0	8 x8	1 x3	3 x4	5 x9	0 x2	7 x3	4 x 1
2 x3	8 x6	0 x5	6 x1	3 x8	1 x 1	9 x0	2 x8	6 x4	0 x7
7 x7	1 x4	6 x2	4 x5	2 x4	4 x 9	7 x0	1 x2	8 x4	6 x5
3 x2	4 x6	1 x9	5 x7	8 x2	0 x8	4 x2	9 x8	3 x6	5 x5
8 x9	3 x7	9 x7	1 x7	6 x0	0 x3	7 x2	1 x5	7 x8	4 x0
8 x3	5 x2	0 x4	9 x5	6 x7	2 x7	6 x3	5 x4	1 x0	9 x 2
7 x 6	1 x 8	9 x6	4 x 4	5 x3	8 x1	3 x3	4 x8	9 x3	2 x0
8 x0	3 x1	6 x8	0 x9	8 x7	2 x 9	9 x4	0 x1	7 x4	5 x8
0 x6	7 x1	2 x5	6 x9	3 x9	1 x6	5 x0	6 x6	2 x1	7 x9

Underline the complete subjectand circle the simple subject.

Baseball season begins soon.

Kim and Karen are on the team.

They usually play infield.

Her birthday was in two weeks.

Both my hat and gloves are blue.

QUIZ

Easy day---work on multiplication facts and getting them all correct.
Copy down any that you miss and say them over and over again.

READING

Your other task for the day is to read a book. At this point you should be able to read for ½ hour to 1 hour each day. Look online for a variety of book lists. You can also check out my site www.plainandnotsoplain.com and see all of the books that we have enjoyed at this grade level.
Write the title of the book you are reading and how long you have read for.

_____

_____

9 x1	2 x2	5 x1	4 x3	0 x0	9 x9	3 x5	8 x5	2 x6	4 x7
5 x6	7 x5	3 x0	8 x8	1 x3	3 x4	5 x9	0 x2	7 x3	4 x 1
2 x3	8 x6	0 x5	6 x1	3 x8	1 x 1	9 x0	2 x8	6 x4	0 x7
7 x7	1 x4	6 x2	4 x5	2 x4	4 x 9	7 x0	1 x2	8 x4	6 x5
3 x2	4 x6	1 x9	5 x7	8 x2	0 x8	4 x2	9 x8	3 x6	5 x5
8 x9	3 x7	9 x7	1 x7	6 x0	0 x3	7 x2	1 x5	7 x8	4 x0
8 x3	5 x2	0 x4	9 x5	6 x7	2 x7	6 x3	5 x4	1 x0	9 x 2
7 x 6	1 x 8	9 x6	4 x 4	5 x3	8 x1	3 x3	4 x8	9 x3	2 x0
8 x0	3 x1	6 x8	0 x9	8 x7	2 x 9	9 x4	0 x1	7 x4	5 x8
0 x6	7 x1	2 x5	6 x9	3 x9	1 x6	5 x0	6 x6	2 x1	7 x9

The predicate of a sentence tells what the subject did or what happened to the subject. The predicate can be one word or many words. It always contains a verb.

We **studied.**
Aaron **will look at the videotapes this weekend.**

Underline the predicate in the following sentences.

Amy lost her ring yesterday.

Denise found the ring today.

One of the stones was missing.

Someone had apparently stepped on it.

A jeweler can replace the stone in Amy's ring.

The main part of the predicate is the verb or verb phrase. The verb or verb phrase in the predicate is the simple predicate.
Jessica **<u>helped</u> her mother in the kitchen.**
Kim **<u>will meet</u> us at the park.**

Underline the predicate. Circle the verb or verb phrase.

Mrs. Maryon gave Austin a surprise birthday party.

Kim's brother Will invited his friends.

Her friends decorated the house.

week 18 copy your words

across

afford

battle

goddess

copper

difference

difficult

gallon

message

official

recess

success

suppose

terrible

traffic

Easy day---work on multiplication facts and getting them all correct.
Copy down any that you miss and say them over and over again.

READING

Your other task for the day is to read a book. At this point you should be able to read for ½ hour to 1 hour each day. Look online for a variety of book lists. You can also check out my site www.plainandnotsoplain.com and see all of the books that we have enjoyed at this grade level. Write the title of the book you are reading and how long you have read for.

_____

_____

100 Multiplication facts

9 x1	2 x2	5 x1	4 x3	0 x0	9 x9	3 x5	8 x5	2 x6	4 x7
5 x6	7 x5	3 x0	8 x8	1 x3	3 x4	5 x9	0 x2	7 x3	4 x 1
2 x3	8 x6	0 x5	6 x1	3 x8	1 x 1	9 x0	2 x8	6 x4	0 x7
7 x7	1 x4	6 x2	4 x5	2 x4	4 x 9	7 x0	1 x2	8 x4	6 x5
3 x2	4 x6	1 x9	5 x7	8 x2	0 x8	4 x2	9 x8	3 x6	5 x5
8 x9	3 x7	9 x7	1 x7	6 x0	0 x3	7 x2	1 x5	7 x8	4 x0
8 x3	5 x2	0 x4	9 x5	6 x7	2 x7	6 x3	5 x4	1 x0	9 x 2
7 x 6	1 x 8	9 x6	4 x 4	5 x3	8 x1	3 x3	4 x8	9 x3	2 x0
8 x0	3 x1	6 x8	0 x9	8 x7	2 x 9	9 x4	0 x1	7 x4	5 x8
0 x6	7 x1	2 x5	6 x9	3 x9	1 x6	5 x0	6 x6	2 x1	7 x9

Usually the predicate comes after the subject.
The whole school **enjoyed the game.**

In a question, part of the predicate comes before the subject.

Did you **bring Sally the tapes?**

Then Aaron **helped his sisters clean up.**

Underline the predicate and circle the verb or verb phrase.

Did you talk to Christy after the party?

Why did Elena leave early?

Maybe she was feeling sick.

Her mother needed her at home.

Because of a computer problem, she was needed in the office.

A verb can be compound. A compound verb is two or more verbs or verb phrases joined by a conjunction.

The parents **clapped** and **cheered.**
The actors **looked** calm but **were** very nervous.

Underline predicate, circle the verb/verb phrase

The big cars cost too much and used too much gas.
The used cars showed rust spots and needed repairs.

```
D  Z  L  A  Z  B  M  A  C  A  T  Y  S  C  I
Q  I  C  R  R  L  K  C  I  S  R  L  D  S  P
W  M  F  I  E  M  B  R  P  S  A  E  U  U  I
M  G  C  F  U  C  I  O  E  W  F  Q  D  P  L
S  E  M  Q  E  D  E  S  Y  B  F  D  O  P  H
S  L  E  A  I  R  X  S  S  V  I  I  P  O  F
H  I  S  U  C  C  E  S  S  F  C  F  H  S  A
K  T  S  J  D  B  E  N  E  Y  Q  F  E  E  X
A  L  A  F  I  D  A  L  C  X  U  I  Q  U  C
F  M  G  H  D  Q  B  T  N  E  H  C  K  O  O
F  J  E  O  L  I  C  R  T  H  Y  U  O  M  P
O  B  G  X  R  C  R  Y  L  L  P  L  U  A  P
R  S  H  R  M  D  R  C  W  C  E  T  K  A  E
D  Q  E  O  J  O  F  F  I  C  I  A  L  Y  R
W  T  J  R  M  G  A  L  L  O  N  U  Q  E  N
```

ACROSS	AFFORD	BATTLE
GODDESS	COPPER	DIFFERENCE
DIFFICULT	GALLON	MESSAGE
OFFICIAL	RECESS	SUCCESS
SUPPOSE	TERRIBLE	TRAFFIC

Easy day---work on multiplication facts and getting them all correct.
Copy down any that you miss and say them over and over again.

READING

Your other task for the day is to read a book. At this point you should be able to read for ½ hour to 1 hour each day. Look online for a variety of book lists. You can also check out my site www.plainandnotsoplain.com and see all of the books that we have enjoyed at this grade level.
Write the title of the book you are reading and how long you have read for.

_____

_____

9 x1	2 x2	5 x1	4 x3	0 x0	9 x9	3 x5	8 x5	2 x6	4 x7
5 x6	7 x5	3 x0	8 x8	1 x3	3 x4	5 x9	0 x2	7 x3	4 x 1
2 x3	8 x6	0 x5	6 x1	3 x8	1 x 1	9 x0	2 x8	6 x4	0 x7
7 x7	1 x4	6 x2	4 x5	2 x4	4 x 9	7 x0	1 x2	8 x4	6 x5
3 x2	4 x6	1 x9	5 x7	8 x2	0 x8	4 x2	9 x8	3 x6	5 x5
8 x9	3 x7	9 x7	1 x7	6 x0	0 x3	7 x2	1 x5	7 x8	4 x0
8 x3	5 x2	0 x4	9 x5	6 x7	2 x7	6 x3	5 x4	1 x0	9 x 2
7 x 6	1 x 8	9 x6	4 x 4	5 x3	8 x1	3 x3	4 x8	9 x3	2 x0
8 x0	3 x1	6 x8	0 x9	8 x7	2 x 9	9 x4	0 x1	7 x4	5 x8
0 x6	7 x1	2 x5	6 x9	3 x9	1 x6	5 x0	6 x6	2 x1	7 x9

Types of sentences
There are four types of sentences
Declarative-makes a statement "Oh, I do declare."—said with southern accent☺
Interrogative—asks a question
Imperative—gives a command or makes a request
Exclamatory—your exclaiming something!

Decide which type of sentences these are:

Are you hungry?_____

I am starved!_____

Bring me my shoes, please._____

We can eat at this restaurant._____

Write your own:
declarative

_____

interrogative

_____

exclamatory

_____

imperative

_____

Write a sentence for each of your words

In this lesson, we will learn a pencil and paper method for dividing a two digit number by a one digit number. We will demonstrate the method as we solve the problem:
The seventy-eight fifth graders at Elm School need to be divided equally among three classrooms. How many students should be in each room?

There are three numbers in this "equal groups" problem: the total number of students, the number of classrooms, and the number of students in each classroom.

Number of groups x number in each group= total

3 classrooms x n (students in each classroom)=78
To find the number of students in each classroom, we divide 78 by 3

For first step, we ignore the 8 and divide 7 by 3. We write the "2" above the 7. Then we multiply 2 by 3 and write "6" below the 7. Then we subtract and write "1".

$$
\begin{array}{r}
2 \\
3\overline{)78} \\
\underline{-6}\downarrow \\
1\ 8
\end{array}
$$

Now we divide 18 by 3 and get 6. We write the 6 above the 8 in 78. Then we multiply 6 by 3 and write "18" below the 18.

$$
\begin{array}{r}
2\ 6 \\
3\overline{)78} \\
\underline{-6}\downarrow \\
1\ \ 8 \\
\underline{-1\ \ 8} \\
0
\end{array}
$$

We subtract and find the remainder is zero. This means that if the students are divided equally among the classrooms, there will be 26 students in each classroom

If you multiply 26 x3=78 to check your answer

Your turn: Do the above method for this 87 divided by 3. Then check your work.

Division facts: 1,2,3, 5

10÷1=	35÷5 =	14÷2=	3÷3=	18÷3=	20÷5=	15÷5=
25÷5=	9÷1=	30÷5=	15÷3=	6÷2=	15÷5=	10÷2=
12÷3=	21÷3=	35÷5=	5÷1=	6÷1=	10÷2=	4÷1=
18÷9=	16÷2=	4÷2=	15÷5=	18÷2=	9÷3=	9÷9=
3÷1=	5÷5=	10÷5=	6÷3=	12÷2=	3÷3=	2÷1=
14÷2=	2÷2=	7÷1=	40÷5=	8÷2=	2÷2=	10÷5=
10÷2=	24÷3=	27÷3=	45÷5=	12÷3=	18÷3=	27÷3=

READING

Your other task for the day is to read a book. At this point you should be able to read for ½ hour to 1 hour each day. Look online for a variety of book lists. You can also check out my site www.plainandnotsoplain.com and see all of the books that we have enjoyed at this grade level. Write the title of the book you are reading and how long you have read for.

_____

_____

Double negatives

Do not write double negatives in a sentence.

 I don't need no money. (no, and not)

Rewrite the sentences below to make them correct.

They won't ask no questions.

_____

She don't never eat vegetables.

_____

There ain't nobody at the door.

_____

I never saw no shooting stars.

_____

QUIZ

Practice these, just take your time and do the same method as yesterday.

3 | 51   4 | 52   5 | 75

Write 406,912 in expanded form

A stop sign has the shape of an octagon. How many sides do seven stops sign have?

One foot equals 12 inches. If each side of a square is 1 foot long, then what is the perimeter of the square in inches?

Some birds sat on the wire at sunup. After 47 more birds came there were 112 birds sitting on the wire. How many birds sat on the wire at sunup?

Division facts: 1,2,3, 5

10÷1=	35÷5 =	14÷2=	3÷3=	18÷3=	20÷5=	15÷5=
25÷5=	9÷1=	30÷5=	15÷3=	6÷2=	15÷5=	10÷2=
12÷3=	21÷3=	35÷5=	5÷1=	6÷1=	10÷2=	4÷1=
18÷9=	16÷2=	4÷2=	15÷5=	18÷2=	9÷3=	9÷9=
3÷1=	5÷5=	10÷5=	6÷3=	12÷2=	3÷3=	2÷1=
14÷2=	2÷2=	7÷1=	40÷5=	8÷2=	2÷2=	10÷5=
10÷2=	24÷3=	27÷3=	45÷5=	12÷3=	18÷3=	27÷3=

READING

Your other task for the day is to read a book. At this point you should be able to read for ½ hour to 1 hour each day. Look online for a variety of book lists. You can also check out my site www.plainandnotsoplain.com and see all of the books that we have enjoyed at this grade level. Write the title of the book you are reading and how long you have read for.

_____

_____

Choose the synonym. Pick the word that is closest in meaning to the underlined word.

1. They felt so **drowsy** after the holiday party.
   a. full
   b. energetic
   c. relaxed
   d. sleepy
2. You can **obtain** samples at the customer service window.
   a. get
   b. purchase
   c. borrow
   d. copy
3. Emergency workers responded to **urgent** calls for help.
   a. casual
   b. critical
   c. noisy
   d. minor
4. We'd like to **extend** our vacation by several days.
   a. limit
   b. cancel
   c. continue
   d. remember
5. People who work **hastily** are more likely to make sloppy mistakes.
   a. speedily
   b. darkly
   c. casually
   d. fearfully
6. When Jadyn gets upset, her lips tend to **quiver.**
   a. tighten
   b. hurt
   c. tremble
   d. troop
7. The new student looked around the room with **envy** over all he had missed.
   a. jealousy
   b. anger
   c. awe
   d. pleasure
8. What is the annoying **clatter** coming from the attic?
   a. odor
   b. conversation
   c. gossip
   d. racket

week 19 copy your spelling words

bare

stair

pane

hall

bury

groan

bear

stare

raise

haul

weight

pain

grown

berry

wait

rays

The numbers in a division problem are named the divisor, the dividend, and the quotient.

Dividend ÷ divisor= quotient

$$\text{Divisor} \overline{\smash{\big)}\,\text{dividend}}^{\text{quotient}}$$

Identify the 8 in each of these problems as the divisor, dividend or quotient:

8÷2=4

$$8\overline{\smash{\big)}\,24}^{\;3}$$

$$\frac{40}{5}=8$$

Divide 525 by 5 and then check your answer

Divide 455 by 7

READING

Your other task for the day is to read a book. At this point you should be able to read for ½ hour to 1 hour each day. Look online for a variety of book lists. You can also check out my site www.plainandnotsoplain.com and see all of the books that we have enjoyed at this grade level. Write the title of the book you are reading and how long you have read for.

_____

_____

Division facts: 1,2,3, 5

10÷1=	35÷5 =	14÷2=	3÷3=	18÷3=	20÷5=	15÷5=
25÷5=	9÷1=	30÷5=	15÷3=	6÷2=	15÷5=	10÷2=
12÷3=	21÷3=	35÷5=	5÷1=	6÷1=	10÷2=	4÷1=
18÷9=	16÷2=	4÷2=	15÷5=	18÷2=	9÷3=	9÷9=
3÷1=	5÷5=	10÷5=	6÷3=	12÷2=	3÷3=	2÷1=
14÷2=	2÷2=	7÷1=	40÷5=	8÷2=	2÷2=	10÷5=
10÷2=	24÷3=	27÷3=	45÷5=	12÷3=	18÷3=	27÷3=

Antonym---pick the word that means the opposite of the bold faced word.

1. The mayor's **loyal** aide takes care of every assignment.
   a. unfaithful
   b. professional
   c. part-time
   d. reliable
2. He is careful never to make **shallow** remarks, especially about key issues.
   a. confusing
   b. thoughtless
   c. deep
   d. supporting
3. In the upcoming election, it isn't clear which candidate will **triumph.**
   a. transfer
   b. vote
   c. win
   d. lose
4. But this **vibrant** mayor has many followers.
   a. disguise
   b. reveal
   c. research
   d. interrupt
5. In last night's speech, the mayor emphasized two **valid** reasons to support her.
   a. sound
   b. unconvincing
   c. important
   d. roundabout
6. The second was her success in cleaning up **toxic** waste from the region.
   a. harmful
   b. filthy
   c. harmless
   d. cluttered
7. Her trusty aide was there to **magnify** all the successes of her term in office.
   a. boost
   b. stress
   c. repeat
   d. lessen

```
Z  Y  W  Z  R  X  P  A  S  Y  P  A  P  J  S
Y  B  E  X  D  H  L  X  K  T  D  F  A  E  T
P  F  W  V  M  Z  G  M  H  G  A  G  N  W  A
W  T  H  C  N  D  I  Q  S  A  G  R  E  L  I
A  C  H  A  T  W  C  Q  K  V  U  M  E  R  R
G  K  O  U  L  H  A  H  F  U  Q  L  A  W  X
W  R  H  O  O  L  Y  I  K  R  T  R  L  Q  D
G  U  O  K  R  Q  P  J  T  Y  K  O  J  P  E
A  I  E  W  S  R  E  K  R  W  L  B  U  R  Y
V  B  F  Y  N  A  R  A  Y  D  M  A  W  P
G  T  A  X  A  T  E  Y  I  C  J  B  D  E  A
B  E  A  R  K  B  A  L  S  T  L  G  L  I  I
D  Z  I  N  K  U  V  F  E  T  W  G  C  G  N
T  O  Q  C  R  D  U  D  D  B  C  V  X  H  F
Q  W  C  O  O  W  L  M  P  C  T  C  M  T  L
```

BARE	STAIR	PANE
HALL	BURY	GROAN
BEAR	STARE	RAISE
HAUL	WEIGHT	PAIN
GROWN	BERRY	WAIT
RAYS		

The chef uses 3 eggs for each omelet. How many omelets can be made with 24 eggs?

Kim wore braces for 3 years. For how many months did she wear braces?

Fred bought a book for $12.89 and a folder for $3.29. How much did he spend?

Each side of a hexagon is 1 cm long. What is the perimeter?

168÷3   564x4

12 x7 x10   100x42

Three quarters are what fraction of a dollar

10÷1=	35÷ 5 =	14÷2=	3÷3=	18÷3=	20÷5=	15÷5=
25÷5=	9÷1=	30÷5=	15÷3=	6÷2=	15÷5=	10÷2=
12÷3=	21÷3=	35÷5=	5÷1=	6÷1=	10÷2=	4÷1=
18÷9=	16÷2=	4÷2=	15÷5=	18÷2=	9÷3=	9÷9=
3÷1=	5÷5=	10÷5=	6÷3=	12÷2=	3÷3=	2÷1=
14÷2=	2÷2=	7÷1=	40÷5=	8÷2=	2÷2=	10÷5=
10÷2=	24÷3=	27÷3=	45÷5=	12÷3=	18÷3=	27÷3=

READING

Your other task for the day is to read a book. At this point you should be able to read for ½ hour to 1 hour each day. Look online for a variety of book lists. You can also check out my site www.plainandnotsoplain.com and see all of the books that we have enjoyed at this grade level. Write the title of the book you are reading and how long you have read for.

_____

_____

Mark the answer that has the same meaning as the expression

1. Don't beat around the bush anymore
   a. avoid the main point
   b. rake the leaves
   c. repeat yourself
   d. get frustrated
2. Let's wait until all this blows over.
   a. comes apart
   b. gets worse
   c. exhales
   d. passes
3. It's an enjoyable way to break the ice.
   a. climb a mountain
   b. relax and interact
   c. chill the room
   d. stop the arguing
4. We must never cut corners on safety.
   a. be foolish
   b. disagree
   c. take shortcuts
   d. get excited
5. Dan got cold feet at the last minute.
   a. became brave
   b. wore heavy socks
   c. lost his nerve
   d. stepped in a puddle
6. I'm totally ready to hit the hay.
   a. go to bed
   b. be a farmer
   c. do my exercises
   d. take a break
7. That attitude makes them see red!
   a. feel embarrassed
   b. get angry
   c. want to read
   d. blush
8. Okay, its time to throw in the towel.
   a. do the laundry
   b. give up
   c. calm down
   d. ask for seconds
9. That movie was really for the birds
   a. about nature
   b. breezy and light
   c. terrible
   d. scary

Write a sentence for each of your words

Seventy-five beans were equally divided into 5 pots. How many beans were in each pot?

The server placed a full pitcher of water on the table. Which of the following is a reasonable estimate of the amount of water in the pitcher?

2 gallons   2 quarts   2 cups   2 ounces

If I were to drink a glass of orange juice for breakfast, what sounds like the reasonable size?

5 gallons   5 cups   6 ounces   6 quarts

A paper clip is closest to what?

An inch   a foot   a yard   a mile

What is closests to 2 pounds?

A book   a door   a pencil   a car

95÷5   234÷2

987,765   -149,384=   409x70

Division facts: 1,2,3, 5

10÷1=	35÷ 5 =	14÷2=	3÷3=	18÷3=	20÷5=	15÷5=
25÷5=	9÷1=	30÷5=	15÷3=	6÷2=	15÷5=	10÷2=
12÷3=	21÷3=	35÷5=	5÷1=	6÷1=	10÷2=	4÷1=
18÷9=	16÷2=	4÷2=	15÷5=	18÷2=	9÷3=	9÷9=
3÷1=	5÷5=	10÷5=	6÷3=	12÷2=	3÷3=	2÷1=
14÷2=	2÷2=	7÷1=	40÷5=	8÷2=	2÷2=	10÷5=
10÷2=	24÷3=	27÷3=	45÷5=	12÷3=	18÷3=	27÷3=

READING

Your other task for the day is to read a book. At this point you should be able to read for ½ hour to 1 hour each day. Look online for a variety of book lists. You can also check out my site www.plainandnotsoplain.com and see all of the books that we have enjoyed at this grade level. Write the title of the book you are reading and how long you have read for.

_____

_____

Explain figures of speech

Think about what the sentences mean—they are not literally they are figures of speech.

1. When my parents saw the damage, they really flew off the handle.

_____

_____

2. That new suit, fits like a glove.

_____

3. I'd really like to join you, but can I take a rain check until later?

_____

_____

4. Dad was sorry, but he said it would cost an arm and a leg.

_____

_____

5. She was feeling slightly under the weather last night.

_____

_____

QUIZ

It took four spoonfuls to make one batch. How many spoonfuls were required to make 40 batches?

Jadyn drew an octagon and a pentagon. What was the total number of sides in the two polygons?

Mount Rainier stands four thousand, three hundred ninety-two meters above sea level. Use digits to write that number of meters

$20- ($8.95+75 cents)

43 cents x 8=

Rewrite this addition problem as a multiplication problem and solve

64+64+64+64+64+64

47x30   60x39

Division facts: 1,2,3,4, 5

10÷1=	35÷5 =	14÷2=	3÷3=	18÷3=	20÷5=	15÷5=
25÷5=	36÷4=	30÷5=	15÷3=	6÷2=	15÷5=	10÷2=
12÷3=	21÷3=	35÷5=	5÷1=	28÷4=	10÷2=	4÷1=
18÷9=	16÷2=	32÷4=	15÷5=	18÷2=	9÷3=	9÷9=
16÷4=	5÷5=	10÷5=	6÷3=	12÷2=	24÷4=	8÷4=
12÷4=	2÷2=	7÷1=	40÷5=	8÷2=	2÷2=	10÷5=
10÷2=	20÷4=	27÷3=	45÷5=	12÷3=	18÷3=	27÷3=

READING

Your other task for the day is to read a book. At this point you should be able to read for ½ hour to 1 hour each day. Look online for a variety of book lists. You can also check out my site www.plainandnotsoplain.com and see all of the books that we have enjoyed at this grade level. Write the title of the book you are reading and how long you have read for.

_____

_____

Add supporting details
Read each sentence. Then write two more sentences that add supporting details.

1. It started out like any other day at home.

_____

_____

_____

2. The artist was preparing to start her latest painting.

_____

_____

_____

3. The roller coaster moved slowly up the steep slope.

_____

_____

_____

4. Each summer, the town holds an all day July 4th festival.

_____

_____

_____

week 20 spelling words copy them

airport

barefoot

birthday

cardboard

downstairs

earthquake

farewell

flyswatter

forenoon

iceberg

landlord

northwest

scarecrow

teakettle

throughout

Millimeters

This line segment is one centimeter long:

_____

If we divide a centimeter into ten equal lengths, each equal length is 1 millimeter long. A dime is about 1 millimeter thick.

The words centimeter and millimeter are based on Latin words. Centum is the Latin word for "hundred". A centimeter is one hundredth of a meter. 1/100. Just as a cent is one hundredth of a dolar. Mille is latin word for thousand. A millimeter is one thousandth 1/1000 of a meter. Just as a milliliter is one thousandth of a liter.

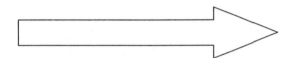

Look at your ruler. And notice the centimeter marks. There are ten millimeters for every centimeter.

How many millimeters long is this

If a paper clip is 3 cm long, how many millimeters long is it?

Measure this in centimeter_____millimeters_____

Sue's house key is 5.2 cm long, how many millimeters is her house key?

Forty-two students could ride in one bus. There were 30 buses. How many students could ride in all the buses?

Division facts: 1,2,3,4, 5

10÷1=	35÷ 5 =	14÷2=	3÷3=	18÷3=	20÷5=	15÷5=
25÷5=	36÷4=	30÷5=	15÷3=	6÷2=	15÷5=	10÷2=
12÷3=	21÷3=	35÷5=	5÷1=	28÷4=	10÷2=	4÷1=
18÷9=	16÷2=	32÷4=	15÷5=	18÷2=	9÷3=	9÷9=
16÷4=	5÷5=	10÷5=	6÷3=	12÷2=	24÷4=	8÷4=
12÷4=	2÷2=	7÷1=	40÷5=	8÷2=	2÷2=	10÷5=
10÷2=	20÷4=	27÷3=	45÷5=	12÷3=	18÷3=	27÷3=

READING

Your other task for the day is to read a book. At this point you should be able to read for ½ hour to 1 hour each day. Look online for a variety of book lists. You can also check out my site www.plainandnotsoplain.com and see all of the books that we have enjoyed at this grade level. Write the title of the book you are reading and how long you have read for.

_____

_____

Prewriting: use story blocks

Plan a story for each title below. Fill in the blocks with your ideas for the story's settings, as well as the beginning, middle, and the end.

Lost in the woods!		
Setting:		
Beginning	middle	end

In the old trunk!		
Setting:		
Beginning	middle	end

```
B  H  M  I  P  O  I  T  T  F  S  Q  U  Z  D
T  I  T  W  U  J  Y  S  E  O  B  Q  R  C  O
U  I  R  P  Q  L  E  Q  Z  R  A  N  L  U  W
Q  A  C  T  Z  W  U  W  T  E  R  F  A  E  N
G  C  A  E  H  U  G  P  H  N  E  L  N  R  S
S  G  E  T  B  D  U  E  R  O  F  Y  D  O  T
R  C  R  A  A  E  A  R  O  O  O  S  L  C  A
G  O  A  D  R  I  R  Y  U  N  O  W  O  A  I
N  J  O  R  O  T  R  G  G  C  T  A  R  R  R
C  G  D  C  E  E  H  P  H  L  D  T  D  D  S
H  J  P  N  Z  C  P  Q  O  T  Q  T  K  B  X
E  G  U  X  Q  A  R  J  U  R  G  E  S  O  P
R  L  R  N  U  Z  C  O  T  A  R  H  A  D
S  M  U  G  L  A  T  J  W  D  K  I  E  R  C
T  E  A  K  E  T  T  L  E  O  T  E  Q  D  J
```

AIRPORT	BAREFOOT	BIRTHDAY
CARDBOARD	DOWNSTAIRS	EARTHQUAKE
FLYSWATTER	FORENOON	ICEBERG
LANDLORD	NORTHWEST	SCARECROW
TEAKETTLE	THROUGHOUT	

We know that the fraction ½ means that a whole has been divided into 2 parts. To find the number in ½ of a group, we divide the total number in the group by 2. To find the number in 1/3 of a group, we divide the total number in the group by 3. To find the number in ¼ of a group, we divide the total number in the group by 4 and so on.

One half of the carrot seeds sprouted. If 84 seeds were planted, how many seeds sprouted?

Draw a figure if you need to

One third of the 27 students earned an A on the test. How many students earned an A?

One fourth of the team's 32 pointes were scored by Austin. Austin scored how many points?

What is 1/5 of 40?

What is 1/3 of 60?

What is ¼ of 60?

Forty-two million is how much greater than twenty-four million?

Division facts: 1,2,3,4, 5

10÷1=	35÷5 =	14÷2=	3÷3=	18÷3=	20÷5=	15÷5=
25÷5=	36÷4=	30÷5=	15÷3=	6÷2=	15÷5=	10÷2=
12÷3=	21÷3=	35÷5=	5÷1=	28÷4=	10÷2=	4÷1=
18÷9=	16÷2=	32÷4=	15÷5=	18÷2=	9÷3=	9÷9=
16÷4=	5÷5=	10÷5=	6÷3=	12÷2=	24÷4=	8÷4=
12÷4=	2÷2=	7÷1=	40÷5=	8÷2=	2÷2=	10÷5=
10÷2=	20÷4=	27÷3=	45÷5=	12÷3=	18÷3=	27÷3=

READING
Your other task for the day is to read a book. At this point you should be able to read for ½ hour to 1 hour each day. Look online for a variety of book lists. You can also check out my site www.plainandnotsoplain.com and see all of the books that we have enjoyed at this grade level. Write the title of the book you are reading and how long you have read for.

_____

_____

Use a character map. Develop a character for a story. Use the character map to figure out what this character is like.

Personality
_____
_____
_____
_____
_____
_____

habits
_____
_____
_____
_____
_____
_____

The character's name:

Age: Gender:

Looks
_____
_____
_____
_____
_____
_____

Feelings
_____
_____
_____
_____
_____
_____

Write a sentence for each of your words

Sometimes division answers end with a zero. It is important to continue the division until all the digits inside the division box have been used.

For example: two hundred pennies are separated into 4 equal piles. How many pennies are in each pile?

```
      5
4 | 200
   -20
     0
```

The division might look complete, but it is not. The answer is not "5 pennies in each pile" that would total only 20 pennies. There is another zero inside the division box to bring down. So we bring down the zero and divide again.

```
      50
4 | 200
   -20↓
     0 0
    -0
       0
```

Check 50 x4=200

Your turn:

Divide 120 by 3   240 by 4

Division facts: 1,2,3,4, 5

10÷1=	35÷5 =	14÷2=	3÷3=	18÷3=	20÷5=	15÷5=
25÷5=	36÷4=	30÷5=	15÷3=	6÷2=	15÷5=	10÷2=
12÷3=	21÷3=	35÷5=	5÷1=	28÷4=	10÷2=	4÷1=
18÷9=	16÷2=	32÷4=	15÷5=	18÷2=	9÷3=	9÷9=
16÷4=	5÷5=	10÷5=	6÷3=	12÷2=	24÷4=	8÷4=
12÷4=	2÷2=	7÷1=	40÷5=	8÷2=	2÷2=	10÷5=
10÷2=	20÷4=	27÷3=	45÷5=	12÷3=	18÷3=	27÷3=

READING

Your other task for the day is to read a book. At this point you should be able to read for ½ hour to 1 hour each day. Look online for a variety of book lists. You can also check out my site www.plainandnotsoplain.com and see all of the books that we have enjoyed at this grade level. Write the title of the book you are reading and how long you have read for.

_____

_____

Prewriting: plan questions
You can gather information by asking good questions. An EMT works in an ambulance, helping people in trouble. Imagine you are going to visit an EMT on a field trip. Write some good questions to ask.

What_____

_____

Who_____

_____

How_____

_____

When_____

_____

Why_____

_____

Where_____

_____

Which_____

_____

QUIZ

Each cookie contains 5 chocolate chips. How many chocolate chips are in 115 cookies?

What is the value of 5 pennies, 3 dimes, 2 quarters, and 3 nickels?

One fourth of the students earned A's. There were 280 students in all. How many students earned A's?

What is ½ of 560

Stephen could hop 72 times in 1 minute. At that rate, how many times could he hop in 9 minutes?

$20- $19,39=   86x40=

Division facts: 1,2,3,4, 5

10÷1=	35÷ 5 =	14÷2=	3÷3=	18÷3=	20÷5=	15÷5=
25÷5=	36÷4=	30÷5=	15÷3=	6÷2=	15÷5=	10÷2=
12÷3=	21÷3=	35÷5=	5÷1=	28÷4=	10÷2=	4÷1=
18÷9=	16÷2=	32÷4=	15÷5=	18÷2=	9÷3=	9÷9=
16÷4=	5÷5=	10÷5=	6÷3=	12÷2=	24÷4=	8÷4=
12÷4=	2÷2=	7÷1=	40÷5=	8÷2=	2÷2=	10÷5=
10÷2=	20÷4=	27÷3=	45÷5=	12÷3=	18÷3=	27÷3=

READING

Your other task for the day is to read a book. At this point you should be able to read for ½ hour to 1 hour each day. Look online for a variety of book lists. You can also check out my site www.plainandnotsoplain.com and see all of the books that we have enjoyed at this grade level. Write the title of the book you are reading and how long you have read for.

_____

_____

Use a chart to plan a book report. The ideas you list can help you write your report fully and thoughtfully. Pick a book you have read or are reading now.

Book title_____

Author_____

Setting_____

_____

Characters_____

_____

_____

Plot_____

_____

_____

_____

Theme_____

_____

spelling list 21 copy them

batteries

cowboys

delays

donkeys

gravies

ivies

ladies

Mondays

pennies

ponies

stories

trays

Tuesdays

valleys

Wednesdays

One half of the 780 fans stood and cheered. How many fans stood and cheered? What percent of fans stood and cheered?

How many years in ten centuries?

A 2-liter bottle contains how many milliliters of soda?

What is the perimeter of a rectangle 6 inch by 4 inch?

8x8x8=   704x9

285 ÷7   439÷5

Which of these is a multiple of 8
4   12   48   84

Division facts: 1-6

10÷1=	35÷5 =	14÷2=	3÷3=	18÷3=	20÷5=	15÷5=
25÷5=	36÷4=	30÷5=	15÷3=	6÷2=	15÷5=	10÷2=
12÷3=	21÷3=	35÷5=	54÷6=	28÷4=	42÷6=	4÷1=
18÷9=	48÷6	32÷4=	15÷5=	18÷2=	9÷3=	9÷9=
24÷6=	16÷2=	5÷5=	5÷1=	36÷6=	10÷2=	18÷6=
16÷4=	30÷6=	10÷5=	6÷3=	12÷2=	24÷4=	8÷4=
12÷4=	2÷2=	7÷1=	40÷5=	8÷2=	2÷2=	10÷5=
10÷2=	20÷4=	27÷3=	45÷5=	12÷6=	18÷3=	27÷3=

READING

Your other task for the day is to read a book. At this point you should be able to read for ½ hour to 1 hour each day. Look online for a variety of book lists. You can also check out my site www.plainandnotsoplain.com and see all of the books that we have enjoyed at this grade level. Write the title of the book you are reading and how long you have read for.

_____

_____

Fact vs Opinion
Write F for fact and O for opinion

_____Cameras bring happiness and pleasure.

_____Joseph Niepce of France took the first photograph in 1827.

_____He tried to phonograph the view from his window.

_____The quality of that first picture wasn't worth the hours he spent on it.

_____But Niepce was the best photographer of his day.

_____1888 was the most important year in camera history.

_____Nowadays, everyone loves to take pictures.

_____Almost anyone can learn to use a camera.

_____Digital cameras are much better than film cameras.

___Being a photographer is one of the best jobs you could have.

```
J  S  J  P  O  N  I  E  S  U  W  Y  L  H  A
J  E  E  H  R  D  J  C  X  V  B  J  H  Q  F
O  N  L  Q  V  N  U  D  O  B  Z  H  R  G  F
F  R  F  J  A  B  L  X  Z  W  I  C  W  F  X
Y  A  H  D  L  A  L  P  B  L  B  U  O  W  G
T  X  I  E  L  T  I  I  P  G  E  O  O  Q  K
R  U  Q  L  E  T  V  U  Y  K  A  Y  Y  C  M
A  G  W  A  Y  E  I  G  R  A  V  I  E  S  F
Y  R  L  Y  S  R  E  M  O  N  D  A  Y  S  A
S  J  A  S  M  I  S  U  V  A  W  A  X  T  Q
W  D  O  N  K  E  Y  S  X  Z  D  W  U  X  D
W  E  D  N  E  S  D  A  Y  S  N  G  T  M  M
H  N  O  P  E  N  N  I  E  S  A  X  Y  Y  E
L  A  D  I  E  S  Y  U  Y  U  I  S  S  P  Z
B  S  A  Y  L  S  T  O  R  I  E  S  B  B  B
```

BATTERIES	COWBOYS	DELAYS
DONKEYS	GRAVIES	IVIES
LADIES	MONDAYS	PENNIES
PONIES	STORIES	TRAYS
TUESDAYS	VALLEYS	WEDNESDAYS

Seven thousand, three hundred ninety-six is how much less than eleven thousand, eight hundred seventy-three?

Shannon has five days to read a 200-page book. If she wants to read the same number of pages each day, how many pages should she read each day?

The prince searched 7 weeks for the princess. How many days did he search?

One third of the books were placed on the first shelf. What fraction of the books were not placed on the first shelf?

In the word HIPPOPOTAMI, what fraction of the letters are P's?

4+8+6+8+2+10+2+1+1+4+7=

Division facts: 1-6

10÷1=	35÷5 =	14÷2=	3÷3=	18÷3=	20÷5=	15÷5=
25÷5=	36÷4=	30÷5=	15÷3=	6÷2=	15÷5=	10÷2=
12÷3=	21÷3=	35÷5=	54÷6=	28÷4=	42÷6=	4÷1=
18÷9=	48÷6	32÷4=	15÷5=	18÷2=	9÷3=	9÷9=
24÷6=	16÷2=	5÷5=	5÷1=	36÷6=	10÷2=	18÷6=
16÷4=	30÷6=	10÷5=	6÷3=	12÷2=	24÷4=	8÷4=
12÷4=	2÷2=	7÷1=	40÷5=	8÷2=	2÷2=	10÷5=
10÷2=	20÷4=	27÷3=	45÷5=	12÷6=	18÷3=	27÷3=

READING

Your other task for the day is to read a book. At this point you should be able to read for ½ hour to 1 hour each day. Look online for a variety of book lists. You can also check out my site www.plainandnotsoplain.com and see all of the books that we have enjoyed at this grade level. Write the title of the book you are reading and how long you have read for.

_____

_____

1. In which section of the library would you find a book about rockets?
   a. fiction
   b. biography
   c. nonfiction
   d. sports
2. Which book would give information about Egyptian painting?
   a. an atlas
   b. a book on deserts
   c. an art book
   d. a dictionary
3. If you want to know who won the first World Cup Soccer tournament. Which resource would you choose?
   a. an encyclopedia
   b. an almanac
   c. a soccer Website
   d. an interview with a soccer coach
4. To know if a book on submarines tells of the sinking of the Kursk check
   a. Chapter 7
   b. the index
   c. the book jacket
   d. a review
5. Every book tells the year in which it was published. This fact is called
   a. the spine
   b. the dedication
   c. the call number
   d. the copyright date
6. Where in a book will you find the name of its author?
   a. in the glossary
   b. in the index
   c. on the title page
   d. in the table of contents
7. To find the capital of Kenya which resource would you check?
   a. an almanac
   b. an encylclopedia
   c. an atlas
   d. all of the above

Write a sentence for each of your words

The units of weight in the US are ounces, pounds, and tons. Remember that we used ounces to describe a fluid measurement, this is difference. This is about weight.

16 oz=1 lb
2000lb=1 ton

A box of cereal weighs 24 oz
Some students weigh 98 pounds
Many cars weigh 1 ton or more

Your school book weighs about 2 pounds. Two pounds is how many ounces?

The rhino weighed 3 tons. Three tons is how many pounds?

The newborn baby weighed 7lb 12 oz. The baby's weight was how much less than 8 pounds?

Simeon weighed 9 pounds when he was born. How many ounces is that?

How many centimeters is this

←——————→

How many millimeters is this

94,417+8,915=   405,321-231,988=

Division facts: 1-6

10÷1=	35÷5 =	14÷2=	3÷3=	18÷3=	20÷5=	15÷5=
25÷5=	36÷4=	30÷5=	15÷3=	6÷2=	15÷5=	10÷2=
12÷3=	21÷3=	35÷5=	54÷6=	28÷4=	42÷6=	4÷1=
18÷9=	48÷6	32÷4=	15÷5=	18÷2=	9÷3=	9÷9=
24÷6=	16÷2=	5÷5=	5÷1=	36÷6=	10÷2=	18÷6=
16÷4=	30÷6=	10÷5=	6÷3=	12÷2=	24÷4=	8÷4=
12÷4=	2÷2=	7÷1=	40÷5=	8÷2=	2÷2=	10÷5=
10÷2=	20÷4=	27÷3=	45÷5=	12÷6=	18÷3=	27÷3=

READING

Your other task for the day is to read a book. At this point you should be able to read for ½ hour to 1 hour each day. Look online for a variety of book lists. You can also check out my site www.plainandnotsoplain.com and see all of the books that we have enjoyed at this grade level. Write the title of the book you are reading and how long you have read for.

_____

_____

1. Sarah wants to know about Sir Arthur Conan Doyle. In which volume of the encyclopedia should she look?
    a. A
    b. C
    c. D
    d. S
2. Ali is writing a report on passenger helicopters. Which book probably won't help?
    a. Into Deep Space
    b. Modern Aircraft
    c. The 'Copter Chronicles
    d. Heliports and Helipads
3. Penny wants to see a map of Easter Island. Which is the best source for her to check?
    a. an atlas
    b. thesaurus
    c. dictionary
    d. a holiday magazine
4. Gabriel wants to find the definition of the word dulcet. To which part of the dictionary should he turn?
    a. beginning
    b. middle
    c. end
    d. cannot tell
5. Rachel wants to see pictures of ancient rock art. Which might be the best place for her to look?
    a. a rock video
    b. a filmstrip about ancestors
    c. a CD ROm on caves
    d. a website on Alaska
6. To learn the symptons of a skin condition called psoriasis, which of these sources probably won't help?
    a. a thesaurus
    b. a medical dictionary
    c. a home health care book
    d. an interview with a doctor
7. You want to know which albums won Grammy awards in 2001. Which resource would be your best choice?
    a. an almanac
    b. a music Website
    c. an encyclopedia
    d. an interview with a guitarist

QUIZ

In nature, we often find balance in the appearance and structure of objects and living things. For example, we can see a balance in the wing pattern of moths and butterflies. We call this kind of balance symmetry.

We draw a line down the middle of an object and that is called the line of symmetry. If both sides are mirror images of each other, we can call them both symmetrical.

Which of the following are symmetrical

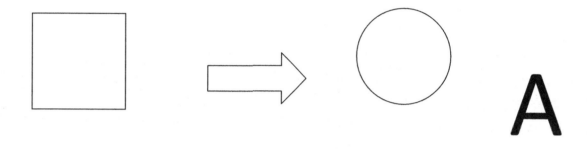

543x 3   642÷2=

326+432+219=   873-213=

Division facts: 1-6

10÷1=	35÷ 5 =	14÷2=	3÷3=	18÷3=	20÷5=	15÷5=
25÷5=	36÷4=	30÷5=	15÷3=	6÷2=	15÷5=	10÷2=
12÷3=	21÷3=	35÷5=	54÷6=	28÷4=	42÷6=	4÷1=
18÷9=	48÷6	32÷4=	15÷5=	18÷2=	9÷3=	9÷9=
24÷6=	16÷2=	5÷5=	5÷1=	36÷6=	10÷2=	18÷6=
16÷4=	30÷6=	10÷5=	6÷3=	12÷2=	24÷4=	8÷4=
12÷4=	2÷2=	7÷1=	40÷5=	8÷2=	2÷2=	10÷5=
10÷2=	20÷4=	27÷3=	45÷5=	12÷6=	18÷3=	27÷3=

READING

Your other task for the day is to read a book. At this point you should be able to read for ½ hour to 1 hour each day. Look online for a variety of book lists. You can also check out my site www.plainandnotsoplain.com and see all of the books that we have enjoyed at this grade level. Write the title of the book you are reading and how long you have read for.

_____

_____

Imagine someone who has never seen a pencil or a pencil sharpener. Give that person step by step written instructions for when and how to sharpen a pencil. Give all details clearly and in order. Use as many steps as you need.

1._____

_____

2._____

_____

3._____

_____

4._____

_____

5._____

_____

6._____

_____

7._____

_____

8._____

_____

9._____

_____

week 22 spelling list copy your words

prearrange

predict

preface

prepay

preview

reappear

rebuild

recover

redecorate

refill

reform

reload

remodel

repaint

restore

If it is not a leap year, what is the total number of days in January, February, and March?

The shoemakers wife made each of the twelve children a pair of pants and 2 shirts. How many pieces of clothing did she make?

John did seven more chin-ups than Paul did. If John did 18 chin ups, how many chin ups did Paul do?

The tally marks for 8 are ⊬⊬⊦ I I I   What are tally for 9?

If each side of an octagon is 1 centimeter long. What is perimeter in millimeters?

One third of the 18 marbles were purple. How many were purple?

Rob picked 46 peaches in one day. At that rate, how many peaches could he pick in 5 days?

Division facts: 1-6

10÷1=	35÷5 =	14÷2=	3÷3=	18÷3=	20÷5=	15÷5=
25÷5=	36÷4=	30÷5=	15÷3=	6÷2=	15÷5=	10÷2=
12÷3=	21÷3=	35÷5=	54÷6=	28÷4=	42÷6=	4÷1=
18÷9=	48÷6	32÷4=	15÷5=	18÷2=	9÷3=	9÷9=
24÷6=	16÷2=	5÷5=	5÷1=	36÷6=	10÷2=	18÷6=
16÷4=	30÷6=	10÷5=	6÷3=	12÷2=	24÷4=	8÷4=
12÷4=	2÷2=	7÷1=	40÷5=	8÷2=	2÷2=	10÷5=
10÷2=	20÷4=	27÷3=	45÷5=	12÷6=	18÷3=	27÷3=

READING

Your other task for the day is to read a book. At this point you should be able to read for ½ hour to 1 hour each day. Look online for a variety of book lists. You can also check out my site www.plainandnotsoplain.com and see all of the books that we have enjoyed at this grade level. Write the title of the book you are reading and how long you have read for.

_____

_____

Write a strong topic sentence that pulls together each group of sentences.

1. The bright hallways smelled of fresh paint.
The bulletin boards were decorated with cheery welcome signs.
Stacks of crisp new books waited in each room.

_____

_____

_____

2. People crowded along both sides of the street.
They waved flags and banners and held colorful balloons.
The distant sound of drums and horns could be heard to the north.

_____

_____

_____

3. We wore our most comfortable shoes for the day.
We hoped to raise money for a worthy cause.
Reporters and photographers were there to cover the event.
Free water stops were set up every few blocks.

_____

_____

_____

4.The cool air smelled salty and damp.
We pulled our rain gear up over our heads and climbed aboard.
Seagulls squawked and flew overhead as we pulled away from the dock.

_____

_____

```
P  R  E  B  U  I  L  D  S  T  I  U  V  N  P
D  R  E  P  A  I  N  T  C  D  N  U  M  P  R
R  Q  E  M  S  S  F  I  O  Q  H  G  D  R  E
U  E  D  A  R  E  D  E  C  O  R  A  T  E  F
X  E  C  Q  R  E  N  T  S  O  R  C  P  P  A
I  M  J  O  R  R  M  U  F  F  E  D  O  A  C
M  Q  E  P  V  G  A  E  S  R  A  Y  R  Y  E
T  G  N  Q  P  E  R  N  K  L  P  C  E  Y  L
V  B  Z  N  R  C  R  A  G  R  P  O  L  F  R
K  N  O  V  E  A  S  Q  Z  E  E  T  O  T  E
M  J  S  I  V  T  F  S  Z  S  A  O  A  R  F
D  U  J  N  I  R  E  C  Q  T  R  D  D  P  I
V  J  G  E  E  K  R  E  M  O  D  E  L  E  L
Z  Y  D  L  W  X  E  G  E  R  Q  J  S  R  L
A  B  W  V  P  B  A  W  T  E  B  W  V  U  Z
```

PREARRANGE	PREDICT	PREFACE
PREPAY	PREVIEW	REAPPEAR
REBUILD	RECOVER	REDECORATE
REFILL	REFOR	RELOAD
REMODEL	REPAINT	RESTORE

Multiplying by ten, hundred, and thousand

Remember when we multiply by ten, we just add a zero to the number

42x10=420

When we multiply by 100, we add two zeros

42x100=4200

When we multiply by 1000, we add three zeros
42x1000=42,000

365x10=   7x1000=   420x100=

Jim saw some pentagons. The pentagons had a total of 100 sides. How many
pentagons did he see?

A full pitcher of orange juice contains about how much juice?
2 ounces   2 liters   2 gallons

46.01- (3.68+10.2)

$3.17x 4=   37x40=

Division facts: 1-7

63÷7=	35÷5 =	14÷2=	3÷3=	18÷3=	20÷5=	15÷5=
25÷5=	36÷4=	56÷7=	49÷7=	6÷2=	15÷5=	10÷2=
12÷3=	21÷3=	35÷5=	54÷6=	28÷4=	42÷6=	4÷1=
18÷9=	48÷6	32÷4=	15÷5=	18÷2=	9÷3=	9÷9=
24÷6=	16÷2=	5÷5=	5÷1=	36÷6=	10÷2=	18÷6=
16÷4=	30÷6=	10÷5=	6÷3=	12÷2=	24÷4=	8÷4=
12÷4=	2÷2=	7÷1=	40÷5=	8÷2=	14÷7=	10÷5=
10÷1=	42÷7=	27÷3=	30÷5=	28÷7=	15÷3=	21÷7=
10:2=	20÷4=	35÷7=	45÷5=	12÷6=	18÷3=	27÷3=

READING

Your other task for the day is to read a book. At this point you should be able to read for ½ hour to 1 hour each day. Look online for a variety of book lists. You can also check out my site www.plainandnotsoplain.com and see all of the books that we have enjoyed at this grade level. Write the title of the book you are reading and how long you have read for.

_____

_____

Your purpose for writing should guide how you write. Read the example below. It shows two sentences on the same topic. But each was written for a different purpose.

Topic: a child in a robot costume
Purpose: to amuse
A kid dressed in boxes and tin cans clanked up our front steps

Purpose: to frighten
A terrifying creature slowly crept up to our doorbell

Write two sentences on each topic. Make each sentence serve a different purpose.

Topic: Soaring in a hang glider

Purpose: to thrill _____

_____

Purpose: to caution against

_____

_____

Topic: your sisters new outfit

Purpose: to flatter

_____

_____

Purpose : to hide your disklike

_____

_____

Write a sentence for each of your words

Multiplying two digit numbers

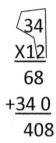

$$\begin{array}{r} 34 \\ \times 12 \\ \hline 68 \end{array}$$

We draw a turtle head around the first part of the problem and multiply as usual. Then that turtle drops an egg(0) and we move over to the next place to do the other place value and multiply.

$$\begin{array}{r} 34 \\ \times 12 \\ \hline 68 \\ +34\ 0 \\ \hline 408 \end{array}$$

Make your turtle head and multiply, then drop a 0 for the egg and multiply the other place value. Then add the two together to get your answer.

Your turn:
$$\begin{array}{r} 31 \\ \times 23 \\ \hline \end{array}$$

$$\begin{array}{r} 32 \\ \times 23 \\ \hline \end{array}$$
$$\begin{array}{r} 43 \\ \times 12 \\ \hline \end{array}$$
$$\begin{array}{r} 34 \\ \times 21 \\ \hline \end{array}$$

Division facts: 1-7

63÷7=	35÷ 5 =	14÷2=	3÷3=	18÷3=	20÷5=	15÷5=
25÷5=	36÷4=	56÷7=	49÷7=	6÷2=	15÷5=	10÷2=
12÷3=	21÷3=	35÷5=	54÷6=	28÷4=	42÷6=	4÷1=
18÷9=	48÷6	32÷4=	15÷5=	18÷2=	9÷3=	9÷9=
24÷6=	16÷2=	5÷5=	5÷1=	36÷6=	10÷2=	18÷6=
16÷4=	30÷6=	10÷5=	6÷3=	12÷2=	24÷4=	8÷4=
12÷4=	2÷2=	7÷1=	40÷5=	8÷2=	14÷7=	10÷5=
10÷1=	42÷7=	27÷3=	30÷5=	28÷7=	15÷3=	21÷7=
10÷2=	20÷4=	35÷7=	45÷5=	12÷6=	18÷3=	27÷3=

READING

Your other task for the day is to read a book. At this point you should be able to read for ½ hour to 1 hour each day. Look online for a variety of book lists. You can also check out my site www.plainandnotsoplain.com and see all of the books that we have enjoyed at this grade level. Write the title of the book you are reading and how long you have read for.

_____

_____

Make each dull sentence better. Add precise nouns and vivid verbs and adjectives

1. The first day of vacation is so good.

_____

_____

2. It's nice to get a chance to be lazy.

_____

_____

3. I don't have to get up early unless I want to.

_____

_____

4. Well, it is harder to see my friends.

_____

_____

5. There will be no homework tonight.

_____

_____

6. Today we went to pick up my new dog.

_____

_____

QUIZ

What is the tally for this number ЈHГ ЈHГ IIII

One half of the 18 players were on the field. How many players were on the field?

A dime is 1/10 of a dollar. What fraction of a dollar is a penny?

$3\overline{)477}$ $5\overline{)2535}$

Practice the division facts to memorize

Division facts: 1-7

63÷7=	35÷5 =	14÷2=	3÷3=	18÷3=	20÷5=	15÷5=
25÷5=	36÷4=	56÷7=	49÷7=	6÷2=	15÷5=	10÷2=
12÷3=	21÷3=	35÷5=	54÷6=	28÷4=	42÷6=	4÷1=
18÷9=	48÷6	32÷4=	15÷5=	18÷2=	9÷3=	9÷9=
24÷6=	16÷2=	5÷5=	5÷1=	36÷6=	10÷2=	18÷6=
16÷4=	30÷6=	10÷5=	6÷3=	12÷2=	24÷4=	8÷4=
12÷4=	2÷2=	7÷1=	40÷5=	8÷2=	14÷7=	10÷5=
10÷1=	42÷7=	27÷3=	30÷5=	28÷7=	15÷3=	21÷7=
10÷2=	20÷4=	35÷7=	45÷5=	12÷6=	18÷3=	27÷3=

READING

Your other task for the day is to read a book. At this point you should be able to read for ½ hour to 1 hour each day. Look online for a variety of book lists. You can also check out my site www.plainandnotsoplain.com and see all of the books that we have enjoyed at this grade level. Write the title of the book you are reading and how long you have read for.

_____

_____

Write the days of the week

_____

_____

_____

_____

_____

_____

_____

Write the months of the year

_____

_____

_____

_____

_____

_____

_____

_____

_____

_____

_____

_____

Spelling list 23 copy them

bicycle

bifocals

bimonthly

binoculars

quadrangle

quadruplet

triangle

tricep

tricolor

tricycle

trio

tripod

unicorn

unicycle

uniform

Let's practice division mostly for the next week☺

READING

Your other task for the day is to read a book. At this point you should be able to read for ½ hour to 1 hour each day. Look online for a variety of book lists. You can also check out my site www.plainandnotsoplain.com and see all of the books that we have enjoyed at this grade level. Write the title of the book you are reading and how long you have read for.

_____

_____

Division facts: 1-7

63÷7=	35÷ 5 =	14÷2=	3÷3=	18÷3=	20÷5=	15÷5=
25÷5=	36÷4=	56÷7=	49÷7=	6÷2=	15÷5=	10÷2=
12÷3=	21÷3=	35÷5=	54÷6=	28÷4=	42÷6=	4÷1=
18÷9=	48÷6	32÷4=	15÷5=	18÷2=	9÷3=	9÷9=
24÷6=	16÷2=	5÷5=	5÷1=	36÷6=	10÷2=	18÷6=
16÷4=	30÷6=	10÷5=	6÷3=	12÷2=	24÷4=	8÷4=
12÷4=	2÷2=	7÷1=	40÷5=	8÷2=	14÷7=	10÷5=
10÷1=	42÷7=	27÷3=	30÷5=	28÷7=	15÷3=	21÷7=
10÷2=	20÷4=	35÷7=	45÷5=	12÷6=	18÷3=	27÷3=

Choose one of the following topics for writing:

- A review of a toothpaste you like or dislike
- A letter of advice to help someone who has a quick temper
- A set of instructions for preparing your favorite meal

_____

_____

_____

_____

_____

_____

_____

_____

_____

_____

_____

```
T  X  D  R  V  T  U  S  P  W  C  Q  I  W  Z
R  F  C  T  X  J  W  F  Q  C  C  J  J  E  R
I  B  B  B  R  Q  U  A  D  R  U  P  L  E  T
C  A  N  I  M  I  Q  N  V  S  M  T  L  U  L
E  S  F  F  M  F  C  E  I  R  T  G  S  N  Q
P  P  X  O  Y  O  W  O  Z  F  N  R  K  I  U
F  R  O  C  I  I  N  Q  L  A  O  W  I  C  A
U  X  O  A  D  P  L  T  I  O  M  R  S  O  D
N  R  P  L  Q  R  S  R  H  N  R  W  M  R  R
I  F  S  S  R  B  T  C  S  L  Q  F  K  N  A
C  C  T  R  I  C  Y  C  L  E  Y  J  P  U  N
Y  V  Z  Z  P  V  K  G  Q  K  Q  X  L  K  G
C  Q  Z  A  B  I  N  O  C  U  L  A  R  S  L
L  T  R  I  P  O  D  Z  B  I  C  Y  C  L  E
E  W  F  X  L  V  A  X  H  D  E  Q  A  T  R
```

BICYCLE	BIFOCALS	BIMONTHLY
BINOCULARS	QUADRANGLE	QUADRUPLET
TRIANGLE	TRICEP	TRICOLOR
TRICYCLE	TRIO	TRIPOD
UNICORN	UNICYCLE	UNIFORM

357

Lets practice division mostly for the next week☺

READING

Your other task for the day is to read a book. At this point you should be able to read for ½ hour to 1 hour each day. Look online for a variety of book lists. You can also check out my site www.plainandnotsoplain.com and see all of the books that we have enjoyed at this grade level. Write the title of the book you are reading and how long you have read for.

_____

_____

Division facts: 1-7

63÷7=	35÷ 5 =	14÷2=	3÷3=	18÷3=	20÷5=	15÷5=
25÷5=	36÷4=	56÷7=	49÷7=	6÷2=	15÷5=	10÷2=
12÷3=	21÷3=	35÷5=	54÷6=	28÷4=	42÷6=	4÷1=
18÷9=	48÷6	32÷4=	15÷5=	18÷2=	9÷3=	9÷9=
24÷6=	16÷2=	5÷5=	5÷1=	36÷6=	10÷2=	18÷6=
16÷4=	30÷6=	10÷5=	6÷3=	12÷2=	24÷4=	8÷4=
12÷4=	2÷2=	7÷1=	40÷5=	8÷2=	14÷7=	10÷5=
10÷1=	42÷7=	27÷3=	30÷5=	28÷7=	15÷3=	21÷7=
10÷2=	20÷4=	35÷7=	45÷5=	12÷6=	18÷3=	27÷3=

Choose one of the following topics to write:
- An evaluation of what makes a good parent
- A summary of the plot of a movie, tv show, book, or story

_____

_____

_____

_____

_____

_____

_____

_____

_____

_____

_____

_____

_____

Write a sentence for each of your words

Lets practice division mostly for the next week☺

READING

Your other task for the day is to read a book. At this point you should be able to read for ½ hour to 1 hour each day. Look online for a variety of book lists. You can also check out my site www.plainandnotsoplain.com and see all of the books that we have enjoyed at this grade level. Write the title of the book you are reading and how long you have read for.

_____

_____

Division facts: 1-8

63÷7=	35÷5 =	72÷8=	3÷3=	18÷3=	20÷5=	15÷5=
14÷2=	64÷8=	10÷5=	54÷6=	48÷8=	9÷3=	27÷3=
25÷5=	36÷4=	56÷7=	49÷7=	6÷2=	15÷5=	10÷2=
12÷3=	21÷3=	35÷5=	56÷8=	28÷4=	42÷6=	4÷1=
18÷9=	48÷6	32÷4=	15÷5=	18÷2=	40÷8=	9÷9=
24÷6=	16÷2=	5÷5=	5÷1=	36÷6=	10÷2=	18÷6=
16÷4=	30÷6=	10÷5=	6÷3=	12÷2=	24÷4=	8÷4=
12÷4=	2÷2=	7÷1=	40÷5=	8÷2=	14÷7=	16÷8=
10÷1=	42÷7=	32÷8=	30÷5=	28÷7=	15÷3=	21÷7=
10÷2=	20÷4=	35÷7=	45÷5=	12÷6=	18÷3=	27÷3=

Choose one of the following topics:

- A story about someone you will never forget
- A story about a funny family episode
- A brief tale that shows your sense of humor

_____

_____

_____

_____

_____

_____

_____

_____

_____

_____

_____

_____

QUIZ

Lets practice division mostly for the next week☺

READING

Your other task for the day is to read a book. At this point you should be able to read for ½ hour to 1 hour each day. Look online for a variety of book lists. You can also check out my site www.plainandnotsoplain.com and see all of the books that we have enjoyed at this grade level. Write the title of the book you are reading and how long you have read for.

_____

_____

Division facts: 1-8

63÷7=	35÷ 5 =	72÷8=	3÷3=	18÷3=	20÷5=	15÷5=
14÷2=	64÷8=	10÷5=	54÷6=	48÷8=	9÷3=	27÷3=
25÷5=	36÷4=	56÷7=	49÷7=	6÷2=	15÷5=	10÷2=
12÷3=	21÷3=	35÷5=	56÷8=	28÷4=	42÷6=	4÷1=
18÷9=	48÷6	32÷4=	15÷5=	18÷2=	40÷8=	9÷9=
24÷6=	16÷2=	5÷5=	5÷1=	36÷6=	10÷2=	18÷6=
16÷4=	30÷6=	10÷5=	6÷3=	12÷2=	24÷4=	8÷4=
12÷4=	2÷2=	7÷1=	40÷5=	8÷2=	14÷7=	16÷8=
10÷1=	42÷7=	32÷8=	30÷5=	28÷7=	15÷3=	21÷7=
10÷2=	20÷4=	35÷7–	45:5=	12÷6=	18÷3=	27÷3=

Choose a topic:
- A description of a beautiful place you have visited
- A description of an important invention
- A memory of a dream or fantasy
- An observation about a unique family member of friend

_____

_____

_____

_____

_____

_____

_____

_____

_____

_____

_____

_____

week 24 spelling list copy them

discolor

dislike

disobey

distrust

nondairy

nonfat

nonsense

unbreakable

uncertain

unfair

unfold

unfriendly

unhappiness

unlucky

unselfish

Lets practice division mostly for the next week☺

READING

Your other task for the day is to read a book. At this point you should be able to read for ½ hour to 1 hour each day. Look online for a variety of book lists. You can also check out my site www.plainandnotsoplain.com and see all of the books that we have enjoyed at this grade level. Write the title of the book you are reading and how long you have read for.

_____

_____

Division facts: 1-8

63÷7=	35÷ 5 =	72÷8=	3÷3=	18÷3=	20÷5=	15÷5=
14÷2=	64÷8=	10÷5=	54÷6=	48÷8=	9÷3=	27÷3=
25÷5=	36÷4=	56÷7=	49÷7=	6÷2=	15÷5=	10÷2=
12÷3=	21÷3=	35÷5=	56÷8=	28÷4=	42÷6=	4÷1=
18÷9=	48÷6	32÷4=	15÷5=	18÷2=	40÷8=	9÷9=
24÷6=	16÷2=	5÷5=	5÷1=	36÷6=	10÷2=	18÷6=
16÷4=	30÷6=	10÷5=	6÷3=	12÷2=	24÷4=	8÷4=
12÷4=	2÷2=	7÷1=	40÷5=	8÷2=	14÷7=	16÷8=
10÷1=	42÷7=	32÷8=	30÷5=	28÷7=	15÷3=	21÷7=
10÷2-	20÷4-	35÷7=	45÷5=	12÷6=	18÷3=	27÷3=

Writing expression
- A time when something unexpected happened to you
- A memory of an event from your early childhood
- An email or letter to a friend you haven't seen or spoken to in a long time.
- A journal entry about something that upset you

```
U  N  O  N  S  E  N  S  E  X  B  X  Y  D  N
N  O  F  N  A  U  R  B  P  P  M  U  F  F  M
H  N  Q  I  Y  F  I  K  D  P  C  B  D  X  H
A  F  T  T  H  N  O  N  D  A  I  R  Y  V  O
P  A  J  U  N  C  E  R  T  A  I  N  Q  U  U
P  T  L  M  K  B  Y  V  V  S  G  G  U  U  N
I  U  N  B  R  E  A  K  A  B  L  E  N  N  F
N  L  D  I  S  O  B  E  Y  A  W  U  L  S  R
E  K  S  D  I  S  C  O  L  O  R  F  U  E  I
S  K  F  Z  L  X  O  B  O  G  O  J  C  L  E
S  X  K  V  U  N  F  A  I  R  S  F  K  F  N
R  X  B  N  G  V  L  H  D  V  J  P  Y  I  D
X  H  P  D  I  S  L  I  K  E  E  B  G  S  L
I  C  E  T  V  D  I  S  T  R  U  S  T  H  Y
J  E  X  K  F  H  B  U  N  F  O  L  D  G  T
```

DISCOLOR	DISLIKE	DISOBEY
DISTRUST	NONDAIRY	NONFAT
NONSENSE	UNBREAKABLE	UNCERTAIN
UNFAIR	UNFOLD	UNFRIENDLY
UNHAPPINESS	UNLUCKY	UNSELFISH

Lets practice division mostly for the next week☺

READING

Your other task for the day is to read a book. At this point you should be able to read for ½ hour to 1 hour each day. Look online for a variety of book lists. You can also check out my site www.plainandnotsoplain.com and see all of the books that we have enjoyed at this grade level. Write the title of the book you are reading and how long you have read for.

_____

_____

Division facts: 1-8

63÷7=	35÷ 5 =	72÷8=	3÷3=	18÷3=	20÷5=	15÷5=
14÷2=	64÷8=	10÷5=	54÷6=	48÷8=	9÷3=	27÷3=
25÷5=	36÷4=	56÷7=	49÷7=	6÷2=	15÷5=	10÷2=
12÷3=	21÷3=	35÷5=	56÷8=	28÷4=	42÷6=	4÷1=
18÷9=	48÷6	32÷4=	15÷5=	18÷2=	40÷8=	9÷9=
24÷6=	16÷2=	5÷5=	5÷1=	36÷6=	10÷2=	18÷6=
16÷4=	30÷6=	10÷5=	6÷3=	12÷2=	24÷4=	8÷4=
12÷4=	2÷2=	7÷1=	40÷5=	8÷2=	14÷7=	16÷8=
10÷1=	42÷7=	32÷8=	30÷5=	28÷7=	15÷3=	21÷7=
10÷2=	20÷4=	35÷7=	45÷5=	12÷6=	18÷3=	27÷3=

Writing persuasion

- A letter to the editor of the newspaper recommending safe new bicycle paths
- A speech you would give if you wanted to be class president
- A public service announcement asking people to clean up their neighborhoods

_____

_____

_____

_____

_____

_____

_____

_____

_____

_____

_____

_____

_____

Write a sentence for each of your words

Lets practice division mostly for the next week☺

READING

Your other task for the day is to read a book. At this point you should be able to read for ½ hour to 1 hour each day. Look online for a variety of book lists. You can also check out my site www.plainandnotsoplain.com and see all of the books that we have enjoyed at this grade level. Write the title of the book you are reading and how long you have read for.

_____

_____

Division facts: 1-8

63÷7=	35÷ 5 =	72÷8=	3÷3=	18÷3=	20÷5=	15÷5=
14÷2=	64÷8=	10÷5=	54÷6=	48÷8=	9÷3=	27÷3=
25÷5=	36÷4=	56÷7=	49÷7=	6÷2=	15÷5=	10÷2=
12÷3=	21÷3=	35÷5=	56÷8=	28÷4=	42÷6=	4÷1=
18÷9=	48÷6	32÷4=	15÷5=	18÷2=	40÷8=	9÷9=
24÷6=	16÷2=	5÷5=	5÷1=	36÷6=	10÷2=	18÷6=
16÷4=	30÷6=	10÷5=	6÷3=	12÷2=	24÷4=	8÷4=
12÷4=	2÷2=	7÷1=	40÷5=	8÷2=	14÷7=	16÷8=
10÷1=	42÷7=	32÷8=	30÷5=	28÷7=	15÷3=	21÷7=
10÷2=	20÷4=	35÷7=	45÷5=	12÷6=	18÷3=	27÷3=

- Advice to a character in a book, or short story
- A letter to an author you liked or disliked
- A critical review of a movie you did not enjoy
- A review of a book for the school newspaper

_____

_____

_____

_____

_____

_____

_____

_____

_____

_____

QUIZ

Lets practice division mostly for the next week☺

READING

Your other task for the day is to read a book. At this point you should be able to read for ½ hour to 1 hour each day. Look online for a variety of book lists. You can also check out my site www.plainandnotsoplain.com and see all of the books that we have enjoyed at this grade level. Write the title of the book you are reading and how long you have read for.

_____

_____

Division facts: 1-8

63÷7=	35÷5 =	72÷8=	3÷3=	18÷3=	20÷5=	15÷5=
14÷2=	64÷8=	10÷5=	54÷6=	48÷8=	9÷3=	27÷3=
25÷5=	36÷4=	56÷7=	49÷7=	6÷2=	15÷5=	10÷2=
12÷3=	21÷3=	35÷5=	56÷8=	28÷4=	42÷6=	4÷1=
18÷9=	48÷6	32÷4=	15÷5=	18÷2=	40÷8=	9÷9=
24÷6=	16÷2=	5÷5=	5÷1=	36÷6=	10÷2=	18÷6=
16÷4=	30÷6=	10÷5=	6÷3=	12÷2=	24÷4=	8÷4=
12÷4=	2÷2=	7÷1=	40÷5=	8÷2=	14÷7=	16÷8=
10÷1=	42÷7=	32÷8=	30÷5=	28÷7=	15÷3=	21÷7=
10÷2=	20÷4=	35÷7=	45÷5=	12÷6=	18÷3=	27÷3=

- Classified ad for selling your old tablet
- A letter to a pet shop offering to work on Saturdays
- An invitation to a party your are having

_____

_____

_____

_____

_____

_____

_____

_____

_____

_____

_____

_____

week 25 spelling list

beliefs

calves

chiefs

cliffs

cuffs

elves

halves

knives

leaves

lives

loaves

roofs

scarves

shelves

wives

Lets practice division mostly for the next week☺

RLADING

Your other task for the day is to read a book. At this point you should be able to read for ½ hour to 1 hour each day. Look online for a variety of book lists. You can also check out my site www.plainandnotsoplain.com and see all of the books that we have enjoyed at this grade level. Write the title of the book you are reading and how long you have read for.

_____

_____

Division facts: 1-9

63÷7=	35÷5 =	72÷8=	3÷3=	18÷3=	20÷5=	15÷5=
18÷9=	81÷9=	12÷6=	5÷5=	28÷4=	54÷9=	45÷9=
14÷2=	64÷8=	10÷5=	54÷6=	48÷8=	9÷3=	27÷3=
25÷5=	36÷4=	56÷7=	49÷7=	6÷2=	15÷5=	10÷2=
12÷3=	21÷3=	35÷5=	56÷8=	63÷9=	42÷6=	4÷1=
72÷9=	48÷6	32÷4=	15÷5=	18÷2=	40÷8=	9÷9=
24÷6=	16÷2=	36÷9=	5÷1=	36÷6=	10÷2=	18÷6=
16÷4=	30÷6=	10÷5=	6÷3=	12÷2=	24÷4=	8÷4=
12÷4=	2÷2=	7÷1=	40÷5=	8÷2=	14÷7=	16÷8=
10÷1=	42÷7=	32÷8=	30÷5=	28÷7=	15÷3=	21÷7=
10÷2=	20÷4=	35÷7=	45÷5=	27÷9=	18÷3=	27÷3=

Sometimes people have difficulty using good, well, sure, surely,real and really correctly.

Adjectives	Adverbs
Good is an adjective when it describes a noun. That was a good dinner.	Good is never used as an adverb.
Well is an adjective when it means in good health or having a good appearance. She looks well.	Well is an adverb when it is used to tell that something is done capably or effectively. She writes well.
Sure is an adjective when it modifies a noun. A robin is a sure sign of spring.	Surely is an adverb. He surely wants a job.
Real is an adjective that means genuine or true. That was a real diamond.	Really is an adverb. Mary really played a good game.

You did a very(good/well) job of writing your book report.

The detective in the story used his skills (well/good).

He (sure/surely) solved the case before anyone else did.

I (real/really)want to read that book now.

Did it take you long to decide who the (real/really) criminal was?

Although the butler looked (well, good) and healthy, he died.

You will (sure/surely) get a good grade on that report.

Detective Sam read the clues (good/well) as he worked on the case.

```
W  K  M  B  U  L  B  Z  Q  J  B  X  R  T  E
N  P  K  H  X  P  J  L  H  W  I  V  E  S  L
W  A  W  A  E  A  S  C  A  K  N  V  I  C  V
L  S  L  B  H  E  N  A  L  K  N  I  I  A  E
O  L  T  E  V  H  G  L  V  C  J  I  Q  R  S
A  E  E  L  A  H  D  V  E  T  D  J  V  V  K
V  I  E  I  U  H  E  S  I  V  R  Y  E  F
E  H  Y  E  B  Y  E  S  J  C  R  M  O  S  S
S  Z  G  F  D  A  F  S  L  W  U  O  M  G  M
H  C  B  S  R  E  B  Q  I  S  M  F  O  O  T
I  L  T  N  I  Y  G  Q  V  E  B  O  F  F  V
R  I  C  H  V  B  E  X  E  E  U  K  T  S  S
F  F  C  Y  Q  K  H  X  S  N  O  R  V  Y  T
R  F  S  V  D  H  Q  D  C  W  S  T  V  D  U
O  S  I  I  S  W  F  R  W  T  G  D  X  E  L
```

BELIEFS	CALVES	CHIEFS
CLIFFS	CUFFS	ELVES
HALVES	KNIVES	LEAVES
LIVES	LOAVES	ROOFS
SCARVES	SHELVES	WIVES

Lets practice division mostly for the next week☺

READING

Your other task for the day is to read a book. At this point you should be able to read for ½ hour to 1 hour each day. Look online for a variety of book lists. You can also check out my site www.plainandnotsoplain.com and see all of the books that we have enjoyed at this grade level. Write the title of the book you are reading and how long you have read for.

_____

_____

Division facts: 1-9

63÷7=	35÷ 5 =	72÷8=	3÷3=	18÷3=	20÷5=	15÷5=
18÷9=	81÷9=	12÷6=	5÷5=	28÷4=	54÷9=	45÷9=
14÷2=	64÷8=	10÷5=	54÷6=	48÷8=	9÷3=	27÷3=
25÷5=	36÷4=	56÷7=	49÷7=	6÷2=	15÷5=	10÷2=
12÷3=	21÷3=	35÷5=	56÷8=	63÷9=	42÷6=	4÷1=
72÷9=	48÷6	32÷4=	15÷5=	18÷2=	40÷8=	9÷9=
24÷6=	16÷2=	36÷9=	5÷1=	36÷6=	10÷2=	18÷6=
16÷4=	30÷6=	10÷5=	6÷3=	12÷2=	24÷4=	8÷4=
12÷4=	2÷2=	7÷1=	40÷5=	8÷2=	14÷7=	16÷8=
10÷1=	42÷7=	32÷8=	30÷5=	28÷7=	15÷3=	21÷7=
10÷2=	20÷4=	35÷7=	45÷5=	27÷9=	18÷3=	27÷3=

For each word given below, write the root word, and prefix/suffix. Remember some root word's spelling have been changed before adding suffixes. Not all words will have a prefix and a suffix.

word	prefix	root word	suffix
resourceful			
accomplishment			
numbness			
convincing			
disobeying			
unmistakable			
disinfecting			
disclaimed			
reopening			
restless			
precaution			

Write a sentence for each of your words

Mixed numbers and improper fractions

Here we show a picture of 1 ½ shaded circles. Each whole circle has been divided into two half circles.

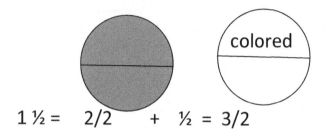

1 ½ =   2/2   +   ½ = 3/2

We see from this picture that 1 ½ is the same as three halves, which is written 3/2. The numerator is greater than the denominator so the fraction 3/2 is greater than 1. Fractions that are greater than or equal to 1 are called improper fractions.

Your turn:
Draw circles to show that 2 ¾ is equal to 11/4

Draw circles to show that 1 ¾ = 7/4

Division facts: 1-9

63÷7=	35÷5 =	72÷8=	3÷3=	18÷3=	20÷5=	15÷5=
18÷9=	81÷9=	12÷6=	5÷5=	28÷4=	54÷9=	45÷9=
14÷2=	64÷8=	10÷5=	54÷6=	48÷8=	9÷3=	27÷3=
25÷5=	36÷4=	56÷7=	49÷7=	6÷2=	15÷5=	10÷2=
12÷3=	21÷3=	35÷5=	56÷8=	63÷9=	42÷6=	4÷1=
72÷9=	48÷6	32÷4=	15÷5=	18÷2=	40÷8=	9÷9=
24÷6=	16÷2=	36÷9=	5÷1=	36÷6=	10÷2=	18÷6=
16÷4=	30÷6=	10÷5=	6÷3=	12÷2=	24÷4=	8÷4=
12÷4=	2÷2=	7÷1=	40÷5=	8÷2=	14÷7=	16÷8=
10÷1=	42÷7=	32÷8=	30÷5=	28÷7=	15÷3=	21÷7=
10÷2=	20÷4=	35÷7=	45÷5=	27÷9=	18÷3=	27÷3=

READING

Your other task for the day is to read a book. At this point you should be able to read for ½ hour to 1 hour each day. Look online for a variety of book lists. You can also check out my site www.plainandnotsoplain.com and see all of the books that we have enjoyed at this grade level. Write the title of the book you are reading and how long you have read for.

_____

_____

Each of these words has more than one meaning. Write the two meanings

word	meaning 1	meaning 2
spring		
run		
ruler		
duck		
cold		
tire		
rose		
face		
train		
pen		
box		
line		
bowl		

QUIZ

Multiply two digit

Remember how to do this—make the turtle head and drop an egg (0)

$$
\begin{array}{r}
^4 \\
46 \\
\times 27 \\
\hline
322
\end{array}
$$

The second step is to multiply the 46 by the 2.

$$
\begin{array}{r}
\cancel{4} \\
46 \\
\times 27 \\
\hline
322 \\
+920 \\
\hline
1242
\end{array}
$$

We ignore that 4 that we carried in the first step. Cross it off so you don't get confused.

Your turn:

$$
\begin{array}{r}
46 \\
\times 72 \\
\hline
\end{array}
\qquad\qquad
\begin{array}{r}
38 \\
\times 26 \\
\hline
\end{array}
$$

Division facts: 1-9

63÷7=	35÷5 =	72÷8=	3÷3=	18÷3=	20÷5=	15÷5=
18÷9=	81÷9=	12÷6=	5÷5=	28÷4=	54÷9=	45÷9=
14÷2=	64÷8=	10÷5=	54÷6=	48÷8=	9÷3=	27÷3=
25÷5=	36÷4=	56÷7=	49÷7=	6÷2=	15÷5=	10÷2=
12÷3=	21÷3=	35÷5=	56÷8=	63÷9=	42÷6=	4÷1=
72÷9=	48÷6	32÷4=	15÷5=	18÷2=	40÷8=	9÷9=
24÷6=	16÷2=	36÷9=	5÷1=	36÷6=	10÷2=	18÷6=
16÷4=	30÷6=	10÷5=	6÷3=	12÷2=	24÷4=	8÷4=
12÷4=	2÷2=	7÷1=	40÷5=	8÷2=	14÷7=	16÷8=
10÷1=	42÷7=	32÷8=	30÷5=	28÷7=	15÷3=	21÷7=
10÷2=	20÷4=	35÷7=	45÷5=	27÷9=	18÷3=	27÷3=

READING

Your other task for the day is to read a book. At this point you should be able to read for ½ hour to 1 hour each day. Look online for a variety of book lists. You can also check out my site www.plainandnotsoplain.com and see all of the books that we have enjoyed at this grade level. Write the title of the book you are reading and how long you have read for.

_____

_____

ABC order

_____hundred

_____cushion

_____generous

_____alabaster

_____delicate

_____peasant

_____humble

_____once

_____stallions

_____silks

_____jade

_____oxen

_____dragonfish

_____ivory

_____chests

week 26 spelling words copy them

ailment

attention

basement

celebration

movement

employment

germination

limitation

measurement

disappointment

multiplication

statement

subtraction

treatment

vacation

Thinking of money can help us understand decimal place value.

Hundreds	tens	ones	decimal point	tenths	hundredths	thousandths
$4	3	2	.	4	9	

Which digit in 12.875 is in the tenths place?

Which digit is in the hundredths place in 4.37?

Compare with < > =   (the wider part points to larger number)

23.25_____23.250   Both numbers have same digits. When you attach a zero at the end it does not add value to the number. So the numbers are equal.

Subtract 4.37-1.146   Line them up vertically first

    4.370—add that zero as a place holder then subtract
    -1.146

What digit is in the hundredths place? 4.370

Name the place value of the 4 in the number 1.234?

Division Facts 0-9

56÷7=	15÷3=	12÷6=	8÷2=	63÷7=	0÷4=
14÷2=	42÷6=	6÷1=	16÷8=	20÷5=	49÷7=
36÷4=	64÷8=	0÷3=	54÷9=	4÷2=	48÷8=
18÷9=	3÷1=	35÷5=	8÷4=	72÷8=	6÷6=
0÷5=	42÷7=	2÷2=	36÷9=	7÷1=	12÷3=
16÷2=	30÷5=	0÷1=	28÷7=	4÷4=	40÷8=
3÷3=	32÷8=	45÷5=	4÷1=	20÷4=	15÷5=
56÷8=	5÷1=	0÷8=	6÷2=	45÷9=	0÷6=
6÷3=	21÷7=	0÷9=	7÷7=	12÷4=	18÷6=
63÷9=	18÷3=	27÷9=	24÷3=	0÷2=	28÷4=
21÷3=	16÷4=	24÷8=	10÷5=	30÷6=	1÷1=
18÷2=	27÷3=	32÷4=	9÷1=	35÷7=	40÷5=
10÷2=	8÷8=	48÷6=	5÷5=	8÷1=	24÷6=
25÷5=	9÷3=	81÷9=	24÷4=	14÷7=	12÷2=
9÷9=	54÷6=	72÷9=	0÷7=	2÷1=	36÷6=

Synonyms and antonyms

synonyms mean the same

antonyms mean the opposite

word	synonyms		word	antonym
beautiful			helpful	
thrilled			lazy	
friendly			quiet	
done			enjoyed	
fair			hot	
wicked			calm	
amazed			tired	

READING

Your other task for the day is to read a book. At this point you should be able to read for ½ hour to 1 hour each day. Look online for a variety of book lists. You can also check out my site www.plainandnotsoplain.com and see all of the books that we have enjoyed at this grade level. Write the title of the book you are reading and how long you have read for.

_____

_____

```
R  G  G  R  L  I  M  I  T  A  T  I  O  N  R
G  E  R  M  I  N  A  T  I  O  N  C  Q  J  D
G  L  V  A  C  A  T  I  O  N  Y  P  P  F  X
A  T  Y  I  A  T  T  E  N  T  I  O  N  I
T  G  H  P  C  S  T  A  T  E  M  E  N  T  A
X  B  A  S  E  M  E  N  T  O  A  Q  K  O  C
D  I  S  A  P  P  O  I  N  T  M  E  N  T  Q
U  I  T  X  C  E  L  E  B  R  A  T  I  O  N
U  M  T  R  E  A  T  M  E  N  T  U  B  H  V
M  U  L  T  I  P  L  I  C  A  T  I  O  N  Z
V  K  X  D  U  R  P  N  V  A  I  E  O  I  C
M  S  U  B  T  R  A  C  T  I  O  N  M  A  P
X  F  Z  T  H  G  M  O  V  E  M  E  N  T  N
Y  I  X  S  M  E  A  S  U  R  E  M  E  N  T
L  E  M  P  L  O  Y  M  E  N  T  P  J  W  N
```

ATTTENTION	BASEMENT	CELEBRATION
MOVEMENT	EMPLOYMENT	GERMINATION
LIMITATION	MEASUREMENT	DISAPPOINTMENT
MULTIPLICATION	STATEMENT	SUBTRACTION
TREATMENT	VACATION	

Compare with < > =

3.25_____ 32.50

3.250_____3.25

12.34_____1.23

Round 5456 to nearest thousand.

Round 2872 to nearest thousand

What is the tally for 10

100x45=   1000x59=

Draw a square with sides 4 cm long

Division Facts 0-9

56÷7=	15÷3=	12÷6=	8÷2=	63÷7=	0÷4=
14÷2=	42÷6=	6÷1=	16÷8=	20÷5=	49÷7=
36÷4=	64÷8=	0÷3=	54÷9=	4÷2=	48÷8=
18÷9=	3÷1=	35÷5=	8÷4=	72÷8=	6÷6=
0÷5=	42÷7=	2÷2=	36÷9=	7÷1=	12÷3=
16÷2=	30÷5=	0÷1=	28÷7=	4÷4=	40÷8=
3÷3=	32÷8=	45÷5=	4÷1=	20÷4=	15÷5=
56÷8=	5÷1=	0÷8=	6÷2=	45÷9=	0÷6=
6÷3=	21÷7=	0÷9=	7÷7=	12÷4=	18÷6=
63÷9=	18÷3=	27÷9=	24÷3=	0÷2=	28÷4=
21÷3=	16÷4=	24÷8=	10÷5=	30÷6=	1÷1=
18÷2=	27÷3=	32÷4=	9÷1=	35÷7=	40÷5=
10÷2=	8÷8=	48÷6=	5÷5=	8÷1=	24÷6=
25÷5=	9÷3=	81÷9=	24÷4=	14÷7=	12÷2=
9÷9=	54÷6=	72÷9=	0÷7=	2÷1=	36÷6=

READING

Your other task for the day is to read a book. At this point you should be able to read for ½ hour to 1 hour each day. Look online for a variety of book lists. You can also check out my site www.plainandnotsoplain.com and see all of the books that we have enjoyed at this grade level. Write the title of the book you are reading and how long you have read for.

_____

_____

syllables---show your child how to clap out syllables. How many syllables in each word

accident   _____

advertise   _____

carpenter   _____

chocolate   _____

harmony   _____

hesitate   _____

marvelous   _____

peppermint   _____

universe   _____

Write a sentence for each of your words

Mary invited 14 friends for lunch. She plans on making 12 tuna sandwiches, 10 bologna sandwiches, and 8 ham sandwiches. How many sandwiches will she make in all?

Including Mary, each person can have how many sandwiches?

If Mary cuts each tuna sandwich in half, how many halves will there be?

Five pounds of grapes cost $2.95. What was the cost per pound?

If each side of a hexagon is 4 inches long, what is the perimeter of the hexagon in feet?

Nine million, four hundred thousand is how much greater than two million, seven hundred thousand?

$25 + $2.75 + $15.44 + 27 cents=

Division Facts 0-9

56÷7=	15÷3=	12÷6=	8÷2=	63÷7=	0÷4=
14÷2=	42÷6=	6÷1=	16÷8=	20÷5=	49÷7=
36÷4=	64÷8=	0÷3=	54÷9=	4÷2=	48÷8=
18÷9=	3÷1=	35÷5=	8÷4=	72÷8=	6÷6=
0÷5=	42÷7=	2÷2=	36÷9=	7÷1=	12÷3=
16÷2=	30÷5=	0÷1=	28÷7=	4÷4=	40÷8=
3÷3=	32÷8=	45÷5=	4÷1=	20÷4=	15÷5=
56÷8=	5÷1=	0÷8=	6÷2=	45÷9=	0÷6=
6÷3=	21÷7=	0÷9=	7÷7=	12÷4=	18÷6=
63÷9=	18÷3=	27÷9=	24÷3=	0÷2=	28÷4=
21÷3=	16÷4=	24÷8=	10÷5=	30÷6=	1÷1=
18÷2=	27÷3=	32÷4=	9÷1=	35÷7=	40÷5=
10÷2=	8÷8=	48÷6=	5÷5=	8÷1=	24÷6=
25÷5=	9÷3=	81÷9=	24÷4=	14÷7=	12÷2=
9÷9=	54÷6=	72÷9=	0÷7=	2÷1=	36÷6=

READING

Your other task for the day is to read a book. At this point you should be able to read for ½ hour to 1 hour each day. Look online for a variety of book lists. You can also check out my site www.plainandnotsoplain.com and see all of the books that we have enjoyed at this grade level. Write the title of the book you are reading and how long you have read for.

_____

_____

Use quotation marks to enclose the exact words of the speaker. The speakers first word must begin with a capital letter. Also follow these rules:

- When the speaker is named before the direct quotation, separate the speaker from the quotation with a comma.
- When the speaker is named after the direct quotation, use a comma or the proper end mark inside the last quotation.

Ex: Mother said, "You must clean your room."

"Sara is cleaning her room, " said Mother.

"Hurry up!" yelled John.

Punctuate these sentences correctly.

1. Father asked John, will you be home for dinner.

_____

_____

2. Hurry up yelled Pete

_____

3. When will you have time to eat asked Dad

_____

_____

QUIZ

6.2-0.26=   31x17=

George Washington was born in 1732 and died in 1799. How many years did he live?

A $1 bill weighs about 1 gram. How much would a $5 bill weigh?

Write tally marks for 14

One half of the 32 chess pieces were still on the board. How many chess pieces were still on the board?

Max left home at 10:30 am. He traveled for 7 hours. What time was it when he arrived?

4.12- (3.6+0.2+0.125)

$18-$15.63

Division Facts 0-9

56÷7=	15÷3=	12÷6=	8÷2=	63÷7=	0÷4=
14÷2=	42÷6=	6÷1=	16÷8=	20÷5=	49÷7=
36÷4=	64÷8=	0÷3=	54÷9=	4÷2=	48÷8=
18÷9=	3÷1=	35÷5=	8÷4=	72÷8=	6÷6=
0÷5=	42÷7=	2÷2=	36÷9=	7÷1=	12÷3=
16÷2=	30÷5=	0÷1=	28÷7=	4÷4=	40÷8=
3÷3=	32÷8=	45÷5=	4÷1=	20÷4=	15÷5=
56÷8=	5÷1=	0÷8=	6÷2=	45÷9=	0÷6=
6÷3=	21÷7=	0÷9=	7÷7=	12÷4=	18÷6=
63÷9=	18÷3=	27÷9=	24÷3=	0÷2=	28÷4=
21÷3=	16÷4=	24÷8=	10÷5=	30÷6=	1÷1=
18÷2=	27÷3=	32÷4=	9÷1=	35÷7=	40÷5=
10÷2=	8÷8=	48÷6=	5÷5=	8÷1=	24÷6=
25÷5=	9÷3=	81÷9=	24÷4=	14÷7=	12÷2=
9÷9=	54÷6=	72÷9=	0÷7=	2÷1=	36÷6=

READING

Your other task for the day is to read a book. At this point you should be able to read for ½ hour to 1 hour each day. Look online for a variety of book lists. You can also check out my site www.plainandnotsoplain.com and see all of the books that we have enjoyed at this grade level. Write the title of the book you are reading and how long you have read for.

_____

_____

Use commas to separate words or groups of words in a series of three or more.

Mom ate fried chicken, beans, and potato salad for dinner.

Your turn:

Place commas to separate the items in a series.

1. John bought buttered popcorn diet soda peanuts and a hot dog at the game.

2. The package of jelly beans held assorted flavors such as banana licorice strawberry watermelon and grape.

3. The picnic basket was filled with sandwiches pickles potato chips orange apples and brownies.

Rewrite the sentences below and add commas.

4. Karen had chocolate ice cream peanut butter cookies and strawberry licorice.

_____

_____

week 27 spelling list copy them

aren't

couldn't

doesn't

hasn't

he'd

I'd

she's

should've

they'll

wasn't

weren't

what's

who'd

won't

you've

Let's work on division problems

READING

Your other task for the day is to read a book. At this point you should be able to read for ½ hour to 1 hour each day. Look online for a variety of book lists. You can also check out my site www.plainandnotsoplain.com and see all of the books that we have enjoyed at this grade level. Write the title of the book you are reading and how long you have read for.

_____

_____

Division Facts 0-9

56÷7=	15÷3=	12÷6=	8÷2=	63÷7=	0÷4=
14÷2=	42÷6=	6÷1=	16÷8=	20÷5=	49÷7=
36÷4=	64÷8=	0÷3=	54÷9=	4÷2=	48÷8=
18÷9=	3÷1=	35÷5=	8÷4=	72÷8=	6÷6=
0÷5=	42÷7=	2÷2=	36÷9=	7÷1=	12÷3=
16÷2=	30÷5=	0÷1=	28÷7=	4÷4=	40÷8=
3÷3=	32÷8=	45÷5=	4÷1=	20÷4=	15÷5=
56÷8=	5÷1=	0÷8=	6÷2=	45÷9=	0÷6=
6÷3=	21÷7=	0÷9=	7÷7=	12÷4=	18÷6=
63÷9=	18÷3=	27÷9=	24÷3=	0÷2=	28÷4=
21÷3=	16÷4=	24÷8=	10÷5=	30÷6=	1÷1=
18÷2=	27÷3=	32÷4=	9÷1=	35÷7=	40÷5=
10÷2=	8÷8=	48÷6=	5÷5=	8÷1=	24÷6=
25÷5=	9÷3=	81÷9=	24÷4=	14÷7=	12÷2=
9÷9=	54÷6=	72÷9=	0÷7=	2÷1=	36÷6=

Subject/verb agreement

These two must agree. If the subject is singular, add s to the verb. If the subject is plural, do not add an ending to the verb.

Lava only **flows** when it is very hot. (singular)

Cinders **shoot** out of an active volcano. (plural)

Write the correct form of the verb.

1. Some volcanoes _____ quietly. (erupt)

2. The ground _____ around a volcano jut before an eruption.(swell)

3. Tremors _____ as magma works its way to the surface. (increase)

4. The sky _____ from the ash and dust that explode out of a volcano. (darken)

5. Steam _____ when molten lava comes in contact with water. (flow)

nothing today☺ for spelling

Let's work on division problems

READING

Your other task for the day is to read a book. At this point you should be able to read for ½ hour to 1 hour each day. Look online for a variety of book lists. You can also check out my site www.plainandnotsoplain.com and see all of the books that we have enjoyed at this grade level. Write the title of the book you are reading and how long you have read for.

_____

_____

56÷7=	15÷3=	12÷6=	8÷2=	63÷7=	0÷4=
14÷2=	42÷6=	6÷1=	16÷8=	20÷5=	49÷7=
36÷4=	64÷8=	0÷3=	54÷9=	4÷2=	48÷8=
18÷9=	3÷1=	35÷5=	8÷4=	72÷8=	6÷6=
0÷5=	42÷7=	2÷2=	36÷9=	7÷1=	12÷3=
16÷2=	30÷5=	0÷1=	28÷7=	4÷4=	40÷8=
3÷3=	32÷8=	45÷5=	4÷1=	20÷4=	15÷5=
56÷8=	5÷1=	0÷8=	6÷2=	45÷9=	0÷6=
6÷3=	21÷7=	0÷9=	7÷7=	12÷4=	18÷6=
63÷9=	18÷3=	27÷9=	24÷3=	0÷2=	28÷4=
21÷3=	16÷4=	24÷8=	10÷5=	30÷6=	1÷1=
18÷2=	27÷3=	32÷4=	9÷1=	35÷7=	40÷5=
10÷2=	8÷8=	48÷6=	5÷5=	8÷1=	24÷6=
25÷5=	9÷3=	81÷9=	24÷4=	14÷7=	12÷2=
9÷9=	54÷6=	72÷9=	0÷7=	2÷1=	36÷6=

Write the pronoun that agrees with the subject.

_____(They, We, He)tries very hard to skate
backwards at the skating rink.

_____(I, She, You) tells everyone about all the fun things
there are to do at the park.

_____(We, YOu,HE) invites a friend every time he goes to the
bicycle acrobatic demonstrations.

_____(It, We, He) send invitations to all our friends whenever
there is a safety seminar at our school.

_____(She,They,He) look both ways very carefully before
crossing the street on their roller-blades.

Write a sentence for each of your words

Let's work on division problems

READING

Your other task for the day is to read a book. At this point you should be able to read for ½ hour to 1 hour each day. Look online for a variety of book lists. You can also check out my site www.plainandnotsoplain.com and see all of the books that we have enjoyed at this grade level. Write the title of the book you are reading and how long you have read for.

_____

_____

Division Facts 0-9

56÷7=	15÷3=	12÷6=	8÷2=	63÷7=	0÷4=
14÷2=	42÷6=	6÷1=	16÷8=	20÷5=	49÷7=
36÷4=	64÷8=	0÷3=	54÷9=	4÷2=	48÷8=
18÷9=	3÷1=	35÷5=	8÷4=	72÷8=	6÷6=
0÷5=	42÷7=	2÷2=	36÷9=	7÷1=	12÷3=
16÷2=	30÷5=	0÷1=	28÷7=	4÷4=	40÷8=
3÷3=	32÷8=	45÷5=	4÷1=	20÷4=	15÷5=
56÷8=	5÷1=	0÷8=	6÷2=	45÷9=	0÷6=
6÷3=	21÷7=	0÷9=	7÷7=	12÷4=	18÷6=
63÷9=	18÷3=	27÷9=	24÷3=	0÷2=	28÷4=
21÷3=	16÷4=	24÷8=	10÷5=	30÷6=	1÷1=
18÷2=	27÷3=	32÷4=	9÷1=	35÷7=	40÷5=
10÷2=	8÷8=	48÷6=	5÷5=	8÷1=	24÷6=
25÷5=	9÷3=	81÷9=	24÷4=	14÷7=	12÷2=
9÷9=	54÷6=	72÷9=	0÷7=	2÷1=	36÷6=

Combining sentences. Two sentences can be written as one sentence by using connector words. Choose one of the words to combine the two sentences into one sentence.

1. We can eat now. We can eat after the game. (while, or, because)

_____

_____

2. We stood on the cabin's deck. The sun rose over the deck. (as, or, but)

_____

_____

3. The concert did not begin on time. The conductor was late arriving. (until, because, while)

_____

_____

4. The baseball teams waited in the dugouts. The rain ended and the field was uncovered. (or, until, after)

_____

_____

QUIZ

Let's work on division problems

READING

Your other task for the day is to read a book. At this point you should be able to read for ½ hour to 1 hour each day. Look online for a variety of book lists. You can also check out my site www.plainandnotsoplain.com and see all of the books that we have enjoyed at this grade level. Write the title of the book you are reading and how long you have read for.

_____

_____

56÷7=	15÷3=	12÷6=	8÷2=	63÷7=	0÷4=
14÷2=	42÷6=	6÷1=	16÷8=	20÷5=	49÷7=
36÷4=	64÷8=	0÷3=	54÷9=	4÷2=	48÷8=
18÷9=	3÷1=	35÷5=	8÷4=	72÷8=	6÷6=
0÷5=	42÷7=	2÷2=	36÷9=	7÷1=	12÷3=
16÷2=	30÷5=	0÷1=	28÷7=	4÷4=	40÷8=
3÷3=	32÷8=	45÷5=	4÷1=	20÷4=	15÷5=
56÷8=	5÷1=	0÷8=	6÷2=	45÷9=	0÷6=
6÷3=	21÷7=	0÷9=	7÷7=	12÷4=	18÷6=
63÷9=	18÷3=	27÷9=	24÷3=	0÷2=	28÷4=
21÷3=	16÷4=	24÷8=	10÷5=	30÷6=	1÷1=
18÷2=	27÷3=	32÷4=	9÷1=	35÷7=	40÷5=
10÷2-	8÷8=	48÷6=	5÷5=	8÷1=	24÷6=
25÷5=	9÷3=	81÷9=	24÷4=	14÷7=	12÷2=
9÷9=	54÷6=	72÷9=	0÷7=	2÷1=	36÷6=

A cause and effect sentence has two parts: a cause, which tells why and effect which tells what happened.

Today is Saturday, (the cause) so I don't have to go to school (the effect)

Combine the two sentences into a cause-effect sentence.

1. I could not eat my dessert. I was full from dinner.

_____

_____

2. I love animals. I want to be a veterinarian someday.

_____

_____

3. The astronomer could not see clearly. The night was cloudy.

_____

_____

write your own cause-effect sentence

_____

_____

week 28 spelling list copy the words

scheme

scholar

school

schooner

scratch

scream

screw

scrimmage

scrub

straight

strainer

strength

string

stripe

struggle

Let's work on division problems

READING

Your other task for the day is to read a book. At this point you should be able to read for ½ hour to 1 hour each day. Look online for a variety of book lists. You can also check out my site www.plainandnotsoplain.com and see all of the books that we have enjoyed at this grade level. Write the title of the book you are reading and how long you have read for.

_____

_____

Division Facts 0-9

56÷7=	15÷3=	12÷6=	8÷2=	63÷7=	0÷4=
14÷2=	42÷6=	6÷1=	16÷8=	20÷5=	49÷7=
36÷4=	64÷8=	0÷3=	54÷9=	4÷2=	48÷8=
18÷9=	3÷1=	35÷5=	8÷4=	72÷8=	6÷6=
0÷5=	42÷7=	2÷2=	36÷9=	7÷1=	12÷3=
16÷2=	30÷5=	0÷1=	28÷7=	4÷4=	40÷8=
3÷3=	32÷8=	45÷5=	4÷1=	20÷4=	15÷5=
56÷8=	5÷1=	0÷8=	6÷2=	45÷9=	0÷6=
6÷3=	21÷7=	0÷9=	7÷7=	12÷4=	18÷6=
63÷9=	18÷3=	27÷9=	24÷3=	0÷2=	28÷4=
21÷3=	16÷4=	24÷8=	10÷5=	30÷6=	1÷1=
18÷2=	27÷3=	32÷4=	9÷1=	35÷7=	40÷5=
10÷2=	8÷8=	48÷6=	5÷5=	8÷1=	24÷6=
25÷5=	9÷3=	81÷9=	24÷4=	14÷7=	12÷2=
9÷9=	54÷6=	72÷9=	0÷7=	2÷1=	36÷6=

One is to once, as two is to _____

Reverse is to forward as sit is to _____

shiny is to dull as foolish is to _____

teacher is to education as judge is to _____

illness is to doctor as crime is to _____

1,2,3 is to count as a,b,c is to _____

```
I   K   X   M   O   W   W   G   W   G   G   S   H   S   C
J   N   O   V   B   V   S   S   D   F   O   J   X   C   J
S   C   W   D   A   B   T   C   C   U   S   S   Q   H   P
D   Q   D   D   U   S   R   R   S   U   C   I   B   O   I
S   O   S   R   S   T   A   A   T   T   H   S   B   O   T
M   A   C   O   C   R   I   T   R   D   O   T   K   N   S
S   S   H   A   R   I   G   C   A   L   L   R   H   E   T
T   R   E   K   E   N   H   H   I   Y   A   E   W   R   R
R   J   M   C   A   G   T   Y   N   W   R   N   O   O   U
I   S   E   N   M   U   H   P   E   J   T   G   O   D   G
P   G   C   W   C   O   Q   D   R   W   H   T   W   J   G
E   S   C   R   I   M   M   A   G   E   O   H   J   N   L
O   V   S   J   E   S   C   H   O   O   L   U   F   S   E
K   E   D   M   Y   W   W   B   Q   X   A   D   Z   H   H
N   G   X   N   X   H   B   A   E   V   K   Y   D   X   N
```

SCHEME	SCHOLAR	SCHOOL
SCHOONER	SCRATCH	SCREAM
SCREW	SCRIMMAGE	SCRUB
STRAIGHT	STRAINER	STRENGTH
STRING	STRIPE	STRUGGLE

Let's work on division problems

READING

Your other task for the day is to read a book. At this point you should be able to read for ½ hour to 1 hour each day. Look online for a variety of book lists. You can also check out my site www.plainandnotsoplain.com and see all of the books that we have enjoyed at this grade level. Write the title of the book you are reading and how long you have read for.

_____

_____

Division Facts 0-9

56÷7=	15÷3=	12÷6=	8÷2=	63÷7=	0÷4=
14÷2=	42÷6=	6÷1=	16÷8=	20÷5=	49÷7=
36÷4=	64÷8=	0÷3=	54÷9=	4÷2=	48÷8=
18÷9=	3÷1=	35÷5=	8÷4=	72÷8=	6÷6=
0÷5=	42÷7=	2÷2=	36÷9=	7÷1=	12÷3=
16÷2=	30÷5=	0÷1=	28÷7=	4÷4=	40÷8=
3÷3=	32÷8=	45÷5=	4÷1=	20÷4=	15÷5=
56÷8=	5÷1=	0÷8=	6÷2=	45÷9=	0÷6=
6÷3=	21÷7=	0÷9=	7÷7=	12÷4=	18÷6=
63÷9=	18÷3=	27÷9=	24÷3=	0÷2=	28÷4=
21÷3=	16÷4=	24÷8=	10÷5=	30÷6=	1÷1=
18÷2=	27÷3=	32÷4=	9÷1=	35÷7=	40÷5=
10÷2=	8÷8=	48÷6=	5÷5=	8÷1=	24÷6=
25÷5=	9÷3=	81÷9=	24÷4=	14÷7=	12÷2=
9÷9=	54÷6=	72÷9=	0÷7=	2÷1=	36÷6=

Use a dictionary (google) to help you answer the questions using complete sentences.

1. Which would you use to treat a sore throat: a gargoyle or gargle?

_____

_____

2. Which is an instrument: calligraphy or calliope?

_____

_____

3. If you trick someone, do you bamboozle him or barcarole him?

_____

_____

4. Which might you wear: argyles or calliopes?

_____

_____

5. In Venice, Italy, would you travel in a gondola or a calamity?

_____

_____

Write a sentence for each of your words

Let's work on division problems

READING

Your other task for the day is to read a book. At this point you should be able to read for ½ hour to 1 hour each day. Look online for a variety of book lists. You can also check out my site www.plainandnotsoplain.com and see all of the books that we have enjoyed at this grade level. Write the title of the book you are reading and how long you have read for.

_____

_____

Division Facts 0-9

56÷7=	15÷3=	12÷6=	8÷2=	63÷7=	0÷4=
14÷2=	42÷6=	6÷1=	16÷8=	20÷5=	49÷7=
36÷4=	64÷8=	0÷3=	54÷9=	4÷2=	48÷8=
18÷9=	3÷1=	35÷5=	8÷4=	72÷8=	6÷6=
0÷5=	42÷7=	2÷2=	36÷9=	7÷1=	12÷3=
16÷2=	30÷5=	0÷1=	28÷7=	4÷4=	40÷8=
3÷3=	32÷8=	45÷5=	4÷1=	20÷4=	15÷5=
56÷8=	5÷1=	0÷8=	6÷2=	45÷9=	0÷6=
6÷3=	21÷7=	0÷9=	7÷7=	12÷4=	18÷6=
63÷9=	18÷3=	27÷9=	24÷3=	0÷2=	28÷4=
21÷3=	16÷4=	24÷8=	10÷5=	30÷6=	1÷1=
18÷2–	27:3=	32÷4=	9÷1–	35÷7=	40÷5=
10÷2=	8÷8=	48÷6=	5÷5=	8÷1=	24÷6=
25÷5=	9÷3=	81÷9=	24÷4=	14÷7=	12÷2=
9÷9=	54÷6=	72÷9=	0÷7=	2÷1=	36÷6=

Remember double negatives? Only use one negative word in a sentence.

1. There wasn't (no, any) snow on our grass this morning.

2. I couldn't find anyone (nowhere, anywhere) who wanted to build a snowman.

3. We shouldn't ask (anyone, no one) to go ice skating with us.

4. Not a single student skiing (anywhere, nowhere) was unhappy yesterday.

5. No one (never, ever) thought it was a waste of time to go ice skating on the pond.

6. There wasn't (anything, nothing) wrong with using the clean, fresh snow to make our fruit drinks.

QUIZ

Let's work on division problems

READING

Your other task for the day is to read a book. At this point you should be able to read for ½ hour to 1 hour each day. Look online for a variety of book lists. You can also check out my site www.plainandnotsoplain.com and see all of the books that we have enjoyed at this grade level. Write the title of the book you are reading and how long you have read for.

_____

_____

Division Facts 0-9

56÷7=	15÷3=	12÷6=	8÷2=	63÷7=	0÷4=
14÷2=	42÷6=	6÷1=	16÷8=	20÷5=	49÷7=
36÷4=	64÷8=	0÷3=	54÷9=	4÷2=	48÷8=
18÷9=	3÷1=	35÷5=	8÷4=	72÷8=	6÷6=
0÷5=	42÷7=	2÷2=	36÷9=	7÷1=	12÷3=
16÷2=	30÷5=	0÷1=	28÷7=	4÷4=	40÷8=
3÷3=	32÷8=	45÷5=	4÷1=	20÷4=	15÷5=
56÷8=	5÷1=	0÷8=	6÷2=	45÷9=	0÷6=
6÷3=	21÷7=	0÷9=	7÷7=	12÷4=	18÷6=
63÷9=	18÷3=	27÷9=	24÷3=	0÷2=	28÷4=
21÷3=	16÷4=	24÷8=	10÷5=	30÷6=	1÷1=
18÷2=	27÷3=	32÷4=	9÷1=	35÷7=	40÷5=
10÷2=	8÷8=	48÷6=	5÷5=	8÷1=	24÷6=
25÷5=	9÷3=	81÷9=	24÷4=	14÷7=	12÷2=
9÷9=	54÷6=	72÷9=	0÷7=	2÷1=	36÷6=

The pronoun I is always capitalized. Each part of a person's or pet's name begins with a capital letter.

An initial is always capitalized and is followed by a period.

Rewrite each sentence with correct capital letters.

1. where did molly parsons get her dog, laddie?

_____

_____

2. the most unusual pet is tom smith's parrot named carl.

_____

_____

3. Write your initials =all three

_____

4. write your dads full name using initials for mister

_____

5. Use the pronoun I to tell what you like to eat best

_____

_____

week 29 spelling list copy your words

biggest

brighter

clumsiest

crazier

cruelest

earlier

firmer

flattest

greener

noisiest

prettier

quietest

simpler

tastiest

widest

Write the tally for 16

Which digit in 1.875 is in the tenths place?

8.3 – (1.74+0.9)

63x1000   37x100

37+24+7+14+11=

52 x 15=   42x88

Draw and shade rectangles to show that 1 2/5 equals 7/5

Division Facts 0-9

56÷7=	15÷3=	12÷6=	8÷2=	63÷7=	0÷4=
14÷2=	42÷6=	6÷1=	16÷8=	20÷5=	49÷7=
36÷4=	64÷8=	0÷3=	54÷9=	4÷2=	48÷8=
18÷9=	3÷1=	35÷5=	8÷4=	72÷8=	6÷6=
0÷5=	42÷7=	2÷2=	36÷9=	7÷1=	12÷3=
16÷2=	30÷5=	0÷1=	28÷7=	4÷4=	40÷8=
3÷3=	32÷8=	45÷5=	4÷1=	20÷4=	15÷5=
56÷8=	5÷1=	0÷8=	6÷2=	45÷9=	0÷6=
6÷3=	21÷7=	0÷9=	7÷7=	12÷4=	18÷6=
63÷9=	18÷3=	27÷9=	24÷3=	0÷2=	28÷4=
21÷3=	16÷4=	24÷8=	10÷5–	30÷6=	1÷1=
18÷2=	27÷3=	32÷4=	9÷1=	35÷7=	40÷5=
10÷2=	8÷8=	48÷6=	5÷5=	8÷1=	24÷6=
25÷5=	9÷3=	81÷9=	24÷4=	14÷7=	12÷2=
9÷9=	54÷6=	72÷9=	0÷7=	2÷1=	36÷6=

Four types of sentences

declarative=makes a statement and ends with a period

exclamatory=exclaims something and ends with a !

interrogative =asks a question and ends with ?

imperative =gives a command or makes a request ends with period.

Write a declarative sentence

Write an exclamatory sentence

Write an interrogative sentence

Write an imperative sentence

READING

Your other task for the day is to read a book. At this point you should be able to read for ½ hour to 1 hour each day. Look online for a variety of book lists. You can also check out my site www.plainandnotsoplain.com and see all of the books that we have enjoyed at this grade level. Write the title of the book you are reading and how long you have read for.

_____

_____

```
R  T  A  S  T  I  E  S  T  E  Y  E  P  P  I
Y  E  A  R  L  I  E  R  C  U  R  K  H  T  R
Y  Q  W  X  N  B  Q  L  J  E  G  J  R  E  U
S  U  R  A  L  W  U  Q  N  T  T  E  I  F  U
C  F  X  T  Y  A  I  E  O  O  L  Z  K  L  B
K  C  D  N  Z  P  E  R  O  P  A  N  I  A  R
L  L  C  O  L  R  T  I  M  R  C  U  Y  T  I
E  U  G  I  G  F  E  I  C  R  R  V  T  T  G
F  M  Y  S  Y  A  S  U  E  K  U  S  E  E  H
L  S  W  I  H  R  T  I  B  L  E  S  Z  S  T
C  I  L  E  X  D  T  U  I  G  L  Y  W  T  E
W  E  L  S  Z  T  T  C  G  U  E  V  F  K  R
U  S  Y  T  E  E  T  I  U  O  S  Y  O  U  Y
T  T  V  R  A  Y  B  R  C  U  T  F  Q  C  I
O  N  P  X  L  B  P  F  I  R  M  E  R  S  E
```

BIGGEST	BRIGHTER	CLUMSIEST
CRAZIER	CRUELEST	EARLIER
FIRMER	FLATTEST	GREENER
NOISIEST	PRETTIER	QUIETEST
SIMPLER	TASTIEST	

453

Which of these letters has two lines of symmetry

V   H   X   Y   O

83 x 40   1000x53

714÷4   1385÷6

Compare 0.05_____0.050

12.599_____13.00

0.001_____1.00

56÷7=	15÷3=	12÷6=	8÷2=	63÷7=	0÷4=
14÷2=	42÷6=	6÷1=	16÷8=	20÷5=	49÷7=
36÷4=	64÷8=	0÷3=	54÷9=	4÷2=	48÷8=
18÷9=	3÷1=	35÷5=	8÷4=	72÷8=	6÷6=
0÷5=	42÷7=	2÷2=	36÷9=	7÷1=	12÷3=
16÷2=	30÷5=	0÷1=	28÷7=	4÷4=	40÷8=
3÷3=	32÷8=	45÷5=	4÷1=	20÷4=	15÷5=
56÷8=	5÷1=	0÷8=	6÷2=	45÷9=	0÷6=
6÷3=	21÷7=	0÷9=	7÷7=	12÷4=	18÷6=
63÷9=	18÷3=	27÷9=	24÷3=	0÷2=	28÷4=
21÷3=	16÷4=	24÷8=	10÷5=	30÷6=	1÷1=
18÷2=	27÷3=	32÷4=	9÷1=	35÷7=	40÷5=
10÷2=	8÷8-	48÷6=	5÷5=	8÷1=	24÷6=
25÷5=	9÷3=	81÷9=	24÷4=	14÷7=	12÷2=
9÷9=	54÷6=	72÷9=	0÷7=	2÷1=	36÷6=

Fact and Opinion

Facts can be proven. Opinions are someones idea about something.

Write me a fact and an opinion about cats

Write me a fact and an opinion about summer

Write me a fact and an opinion about snow

READING

Your other task for the day is to read a book. At this point you should be able to read for ½ hour to 1 hour each day. Look online for a variety of book lists. You can also check out my site www.plainandnotsoplain.com and see all of the books that we have enjoyed at this grade level. Write the title of the book you are reading and how long you have read for.

_____

_____

Write a sentence for each of your words

Finding the average

To find the average of something, we add up all the numbers and divide by the number we are adding.

If I want to know the average age of my children, I would first add up all the ages of my children:

18, 13, 10, 5, 4

Added up you get 50. Then divide by 5—the number of numbers I'm adding and I get 10. That is the average age of my children.

Four vans carried the team to the soccer field. There were 5 players in the first van, 4 players in the second van, 3 players in the third van, and 8 players in the fourth van. What was the average number of players per van?

In three classrooms there were 24,26, and 28 children. What was the average number of children per classroom?

For five days the temperatures were: 79, 82, 84, 81, and 74 degrees. What was the average for those five days?

Division Facts 0-9

56÷7=	15÷3=	12÷6=	8÷2=	63÷7=	0÷4=
14÷2=	42÷6=	6÷1=	16÷8=	20÷5=	49÷7=
36÷4=	64÷8=	0÷3=	54÷9=	4÷2=	48÷8=
18÷9=	3÷1=	35÷5=	8÷4=	72÷8=	6÷6=
0÷5=	42÷7=	2÷2=	36÷9=	7÷1=	12÷3=
16÷2=	30÷5=	0÷1=	28÷7=	4÷4=	40÷8=
3÷3=	32÷8=	45÷5=	4÷1=	20÷4=	15÷5=
56÷8=	5÷1=	0÷8=	6÷2=	45÷9=	0÷6=
6÷3=	21÷7=	0÷9=	7÷7=	12÷4=	18÷6=
63÷9=	18÷3=	27÷9=	24÷3=	0÷2=	28÷4=
21÷3=	16÷4=	24÷8=	10÷5=	30÷6=	1÷1=
18÷2=	27÷3=	32÷4=	9÷1=	35÷7=	40÷5=
10÷2=	8÷8=	48÷6=	5÷5=	8÷1=	24÷6=
25÷5=	9÷3=	81÷9=	24÷4=	14÷7=	12÷2=
9÷9=	54÷6=	72÷9=	0÷7=	2÷1=	36÷6=

Fiction and nonfiction (fiction books are made up stories and nonfiction books are facts)

Write fiction or nonfiction for the descriptions below

1. The Planets. This book describes the planets in our solar system. Descriptions and pictures of each planet are included.

_____

2. Explorers Go To America. This book gives the routes the explorers took to America. Maps and illustrations are given.

_____

3. The Chicken and the Dragon. This is the story of a dragon who helps a chicken remember his way home.

_____

4.The Mouse and the Motorcycle. This is the story about Ralph the mouse and his adventures in a hotel.

_____

5. Sports Legends. This book describes the lives of famous sports stars.

_____

READING

Your other task for the day is to read a book. At this point you should be able to read for ½ hour to 1 hour each day. Look online for a variety of book lists. You can also check out my site www.plainandnotsoplain.com and see all of the books that we have enjoyed at this grade level. Write the title of the book you are reading and how long you have read for.

_____

_____

QUIZ

Average—to find the average of a set of numbers, we added the numbers and then divided by the number of numbers. Another name for the average is the mean.

Find the mean of Tim's seven test scores:
80,85,85, 10,90,85, 90

_____

The median of a set of numbers is the middle number when the numbers are arranged in order of size.

The range of a set of numbers is the difference between the largest and the smallest numbers. We subtract the smallest from largest number.

What is the median and the range of Tim's seven test scores:
Write them again in order if that will help

Mode—of a set of numbers is the number that occurs most often. What was the mode of Tim's test scores_____

Find the mean_____median_____mode_____range_____

31, 28, 31, 30, 25

Division Facts 0-9

56÷7=	15÷3=	12÷6=	8÷2=	63÷7=	0÷4=
14÷2=	42÷6=	6÷1=	16÷8=	20÷5=	49÷7=
36÷4=	64÷8=	0÷3=	54÷9=	4÷2=	48÷8=
18÷9=	3÷1=	35÷5=	8÷4=	72÷8=	6÷6=
0÷5=	42÷7=	2÷2=	36÷9=	7÷1=	12÷3=
16÷2=	30÷5=	0÷1=	28÷7=	4÷4=	40÷8=
3÷3=	32÷8=	45÷5=	4÷1=	20÷4=	15÷5=
56÷8=	5÷1=	0÷8=	6÷2=	45÷9=	0÷6=
6÷3=	21÷7=	0÷9=	7÷7=	12÷4=	18÷6=
63÷9=	18÷3=	27÷9=	24÷3=	0÷2=	28÷4=
21÷3=	16÷4=	24÷8=	10÷5=	30÷6=	1÷1=
18÷2=	27÷3=	32÷4=	9÷1=	35÷7=	40÷5=
10÷2=	8÷8=	48÷6=	5÷5=	8÷1=	24÷6=
25÷5=	9÷3=	81÷9=	24÷4=	14÷7=	12÷2=
9÷9=	54÷6=	72÷9=	0÷7=	2÷1=	36÷6=

Google the US map and locate your state. Write the names of the states or bodies of water bordering your state

Your other task for the day is to read a book. At this point you should be able to read for ½ hour to 1

northwest	north	northeast
west	my state	east
southwest	south	southeast

hour each day. Look online for a variety of book lists. You can also check out my site
www.plainandnotsoplain.com and see all of the books that we have enjoyed at this grade level.
Write the title of the book you are reading and how long you have read for.

_____

_____

week 30 spelling words

bass

bowl

close

cobbler

does

file

flounder

grave

hawk

list

minute

object

paddle

present

sow

Shapes such as triangles, rectangles, and circles are flat shapes that cover an area but do not take up space. They have length and width but not depth. Objects that take up space are things such as cars, basketballs, desks, houses, and people. Geometric shapes that take up space are called geometric solids.

Here are some common ones:

Cube   cylinder   sphere   pyramid   cone

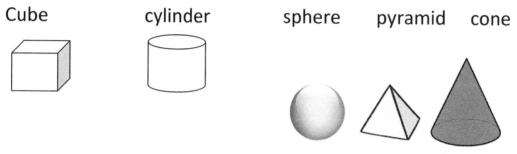

What is the shape of soup can?

What shape is a basketball?

What shape is funnel?

Use word to write 7.69

Use words to write 421.9

There were 24 people in one line and 16 people in another. What was the average number of people in line?

Division Facts 0-9

56÷7=	15÷3=	12÷6=	8÷2=	63÷7=	0÷4=
14÷2=	42÷6=	6÷1=	16÷8=	20÷5=	49÷7=
36÷4=	64÷8=	0÷3=	54÷9=	4÷2=	48÷8=
18÷9=	3÷1=	35÷5=	8÷4=	72÷8=	6÷6=
0÷5=	42÷7=	2÷2=	36÷9=	7÷1=	12÷3=
16÷2=	30÷5=	0÷1=	28÷7=	4÷4=	40÷8=
3÷3=	32÷8=	45÷5=	4÷1=	20÷4=	15÷5=
56÷8=	5÷1=	0÷8=	6÷2=	45÷9=	0÷6=
6÷3=	21÷7=	0÷9=	7÷7=	12÷4=	18÷6=
63÷9=	18÷3=	27÷9=	24÷3=	0÷2=	28÷4=
21÷3=	16÷4=	24÷8=	10÷5=	30÷6=	1÷1=
18÷2=	27÷3=	32÷4=	9÷1=	35÷7=	40÷5=
10÷2–	8÷8–	48÷6=	5÷5=	8÷1=	24÷6=
25÷5=	9÷3=	81÷9=	24÷4=	14÷7=	12÷2=
9÷9=	54÷6=	72÷9=	0÷7=	2÷1=	36÷6=

Write two sentences about the topics listed below. Both sentences should support and be about the same thing.

winter

_____

_____

dogs

_____

_____

books

_____

_____

swimming

_____

_____

READING

Your other task for the day is to read a book. At this point you should be able to read for ½ hour to 1 hour each day. Look online for a variety of book lists. You can also check out my site www.plainandnotsoplain.com and see all of the books that we have enjoyed at this grade level. Write the title of the book you are reading and how long you have read for.

_____

_____

Write a sentence for each of your words

One hundred fifty feet equals how many yards

Use words to write 8.75

The first five odd counting numbers are: 1,3,5,7,9
Find the mean and the median of these five numbers

What geometric shape is a roll of paper towels

3625÷5   3000÷5

Draw and shade a circle to show that 8/8 = 1

9 x1	2 x2	5 x1	4 x3	0 x0	9 x9	3 x5	8 x5	2 x6	4 x7
5 x6	7 x5	3 x0	8 x8	1 x3	3 x4	5 x9	0 x2	7 x3	4 x 1
2 x3	8 x6	0 x5	6 x1	3 x8	1 x 1	9 x0	2 x8	6 x4	0 x7
7 x7	1 x4	6 x2	4 x5	2 x4	4 x 9	7 x0	1 x2	8 x4	6 x5
3 x2	4 x6	1 x9	5 x7	8 x2	0 x8	4 x2	9 x8	3 x6	5 x5
8 x9	3 x7	9 x7	1 x7	6 x0	0 x3	7 x2	1 x5	7 x8	4 x0
8 x3	5 x2	0 x4	9 x5	6 x7	2 x7	6 x3	5 x4	1 x0	9 x 2
7 x 6	1 x 8	9 x6	4 x 4	5 x3	8 x1	3 x3	4 x8	9 x3	2 x0
8 x0	3 x1	6 x8	0 x9	8 x7	2 x 9	9 x4	0 x1	7 x4	5 x8
0 x6	7 x1	2 x5	6 x9	3 x9	1 x6	5 x0	6 x6	2 x1	7 x9

The topic sentence gives the main idea of a paragraph. The support sentences give the details about the main idea. Each sentence must relate to the main idea.

Write three support sentences to go with each topic sentence.

Giving a dog a bath can be a real challenge!

1_____

2._____

3_____

A daily newspaper features many kinds of news.

1_____

2._____

3_____

I can still remember how embarrassed I was that day!

1_____

2._____

3_____

READING
Your other task for the day is to read a book. At this point you should be able to read for ½ hour to 1 hour each day. Look online for a variety of book lists. You can also check out my site www.plainandnotsoplain.com and see all of the books that we have enjoyed at this grade level. Write the title of the book you are reading and how long you have read for.

_____

_____

```
S  E  B  K  U  U  Y  Q  Q  T  T  V  P  Z  T
B  S  A  J  B  G  Q  V  Z  W  E  M  Q  J  T
Z  J  S  Z  P  O  Q  S  M  S  L  I  T  W  N
G  P  S  B  A  L  W  B  O  N  O  N  Z  D  F
S  R  D  J  D  N  P  L  F  R  E  U  T  U  O
O  D  A  J  D  D  C  K  K  S  T  T  C  L  G
W  D  C  V  L  O  W  S  E  E  S  E  S  V  C
G  G  K  A  E  A  E  R  R  J  L  C  T  D  C
W  S  X  A  H  Y  P  S  Q  I  H  Y  K  O  F
U  C  O  B  B  L  E  R  F  H  S  F  R  M  A
L  Y  D  A  F  T  O  B  J  E  C  T  C  A  E
O  I  B  W  P  O  W  G  B  E  S  S  D  G  R
T  K  S  M  F  R  D  K  B  X  B  F  M  B  D
V  Y  M  T  F  L  O  U  N  D  E  R  L  X  W
H  V  A  X  Y  G  K  A  N  D  B  U  X  L  O
```

BASS	BOWL	CLOSE
COBBLER	DOES	FILE
FLOUNDER	GRAVE	HAWK
LIST	MINUTE	OBJECT
PADDLE	PRESENT	SOW

473

We remember that there are two forms for writing money amounts.
25 ¢ or you can write it $0.25

Abe Lincoln was born in 1809 and died in 1865. How many years did he live?

What is the value of 3 ten dollar bills, 4 one dollar bills, 5 dimes, and 2 pennies?

Use words to write 6412.5

James opened a one gallon bottle of milk and poured out 1 quart. How many quarts of milk were left in the bottle?

$68.47+$36.99= $100- $5.43=

33x26=   50x51=

Division Facts 0-9

56÷7=	15÷3=	12÷6=	8÷2=	63÷7=	0÷4=
14÷2=	42÷6=	6÷1=	16÷8=	20÷5=	49÷7=
36÷4=	64÷8=	0÷3=	54÷9=	4÷2=	48÷8=
18÷9=	3÷1=	35÷5=	8÷4=	72÷8=	6÷6=
0÷5=	42÷7=	2÷2=	36÷9=	7÷1=	12÷3=
16÷2=	30÷5=	0÷1=	28÷7=	4÷4=	40÷8=
3÷3=	32÷8=	45÷5=	4÷1=	20÷4=	15÷5=
56÷8=	5÷1=	0÷8=	6÷2=	45÷9=	0÷6=
6÷3=	21÷7=	0÷9=	7÷7=	12÷4=	18÷6=
63÷9=	18÷3=	27÷9=	24÷3=	0÷2=	28÷4=
21÷3=	16÷4=	24÷8=	10÷5=	30÷6=	1÷1=
18÷2=	27÷3=	32÷4=	9÷1=	35÷7=	40÷5=
10÷2=	8÷8=	48÷6=	5÷5=	8÷1=	24÷6=
25÷5=	9÷3=	81÷9=	24÷4=	14÷7=	12÷2=
9÷9=	54÷6=	72÷9=	0÷7=	2÷1=	36÷6=

READING

Your other task for the day is to read a book. At this point you should be able to read for ½ hour to 1 hour each day. Look online for a variety of book lists. You can also check out my site www.plainandnotsoplain.com and see all of the books that we have enjoyed at this grade level. Write the title of the book you are reading and how long you have read for.

_____

_____

A personal letter has 5 parts. The heading, greeting, body, closing and signature.

Begin by putting the date in the right hand corner at top. After the day put a comma.--heading

Use hand motions to explain this----

Then you have the greeting—dear tony,----put a comma after the persons name.
Then the body—your letter
The closing----your friend,----put a comma after the persons name.
The signature Amy

                                                    January 4, 2015

Dear Jan,

I am planning on coming for a visit this summer to Michigan. I can't wait until we can spend a whole week together. We will have so much fun. I would like to go swimming at the lake. Can we go to the zoo? I look forward to visiting.

Your friend,
Amy
Write your own letter to your friend about coming for the summer.

_____

_____

_____
_____
_____
_____
_____
_____
_____

_____

Quiz

Each circle below is divided into parts. Together the parts of each circle make up a whole. We see that 2 halves is the same as 1 whole. We also see that 4 quarters is the same as one whole. As well as 8-eighths equal one whole.

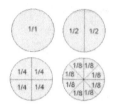

1 whole=2/2   4/4=1 whole   8/8=1 whole

If the numerator of a fraction is the same as the denominator, the fraction equals 1.

Which of these fractions equals 1?
1/6   6/6   7/6

Write a fraction equal to 1 that has a denominator of 7?

How many minutes are in 3 hours?

Bill has $8. Mary has $2 less than Bill. How much money do they have altogether?

59x61=   400÷5=

READING
Your other task for the day is to read a book. At this point you should be able to read for ½ hour to 1 hour each day. Look online for a variety of book lists. You can also check out my site www.plainandnotsoplain.com and see all of the books that we have enjoyed at this grade level. Write the title of the book you are reading and how long you have read for.

_____

_____

9 x1	2 x2	5 x1	4 x3	0 x0	9 x9	3 x5	8 x5	2 x6	4 x7
5 x6	7 x5	3 x0	8 x8	1 x3	3 x4	5 x9	0 x2	7 x3	4 x 1
2 x3	8 x6	0 x5	6 x1	3 x8	1 x 1	9 x0	2 x8	6 x4	0 x7
7 x7	1 x4	6 x2	4 x5	2 x4	4 x 9	7 x0	1 x2	8 x4	6 x5
3 x2	4 x6	1 x9	5 x7	8 x2	0 x8	4 x2	9 x8	3 x6	5 x5
8 x9	3 x7	9 x7	1 x7	6 x0	0 x3	7 x2	1 x5	7 x8	4 x0
8 x3	5 x2	0 x4	9 x5	6 x7	2 x7	6 x3	5 x4	1 x0	9 x 2
7 x 6	1 x 8	9 x6	4 x 4	5 x3	8 x1	3 x3	4 x8	9 x3	2 x0
8 x0	3 x1	6 x8	0 x9	8 x7	2 x 9	9 x4	0 x1	7 x4	5 x8
0 x6	7 x1	2 x5	6 x9	3 x9	1 x6	5 x0	6 x6	2 x1	7 x9

Writing letters to your friends. When you write letters to people, you want to begin the letter with something positive. A bible verse or a positive greeting is a great way to begin. In your letter you want to share something that has happened in your life. Keep it positive, this is not the time to bring negative information. Inform them of something and let it put a smile on their face. No need to puff yourself up, but share what you are learning, maybe a new skill or something that has encouraged you lately. Ask only a few questions, as you don't want them to feel they have to respond to empty ended questions. Include something small in the letter a trinket, piece of candy, or perhaps a sticker. End it with a positive note and let them know you miss them.

week 31 spelling words

board

bored

coarse

course

council

counsel

creak

creek

knot

not

lead

led

ring

wring

who's

whose

If the numerator of a fraction is equal to or greater than the denominator, the fraction is an improper fraction. All of these fractions are improper fractions:

$$\frac{12}{4} \qquad \frac{10}{3} \qquad \frac{9}{4} \qquad \frac{3}{2} \qquad \frac{5}{5}$$

To write an improper fraction as a whole or mixed number, we divide to find out how many wholes the improper fraction contains. If there is no remainder, we write the improper fraction as a whole number. If there is a remainder, the remainder becomes the numerator in a mixed number.

Write $\frac{13}{5}$ as a mixed number. Draw a picture to show that the improper fraction and mixed number are equal. Make circles and divide them into 5 parts. Shade 13 of them.

Write $\frac{10}{3}$ as a mixed number. Then draw a picture to show that the improper fraction and mixed number are equal.

Write $\frac{12}{4}$ as a whole number. Then draw a picture to show that the improper fraction and whole number are equal.

100 Multiplication facts

9 x1	2 x2	5 x1	4 x3	0 x0	9 x9	3 x5	8 x5	2 x6	4 x7
5 x6	7 x5	3 x0	8 x8	1 x3	3 x4	5 x9	0 x2	7 x3	4 x 1
2 x3	8 x6	0 x5	6 x1	3 x8	1 x 1	9 x0	2 x8	6 x4	0 x7
7 x7	1 x4	6 x2	4 x5	2 x4	4 x 9	7 x0	1 x2	8 x4	6 x5
3 x2	4 x6	1 x9	5 x7	8 x2	0 x8	4 x2	9 x8	3 x6	5 x5
8 x9	3 x7	9 x7	1 x7	6 x0	0 x3	7 x2	1 x5	7 x8	4 x0
8 x3	5 x2	0 x4	9 x5	6 x7	2 x7	6 x3	5 x4	1 x0	9 x 2
7 x 6	1 x 8	9 x6	4 x 4	5 x3	8 x1	3 x3	4 x8	9 x3	2 x0
8 x0	3 x1	6 x8	0 x9	8 x7	2 x 9	9 x4	0 x1	7 x4	5 x8
0 x6	7 x1	2 x5	6 x9	3 x9	1 x6	5 x0	6 x6	2 x1	7 x9

Creative endings

Many events occur in the story because of well thought-out plans. Now it is your turn to do the thinking. Each of the following events have been given a new twist. Write what happens.

Uncle Mark was really a German Spy. With all of the gold he.... _____

_____

_____

Mark Waters was wrong about the rain changing to snow. It really changed to... _____

_____

_____

_____

The Commander ordered his doctor to examine the patients... _____

_____

_____

_____

READING

Your other task for the day is to read a book. At this point you should be able to read for ½ hour to 1 hour each day. Look online for a variety of book lists. You can also check out my site www.plainandnotsoplain.com and see all of the books that we have enjoyed at this grade level. Write the title of the book you are reading and how long you have read for.

_____

_____

```
H  Y  I  T  L  A  J  I  B  E  Y  Z  I  N  D
M  Y  P  O  G  E  Y  K  P  B  H  V  X  Y  B
B  Q  O  R  B  H  J  O  X  X  Z  N  O  D  C
J  A  R  E  Q  L  Y  C  K  W  T  P  C  T  C
T  Y  D  V  Z  M  S  G  O  E  G  X  O  Q  L
H  M  Q  N  X  L  N  Y  E  U  C  N  A  C  S
H  E  T  U  E  I  D  H  Q  L  R  G  R  R  B
A  H  B  O  R  E  D  S  I  U  N  S  S  P  O
L  E  D  W  C  H  G  C  A  I  D  V  E  C  A
Q  C  R  E  E  K  U  O  R  S  Q  S  Z  O  R
A  L  Z  U  L  N  H  U  X  E  O  M  F  U  D
Q  J  S  I  R  O  A  N  W  H  A  I  L  N  D
L  I  W  C  G  T  F  C  W  J  V  K  B  S  B
T  E  H  Q  X  P  D  I  H  J  X  P  A  E  Z
L  D  D  L  E  A  D  L  Q  A  R  S  G  L  S
```

BOARD	BORED	COURSE
COARSE	COUNCIL	COUNSEL
CREAK	CREEK	KNOT
NOT	LEAD	LED
RING	WRING	WHOSE

Change each improper fraction to a whole number or to a mixed number. Then draw a picture to show that the improper fraction is equal to the number you wrote.

$\dfrac{7}{2}$ $\dfrac{12}{3}$ $\dfrac{15}{5}$

If the perimeter of a square is 280 feet, how long is each side of the square?

There are 365 days in a common year. How many full weeks are there in 365 days?

Brook passed out cookies to her 6 friends. Each of her friends received 3 cookies. There were 2 cookies left for Brook. How many cookies did Brook have when she began?

Measure this segment in millimeters_____ and centimeters_____

****

100 Multiplication facts

9 x1	2 x2	5 x1	4 x3	0 x0	9 x9	3 x5	8 x5	2 x6	4 x7
5 x6	7 x5	3 x0	8 x8	1 x3	3 x4	5 x9	0 x2	7 x3	4 x 1
2 x3	8 x6	0 x5	6 x1	3 x8	1 x 1	9 x0	2 x8	6 x4	0 x7
7 x7	1 x4	6 x2	4 x5	2 x4	4 x 9	7 x0	1 x2	8 x4	6 x5
3 x2	4 x6	1 x9	5 x7	8 x2	0 x8	4 x2	9 x8	3 x6	5 x5
8 x9	3 x7	9 x7	1 x7	6 x0	0 x3	7 x2	1 x5	7 x8	4 x0
8 x3	5 x2	0 x4	9 x5	6 x7	2 x7	6 x3	5 x4	1 x0	9 x 2
7 x 6	1 x 8	9 x6	4 x 4	5 x3	8 x1	3 x3	4 x8	9 x3	2 x0
8 x0	3 x1	6 x8	0 x9	8 x7	2 x 9	9 x4	0 x1	7 x4	5 x8
0 x6	7 x1	2 x5	6 x9	3 x9	1 x6	5 x0	6 x6	2 x1	7 x9

Write a complete sentence in response to the questions

What does our family do just for fun?

What makes you a good friend to others?

What do you admire most in someone famous?

What do you hope to be doing in the year 2030?

What did you eat for dinner last night?

READING
Your other task for the day is to read a book. At this point you should be able to read for ½ hour to 1 hour each day. Look online for a variety of book lists. You can also check out my site www.plainandnotsoplain.com and see all of the books that we have enjoyed at this grade level. Write the title of the book you are reading and how long you have read for.

_____

_____

Write a sentence for each of your words

Change the improper fraction $\frac{5}{4}$ to a mixed number. Draw a picture to show that the improper fraction and the mixed number are equal.

The cook used 30 pounds of flour each day to make pancakes and bread. How many pounds of flour did the cook use in 63 days?

3.65+2.7+0.454+2.0=

$80-($63.72+$2)

24x1000   47x63=

50x50=   2304÷4

100 Multiplication facts

9 x1	2 x2	5 x1	4 x3	0 x0	9 x9	3 x5	8 x5	2 x6	4 x7
5 x6	7 x5	3 x0	8 x8	1 x3	3 x4	5 x9	0 x2	7 x3	4 x 1
2 x3	8 x6	0 x5	6 x1	3 x8	1 x 1	9 x0	2 x8	6 x4	0 x7
7 x7	1 x4	6 x2	4 x5	2 x4	4 x 9	7 x0	1 x2	8 x4	6 x5
3 x2	4 x6	1 x9	5 x7	8 x2	0 x8	4 x2	9 x8	3 x6	5 x5
8 x9	3 x7	9 x7	1 x7	6 x0	0 x3	7 x2	1 x5	7 x8	4 x0
8 x3	5 x2	0 x4	9 x5	6 x7	2 x7	6 x3	5 x4	1 x0	9 x 2
7 x 6	1 x 8	9 x6	4 x 4	5 x3	8 x1	3 x3	4 x8	9 x3	2 x0
8 x0	3 x1	6 x8	0 x9	8 x7	2 x 9	9 x4	0 x1	7 x4	5 x8
0 x6	7 x1	2 x5	6 x9	3 x9	1 x6	5 x0	6 x6	2 x1	7 x9

Write two topic sentences about the following:

My birthday

A pet

My bedroom

Games I play

READING

Your other task for the day is to read a book. At this point you should be able to read for ½ hour to 1 hour each day. Look online for a variety of book lists. You can also check out my site www.plainandnotsoplain.com and see all of the books that we have enjoyed at this grade level. Write the title of the book you are reading and how long you have read for.

_____

_____

QUIZ

Jason has $8. David has $2 more than Jason. How much money do they have altogether?

Write a fraction equal to one and that has a denominator of 10.

Write 86.743 with words.

Change each improper fraction to a whole number or a mixed number:

$$\frac{9}{5} \qquad\qquad \frac{9}{3} \qquad\qquad \frac{9}{2}$$

Which digit in 86.743 is in the tenths place?

54x29

$12.49 x 8

$50.00-$49.49=

100 Multiplication facts

9 x1	2 x2	5 x1	4 x3	0 x0	9 x9	3 x5	8 x5	2 x6	4 x7
5 x6	7 x5	3 x0	8 x8	1 x3	3 x4	5 x9	0 x2	7 x3	4 x 1
2 x3	8 x6	0 x5	6 x1	3 x8	1 x 1	9 x0	2 x8	6 x4	0 x7
7 x7	1 x4	6 x2	4 x5	2 x4	4 x 9	7 x0	1 x2	8 x4	6 x5
3 x2	4 x6	1 x9	5 x7	8 x2	0 x8	4 x2	9 x8	3 x6	5 x5
8 x9	3 x7	9 x7	1 x7	6 x0	0 x3	7 x2	1 x5	7 x8	4 x0
8 x3	5 x2	0 x4	9 x5	6 x7	2 x7	6 x3	5 x4	1 x0	9 x 2
7 x 6	1 x 8	9 x6	4 x 4	5 x3	8 x1	3 x3	4 x8	9 x3	2 x0
8 x0	3 x1	6 x8	0 x9	8 x7	2 x 9	9 x4	0 x1	7 x4	5 x8
0 x6	7 x1	2 x5	6 x9	3 x9	1 x6	5 x0	6 x6	2 x1	7 x9

A book review is a good way to share about a favorite book. Most good book reviews give facts about the book as well as the writer's opinion.

Choose a favorite book and use the plan below to write a short book review.

Facts

Title:

author:

setting:

main characters:

basic plot:

special features:

what kind of book:

READING

Your other task for the day is to read a book. At this point you should be able to read for ½ hour to 1 hour each day. Look online for a variety of book lists. You can also check out my site www.plainandnotsoplain.com and see all of the books that we have enjoyed at this grade level. Write the title of the book you are reading and how long you have read for.

_____

_____

week 32 spelling list

accepted

admiring

captured

choking

dining

dozed

fanning

guarded

hoping

invited

pledged

practicing

proving

rearranged

squeezing

We find the area of a rectangle or square by multiplying its length by its width. This is helpful if you want to figure out how much floor space or wall space that you need.

Area = length x width

2 ft

6ft

The area of the above is 6ft x 2ft= ?_____What is the perimeter?_____

3inch

What is the area?_____perimeter_____

2cm

9cm

What is the area_____perimeter_____

9 x1	2 x2	5 x1	4 x3	0 x0	9 x9	3 x5	8 x5	2 x6	4 x7
5 x6	7 x5	3 x0	8 x8	1 x3	3 x4	5 x9	0 x2	7 x3	4 x 1
2 x3	8 x6	0 x5	6 x1	3 x8	1 x 1	9 x0	2 x8	6 x4	0 x7
7 x7	1 x4	6 x2	4 x5	2 x4	4 x 9	7 x0	1 x2	8 x4	6 x5
3 x2	4 x6	1 x9	5 x7	8 x2	0 x8	4 x2	9 x8	3 x6	5 x5
8 x9	3 x7	9 x7	1 x7	6 x0	0 x3	7 x2	1 x5	7 x8	4 x0
8 x3	5 x2	0 x4	9 x5	6 x7	2 x7	6 x3	5 x4	1 x0	9 x 2
7 x 6	1 x 8	9 x6	4 x 4	5 x3	8 x1	3 x3	4 x8	9 x3	2 x0
8 x0	3 x1	6 x8	0 x9	8 x7	2 x 9	9 x4	0 x1	7 x4	5 x8
0 x6	7 x1	2 x5	6 x9	3 x9	1 x6	5 x0	6 x6	2 x1	7 x9

Do a book review like yesterday but today is on your Opinion.

Which character did I like best and why?

Was the plot interesting?

What was my favorite part?

Other things I liked about the book:

Some things I did not like:

READING

Your other task for the day is to read a book. At this point you should be able to read for ½ hour to 1 hour each day. Look online for a variety of book lists. You can also check out my site www.plainandnotsoplain.com and see all of the books that we have enjoyed at this grade level. Write the title of the book you are reading and how long you have read for.

_____

_____

```
F  A  N  N  I  N  G  U  A  R  D  E  D  S  D
C  X  A  K  Q  K  Z  G  J  Y  P  N  M  E  O
B  K  B  A  H  R  F  R  P  T  H  Z  R  R  Z
U  D  H  A  D  M  I  R  I  N  G  U  C  S  E
T  P  R  O  V  I  N  G  K  F  T  P  B  K  D
F  S  N  G  R  V  B  S  D  P  G  W  D  E  X
Z  B  Q  R  E  A  R  R  A  N  G  E  D  K  N
I  U  V  U  X  R  Y  C  I  Z  G  A  D  C  W
N  D  P  Z  E  P  O  C  F  D  O  E  K  H  W
V  M  F  F  R  E  I  N  E  G  T  Z  V  O  B
I  P  V  L  O  T  Z  L  N  P  V  Y  V  K  F
T  N  G  K  C  L  P  I  E  S  T  U  Q  I  C
E  Q  V  A  P  V  P  C  N  G  F  Y  S  N  D
D  T  R  K  N  O  C  D  W  G  C  Z  E  G  W
O  P  G  I  H  A  U  U  O  D  I  N  I  N  G
```

ACCEPTED	ADMIRING	CAPTURED
CHOKING	DINING	DOZED
FANNING	GUARDED	HOPING
INVITED	PLEDGED	PRACTICING
PROVING	REARRANGED	SQUEEZING

501

Mary had a dozen cookies. She ate two cookies and then gave half of the rest to a friend. How many cookies did she have left?

Write a fraction equal to 1 and that has a denominator of 5

Use words to write 397 ¾

The hiking club went on a hike of 8 miles, 15 miles, 11 miles, and 18 miles. What was the average length of the club's hikes?

41.6+13.17+9.2=

The ranch market sold 54 dozen eggs in the morning. How many eggs is that?

82x 43=   43x22=

Division Facts 0-9

56÷7=	15÷3=	12÷6=	8÷2=	63÷7=	0÷4=
14÷2=	42÷6=	6÷1=	16÷8=	20÷5=	49÷7=
36÷4=	64÷8=	0÷3=	54÷9=	4÷2=	48÷8=
18÷9=	3÷1=	35÷5=	8÷4=	72÷8=	6÷6=
0÷5=	42÷7=	2÷2=	36÷9=	7÷1=	12÷3=
16÷2=	30÷5=	0÷1=	28÷7=	4÷4=	40÷8=
3÷3=	32÷8=	45÷5=	4÷1=	20÷4=	15÷5=
56÷8=	5÷1=	0÷8=	6÷2=	45÷9=	0÷6=
6÷3=	21÷7=	0÷9=	7÷7=	12÷4=	18÷6=
63÷9=	18÷3=	27÷9=	24÷3=	0÷2=	28÷4=
21÷3=	16÷4=	24÷8=	10÷5=	30÷6=	1÷1=
18÷2=	27÷3=	32÷4=	9÷1=	35÷7=	40÷5=
10÷2=	8:8=	18÷6=	5÷5=	8÷1=	24÷6=
25÷5=	9÷3=	81÷9=	24÷4=	14÷7=	12÷2=
9÷9=	54÷6=	72÷9=	0÷7=	2÷1=	36÷6=

READING

Your other task for the day is to read a book. At this point you should be able to read for ½ hour to 1 hour each day. Look online for a variety of book lists. You can also check out my site www.plainandnotsoplain.com and see all of the books that we have enjoyed at this grade level. Write the title of the book you are reading and how long you have read for.

_____

_____

Fact and Opinion

A fact is something that is proven to be true. An opinion is what someone believes. People hold differing opinion, some of which are unfair or untrue.

Label each as a Fact (F) or opinion (O)

1. _____Girls are odd because they like to play with dolls.

2. _____Sarah has blonde hair and a flat nose.

3._____Timothy was saving all the water for himself.

4._____Chris is strange because he doesn't know what rock music is.

5. _____Fish swim in the water.

6._____Cats have long tails.

7._____North Carolina is a mountainous state.

8. _____North Carolina is the prettiest state ever.

9._____We should always wash our hands.

10._____We should always walk if we can.

11. _____Walking is good for our hearts.

12._____Walking up a mountain is harder than walking in the woods.

13. _____Running is better than walking.

14. _____Tablets are cooler than laptops.

15. _____Everyone should have a cell phone.

Write a fact:

_____

Write an opinion:

_____

Write a sentence for each of your words

Fill in the chart with tally marks and the real number

how many windows in your home		
how many beds in your home		
how many tables in your home		
how many people in your home		
how many tvs in your home		
how many phones in your home		
how many pets in your home		
how many doors in your home		

Division Facts 0-9

56÷7=	15÷3=	12÷6=	8÷2=	63÷7=	0÷4=
14÷2=	42÷6=	6÷1=	16÷8=	20÷5=	49÷7=
36÷4=	64÷8=	0÷3=	54÷9=	4÷2=	48÷8=
18÷9=	3÷1=	35÷5=	8÷4=	72÷8=	6÷6=
0÷5=	42÷7=	2÷2=	36÷9=	7÷1=	12÷3=
16÷2=	30÷5=	0÷1=	28÷7=	4÷4=	40÷8=
3÷3=	32÷8=	45÷5=	4÷1=	20÷4=	15÷5=
56÷8=	5÷1=	0÷8=	6÷2=	45÷9=	0÷6=
6÷3=	21÷7=	0÷9=	7÷7=	12÷4=	18÷6=
63÷9=	18÷3=	27÷9=	24÷3=	0÷2=	28÷4=
21÷3=	16÷4=	24÷8=	10÷5=	30÷6=	1÷1=
18÷2=	27÷3=	32÷4=	9÷1=	35÷7=	40÷5=
10÷2=	8÷8=	48÷6=	5÷5=	8÷1=	24÷6=
25÷5=	9÷3=	81÷9=	24÷4=	14÷7=	12÷2=
9÷9=	54÷6=	72÷9=	0÷7=	2÷1=	36÷6=

READING

Your other task for the day is to read a book. At this point you should be able to read for ½ hour to 1 hour each day. Look online for a variety of book lists. You can also check out my site www.plainandnotsoplain.com and see all of the books that we have enjoyed at this grade level. Write the title of the book you are reading and how long you have read for.

_____

_____

Writing a paragraph

A paragraph is made up of a group of sentences. A paragraph should have, and stick to, a single topic. Each sentence should focus on the topic with plenty of information and supporting details related to the topic.

Elements of a paragraph: There are 3 parts to a paragraph

1. Beginning : The topic sentence is the beginning of the paragraph. It tells what the paragraph is going to be about. It also expresses the feeling of the paragraph.

2. Middle: The middle is the main part of the paragraph. The sentences here give more information and supporting details about the topic sentence.

3. End: After all of the information and details are writing, the ending sentence concludes, or sums up, the paragraph's main idea.

Choose one of the following topic sentences and write a paragraph. Follow the rules above. 1-topic sentence, 2-3 middle, supporting sentences, and 1 ending sentence to sum it all up.

1. There are several reasons why I like Saturdays.
2. It is fun to take a walk in the snow.
3. Some movies are really funny.
4. Swimming in the lake is fun.

QUIZ

26x30

4x3x2x1

43x200

88x26

99x11

76x32

READING

Your other task for the day is to read a book. At this point you should be able to read for ½ hour to 1 hour each day. Look online for a variety of book lists. You can also check out my site www.plainandnotsoplain.com and see all of the books that we have enjoyed at this grade level. Write the title of the book you are reading and how long you have read for.

_____

_____

Division Facts 0-9

56÷7=	15÷3=	12÷6=	8÷2=	63÷7=	0÷4=
14÷2=	42÷6=	6÷1=	16÷8=	20÷5=	49÷7=
36÷4=	64÷8=	0÷3=	54÷9=	4÷2=	48÷8=
18÷9=	3÷1=	35÷5=	8÷4=	72÷8=	6÷6=
0÷5=	42÷7=	2÷2=	36÷9=	7÷1=	12÷3=
16÷2=	30÷5=	0÷1=	28÷7=	4÷4=	40÷8=
3÷3=	32÷8=	45÷5=	4÷1=	20÷4=	15÷5=
56÷8=	5÷1=	0÷8=	6÷2=	45÷9=	0÷6=
6÷3=	21÷7=	0÷9=	7÷7=	12÷4=	18÷6=
63÷9=	18÷3=	27÷9=	24÷3=	0÷2=	28÷4=
21÷3=	16÷4=	24÷8=	10÷5=	30÷6=	1÷1=
18÷2=	27÷3=	32÷4=	9÷1=	35÷7=	40÷5=
10÷2=	8÷8=	48÷6=	5÷5=	8÷1=	24÷6=
25÷5=	9÷3=	81÷9=	24÷4=	14÷7=	12÷2=
9÷9=	54÷6=	72÷9=	0÷7=	2÷1=	36÷6=

Descriptive writing

You may be asked one day to describe something. When you are describing something use images and sense words to make your descriptive writing come alive.

Write a good main idea sentence or topic sentence. This tells what your paragraph will be about.

Develop and elaborate ideas. Use different sentences that tell about your main sentence. Try and "paint a picture" in the mind of your reader.

Choose one of the following and write a paragraph about it

Describe a favorite person
Describe your favorite place to visit
Describe your favorite outfit
Describe what it feels like to eat ice cream
Describe what it is like to cook a marshmallow.

_____
_____
_____
_____
_____
_____
_____
_____
_____
_____
_____
_____
_____
_____
_____
_____
_____

Week 33

Circle the word in each row that rhymes with the word in column one.

self	shelf	leaf	elephant
theft	crest	left	last
bat	float	plate	flat
stand	bond	ban	band
chum	sum	swam	same
dash	cash	floss	cost
clock	choke	dock	deck
bunch	crunch	crank	Grinch
blot	plate	plot	pluck
trim	groom	lime	grim
glint	gain	hint	line
rod	add	odd	told
health	wealth	wheeze	weather
filled	told	build	bold
tot	blip	bloat	blot
pill	mile	mall	mill
last	post	past	chapped
dumb	plume	plum	elm
tell	toll	stall	bell

What geometric shape is the following:
A baseball_____
A party hat_____
A can of corn_____

What is 589 plus 398

7x6x5x9x0

743.898+54.90

Three hundred seconds is how many minutes. (there are 60 seconds in each minute)

On each of the 5 bookshelves, there are 44 books. How many books are on all 5 bookshelves?

Division Facts 0-9

56÷7=	15÷3=	12÷6=	8÷2=	63÷7=	0÷4=
14÷2=	42÷6=	6÷1=	16÷8=	20÷5=	49÷7=
36÷4=	64÷8=	0÷3=	54÷9=	4÷2=	48÷8=
18÷9=	3÷1=	35÷5=	8÷4=	72÷8=	6÷6=
0÷5=	42÷7=	2÷2=	36÷9=	7÷1=	12÷3=
16÷2=	30÷5=	0÷1=	28÷7=	4÷4=	40÷8=
3÷3=	32÷8=	45÷5=	4÷1=	20÷4=	15÷5=
56÷8=	5÷1=	0÷8=	6÷2=	45÷9=	0÷6=
6÷3=	21÷7=	0÷9=	7÷7=	12÷4=	18÷6=
63÷9=	18÷3=	27÷9=	24÷3=	0÷2=	28÷4=
21÷3=	16÷4=	24÷8=	10÷5=	30÷6=	1÷1=
18÷2=	27÷3=	32÷4=	9÷1=	35÷7=	40÷5=
10÷2=	8÷8=	48÷6=	5÷5=	8÷1=	24÷6=
25÷5=	9÷3=	81÷9=	24÷4=	14÷7=	12÷2=
9÷9=	54÷6=	72÷9=	0÷7=	2÷1=	36÷6=

Write the days of the week

Write the months of the year

READING

Your other task for the day is to read a book. At this point you should be able to read for ½ hour to 1 hour each day. Look online for a variety of book lists. You can also check out my site www.plainandnotsoplain.com and see all of the books that we have enjoyed at this grade level. Write the title of the book you are reading and how long you have read for.

_____

_____

Circle the word that is spelled correctly in each row

rock	rokk	rokc	rok
clap	clapp	clappe	clape
bluf	bluff	blufe	blough
walth	wealth	weallth	weilth
aud	oud	odd	od
chelf	shelf	shealf	shief
flatte	flatt	flate	flat
buld	bueld	build	beeld
sum	sum	som	sourn
plot	ploat	plete	ploit
krunch	crunkc	crunch	cruinch
hint	hult	huint	hunit
bel	bell	belle	blle
doak	dock	docke	doik
bant	baunde	band	baind
grimm	grimn	grim	grum

Lets practice just multiplication test this week☺

READING

Your other task for the day is to read a book. At this point you should be able to read for ½ hour to 1 hour each day. Look online for a variety of book lists. You can also check out my site www.plainandnotsoplain.com and see all of the books that we have enjoyed at this grade level. Write the title of the book you are reading and how long you have read for.

_____

_____

100 Multiplication facts

9 x1	2 x2	5 x1	4 x3	0 x0	9 x9	3 x5	8 x5	2 x6	4 x7
5 x6	7 x5	3 x0	8 x8	1 x3	3 x4	5 x9	0 x2	7 x3	4 x1
2 x3	8 x6	0 x5	6 x1	3 x8	1 x1	9 x0	2 x8	6 x4	0 x7
7 x7	1 x4	6 x2	4 x5	2 x4	4 x9	7 x0	1 x2	8 x4	6 x5
3 x2	4 x6	1 x9	5 x7	8 x2	0 x8	4 x2	9 x8	3 x6	5 x5
8 x9	3 x7	9 x7	1 x7	6 x0	0 x3	7 x2	1 x5	7 x8	4 x0
8 x3	5 x2	0 x4	9 x5	6 x7	2 x7	6 x3	5 x4	1 x0	9 x2
7 x6	1 x8	9 x6	4 x4	5 x3	8 x1	3 x3	4 x8	9 x3	2 x0
8 x0	3 x1	6 x8	0 x9	8 x7	2 x9	9 x4	0 x1	7 x4	5 x8
0 x6	7 x1	2 x5	6 x9	3 x9	1 x6	5 x0	6 x6	2 x1	7 x9

Cross out the word that does not belong in each group

filter, mixture, sieve

polish, claw, rip

rope, leather, cord

college, academy, apartment

soil, wash, clean

power, weakness, force

laugh, yell, cry

nail, bolt, hammer

plan, vacation, plot

Circle the word that is spelled correctly in each row

years	yeers	yeares	yeres
mossus	mossis	mosses	mosss
babies	babyes	babys	baibies
cavees	cavies	caves	kaves
clames	klams	clams	klames
dresss	dresses	dressus	dressis
hobbys	hobbyes	hobbies	hobbis
mintz	mintes	mints	ments
props	propse	propes	propps
parents	pairents	parentes	parinse
mistakees	mistakes	mistackes	misstakes
ranchs	ransches	ranshs	ranches
berries	berryes	berrys	berris
armies	armeez	armys	armees
airoes	arrows	arrowes	airoes
patchs	paches	pachs	patches
couchs	kowches	cowches	couches

Lets practice just multiplication test this week☺

READING

Your other task for the day is to read a book. At this point you should be able to read for ½ hour to 1 hour each day. Look online for a variety of book lists. You can also check out my site www.plainandnotsoplain.com and see all of the books that we have enjoyed at this grade level. Write the title of the book you are reading and how long you have read for.

_____

_____

100 Multiplication facts

9 <u>x1</u>	2 <u>x2</u>	5 <u>x1</u>	4 <u>x3</u>	0 <u>x0</u>	9 <u>x9</u>	3 <u>x5</u>	8 <u>x5</u>	2 <u>x6</u>	4 <u>x7</u>
5 <u>x6</u>	7 <u>x5</u>	3 <u>x0</u>	8 <u>x8</u>	1 <u>x3</u>	3 <u>x4</u>	5 <u>x9</u>	0 <u>x2</u>	7 <u>x3</u>	4 <u>x 1</u>
2 <u>x3</u>	8 <u>x6</u>	0 <u>x5</u>	6 <u>x1</u>	3 <u>x8</u>	1 <u>x 1</u>	9 <u>x0</u>	2 <u>x8</u>	6 <u>x4</u>	0 <u>x7</u>
7 <u>x7</u>	1 <u>x4</u>	6 <u>x2</u>	4 <u>x5</u>	2 <u>x4</u>	4 <u>x 9</u>	7 <u>x0</u>	1 <u>x2</u>	8 <u>x4</u>	6 <u>x5</u>
3 <u>x2</u>	4 <u>x6</u>	1 <u>x9</u>	5 <u>x7</u>	8 <u>x2</u>	0 <u>x8</u>	4 <u>x2</u>	9 <u>x8</u>	3 <u>x6</u>	5 <u>x5</u>
8 <u>x9</u>	3 <u>x7</u>	9 <u>x7</u>	1 <u>x7</u>	6 <u>x0</u>	0 <u>x3</u>	7 <u>x2</u>	1 <u>x5</u>	7 <u>x8</u>	4 <u>x0</u>
8 <u>x3</u>	5 <u>x2</u>	0 <u>x4</u>	9 <u>x5</u>	6 <u>x7</u>	2 <u>x7</u>	6 <u>x3</u>	5 <u>x4</u>	1 <u>x0</u>	9 <u>x 2</u>
7 <u>x 6</u>	1 <u>x 8</u>	9 <u>x6</u>	4 <u>x 4</u>	5 <u>x3</u>	8 <u>x1</u>	3 <u>x3</u>	4 <u>x8</u>	9 <u>x3</u>	2 <u>x0</u>
8 <u>x0</u>	3 <u>x1</u>	6 <u>x8</u>	0 <u>x9</u>	8 <u>x7</u>	2 <u>x 9</u>	9 <u>x4</u>	0 <u>x1</u>	7 <u>x4</u>	5 <u>x8</u>
0 <u>x6</u>	7 <u>x1</u>	2 <u>x5</u>	6 <u>x9</u>	3 <u>x9</u>	1 <u>x6</u>	5 <u>x0</u>	6 <u>x6</u>	2 <u>x1</u>	7 <u>x9</u>

Fill in the blanks.

1. The United States celebrates Independence Day on _____4th.
2. We celebrate _____in the month of December.
3. Fools come out to play on this _____day.
4. _____is the shortest month of the year.
5. Summer begins in the month of _____.
6. Farmers bring in their crops, including pumpkins in the month of _____.
7. Winter begins in _____.
8. Your birthday is in _____.
9. We celebrate what in November?_____
10. Which day of the week is the Lord's day?_____
11. Which day of the week do they consider hump day?_____
12. Which two days are the weekend?_____ _____
13. Which day do we start school on?_____
14. Which month is Valentines Day?_____
15. What do we celebrate at the beginning of the year?_____

How many days in the following:

January _____   February _____
March _____   April   _____
May _____   June   _____
July _____   August   _____
September _____   October   _____
November _____   December _____

Circle the word in each row that is spelled correctly.

bakyard	backyard	bakeyard	bacyard
beadspred	bedspred	bedsprede	bedspread
bedroom	berdoom	bedrom	berodom
kampfire	campfyre	kampfyre	campfire
clothesline	closeline	clowsline	closelyne
lookout	lokout	loukout	lookowt
blinedbold	blyndfold	blindfold	fliindfould
grandparent	grandpairent	grandparent	grandparint
fishboll	fishbowl	fichbowl	fishbole
deasktop	desktop	disktop	desktopp
loudspeaker	lowdspeaker	loudspeeeker	lowdspeeker
overdo	overdoo	overdew	ovredo
overhed	overhead	ovurhead	overhede
boukcase	bookcase	bookase	bookcaise
raleroad	railroad	railrode	ralerode
nueborn	newborn	noobron	newebom
snostorm	snoestorm	snowstoorm	snowstorm
watterproof	waterproof	waterprouf	watterprouf
yurkself	yourcelf	yourself	yorself

525

Lets practice just multiplication test this week☺

READING

Your other task for the day is to read a book. At this point you should be able to read for ½ hour to 1 hour each day. Look online for a variety of book lists. You can also check out my site www.plainandnotsoplain.com and see all of the books that we have enjoyed at this grade level. Write the title of the book you are reading and how long you have read for.

_____

_____

100 Multiplication facts

9 x1	2 x2	5 x1	4 x3	0 x0	9 x9	3 x5	8 x5	2 x6	4 x7
5 x6	7 x5	3 x0	8 x8	1 x3	3 x4	5 x9	0 x2	7 x3	4 x 1
2 x3	8 x6	0 x5	6 x1	3 x8	1 x 1	9 x0	2 x8	6 x4	0 x7
7 x7	1 x4	6 x2	4 x5	2 x4	4 x 9	7 x0	1 x2	8 x4	6 x5
3 x2	4 x6	1 x9	5 x7	8 x2	0 x8	4 x2	9 x8	3 x6	5 x5
8 x9	3 x7	9 x7	1 x7	6 x0	0 x3	7 x2	1 x5	7 x8	4 x0
8 x3	5 x2	0 x4	9 x5	6 x7	2 x7	6 x3	5 x4	1 x0	9 x 2
7 x 6	1 x 8	9 x6	4 x 4	5 x3	8 x1	3 x3	4 x8	9 x3	2 x0
8 x0	3 x1	6 x8	0 x9	8 x7	2 x 9	9 x4	0 x1	7 x4	5 x8
0 x6	7 x1	2 x5	6 x9	3 x9	1 x6	5 x0	6 x6	2 x1	7 x9

Sayings---what does this really mean

1. Time heals all wounds.
_____
_____

2. She invited Tom, Dick , and Harry to the party.
_____
_____

3. We will be eating this pot of soup till the cows come home.
_____
_____

4. Out of the frying pan and into the fire.
_____
_____

5. A penny saved is a penny earned.
_____
_____

List your favorite movie:
_____

List your favorite book:
_____

List your favorite two songs:
_____
_____

What is your favorite subject in school:
_____

What are the names of the seven continents:
_____
_____
_____
_____
_____
_____
_____

Name two cities close to us:_____ _____
_____

week 34

circle the word that is spelled correctly in each row

named	nameed	naimed	namede
hopeing	hoppeing	hoping	hopin
ripped	ript	riped	rippt
riping	ripping	ripin	rippin
careed	kared	cared	kareed
karing	careing	kareing	caring
fliping	flipping	flippin	flipin
flaged	flagd	flagged	flaggd
flaging	flageing	flagging	flagin
forced	forseed	forsed	forceed
taisting	tasteing	tasting	taisteing
tasted	tasteed	taisted	taisteed
tappin	tapin	tapping	taipping
tapt	tapped	tappt	taipped
scipping	skipping	skiping	sciping
scaved	saved	saveed	savd
saveing	scaving	savein	saving
discused	discussed	diskussed	diskused
flipped	fliped	flipt	flippt
forsing	forceing	forcing	forseing
skipt	skiped	scipped	skipped

Lets practice just multiplication test this week☺

READING

Your other task for the day is to read a book. At this point you should be able to read for ½ hour to 1 hour each day. Look online for a variety of book lists. You can also check out my site www.plainandnotsoplain.com and see all of the books that we have enjoyed at this grade level. Write the title of the book you are reading and how long you have read for.

_____

_____

100 Multiplication facts

9 x1	2 x2	5 x1	4 x3	0 x0	9 x9	3 x5	8 x5	2 x6	4 x7
5 x6	7 x5	3 x0	8 x8	1 x3	3 x4	5 x9	0 x2	7 x3	4 x1
2 x3	8 x6	0 x5	6 x1	3 x8	1 x1	9 x0	2 x8	6 x4	0 x7
7 x7	1 x4	6 x2	4 x5	2 x4	4 x9	7 x0	1 x2	8 x4	6 x5
3 x2	4 x6	1 x9	5 x7	8 x2	0 x8	4 x2	9 x8	3 x6	5 x5
8 x9	3 x7	9 x7	1 x7	6 x0	0 x3	7 x2	1 x5	7 x8	4 x0
8 x3	5 x2	0 x4	9 x5	6 x7	2 x7	6 x3	5 x4	1 x0	9 x2
7 x6	1 x8	9 x6	4 x4	5 x3	8 x1	3 x3	4 x8	9 x3	2 x0
8 x0	3 x1	6 x8	0 x9	8 x7	2 x9	9 x4	0 x1	7 x4	5 x8
0 x6	7 x1	2 x5	6 x9	3 x9	1 x6	5 x0	6 x6	2 x1	7 x9

Rewrite the following words correctly. Use capitalization, spelling, and commas.

march 22 2012 _____

september 22 1998 _____

sunday janary 12 _____

tuesday april 16_____

june 11 1876 _____

july 7 1998 _____

detroit michigan_____

raleigh north carolina_____

greenville south carolina _____

miami florida _____

hendersonville north carolina _____

dear michael_____

your daughter amy_____

february 10 1976_____

Circle the word that is spelled correctly in each row

trys	trise	tryes	tries
studdied	studied	studeed	studede
pennys	pennyes	pennies	pennees
cozily	cozylie	cozile	cozyly
lazyer	lazyr	lazir	lazier
replyd	replyed	replied	replide
marys	marries	maryes	marryes
caries	carries	carrys	carryes
easily	eesilie	easylie	eazly
sillist	sillyist	silliest	sillyest
prettilie	prettyly	prettily	pretily
happyest	happiest	hapiest	happyist
emtier	emptyer	emptier	emptyer
sorriest	sorryist	sorrist	sorryest
merryer	maryer	marier	merrier
dizzyist	dizziest	dizzyest	diziest
funier	funnyer	funnyier	funnier
jumpyer	jumpyier	jumpier	jumpyr

Lets practice just multiplication test this week☺

READING

Your other task for the day is to read a book. At this point you should be able to read for ½ hour to 1 hour each day. Look online for a variety of book lists. You can also check out my site www.plainandnotsoplain.com and see all of the books that we have enjoyed at this grade level. Write the title of the book you are reading and how long you have read for.

_____

_____

100 Multiplication facts

9 x1	2 x2	5 x1	4 x3	0 x0	9 x9	3 x5	8 x5	2 x6	4 x7
5 x6	7 x5	3 x0	8 x8	1 x3	3 x4	5 x9	0 x2	7 x3	4 x 1
2 x3	8 x6	0 x5	6 x1	3 x8	1 x 1	9 x0	2 x8	6 x4	0 x7
7 x7	1 x4	6 x2	4 x5	2 x4	4 x 9	7 x0	1 x2	8 x4	6 x5
3 x2	4 x6	1 x9	5 x7	8 x2	0 x8	4 x2	9 x8	3 x6	5 x5
8 x9	3 x7	9 x7	1 x7	6 x0	0 x3	7 x2	1 x5	7 x8	4 x0
8 x3	5 x2	0 x4	9 x5	6 x7	2 x7	6 x3	5 x4	1 x0	9 x 2
7 x 6	1 x 8	9 x6	4 x 4	5 x3	8 x1	3 x3	4 x8	9 x3	2 x0
8 x0	3 x1	6 x8	0 x9	8 x7	2 x 9	9 x4	0 x1	7 x4	5 x8
0 x6	7 x1	2 x5	6 x9	3 x9	1 x6	5 x0	6 x6	2 x1	7 x9

Circle the correct word in parentheses.

1. Of the three bats, Sam's is the (light, lightest)
2. Lauren has a very (cute, cuter) kitten.
3. My notebook is (bigger, biggest) than yours.
4. (Light, lightest) rain fell on the roof.
5. Every mother thinks her child is the (cute, cutest) in the class.
6. After playing soccer, Aaron has a (big, bigger) appetite.
7. I think the cartoon at 9:00 is (cuter, cutest) than the cartoon at 9:30.
8. Adam has a (bigger, biggest) lead in the race than Samuel.
9. Of all the boxes, Joe picked the (lighter, lightest) to carry.

Fill in the blanks with correct word: more, most, good, better, best, bad, worse, worst.

1. I like my ice cream cone _____than your ice cream cone.
2. This is the _____banana in the bunch.
3. That was a _____book.
4. Paula has _____pencils than Sam.
5. Alicia has a _____cold.

MORE	MOST	GOOD	BETTER	BEST
BAD	WORSE	WORST		

```
M X Q U W D O O G Q
M B E S T E N T O C
N O W O N P S W Y N
D V R L K O O Z V Q
E B Y E M R P F W I
S A Q S S H B E O L
R D Z T B E T T E R
O P Q V T Q X F T B
W C E H P I Y R U S
U F Q Q N O I Z I T
```

circle the word that is spelled correctly in each row

tube	tueb	toob	toub
spoune	spewn	spoon	spoone
shoud	should	shude	shood
zume	zoom	zuem	zoum
toons	tuens	twens	tunes
wool	woul	wull	woll
mewd	mude	mood	moud
soots	souts	suets	suits
stoul	stule	stool	stewl
kookie	cooky	cukie	cookie
fude	food	foud	fewd
groop	grewp	group	grupe
stoop	stupe	stoup	stewp
moove	move	mouve	muve
stoo	stue	stew	stou
huje	hooge	huge	hewg
grew	grue	groo	grou
spoul	spool	spewl	spule
you'll	yoe'll	yue'll	you'l
brukes	brueks	brooks	brouks
croo	crew	crou	crue
yewsed	used	uzed	uced

Lets practice just multiplication test this week☺

READING
Your other task for the day is to read a book. At this point you should be able to read for ½ hour to 1 hour each day. Look online for a variety of book lists. You can also check out my site www.plainandnotsoplain.com and see all of the books that we have enjoyed at this grade level. Write the title of the book you are reading and how long you have read for.

_____

_____

100 Multiplication facts

9 x1	2 x2	5 x1	4 x3	0 x0	9 x9	3 x5	8 x5	2 x6	4 x7
5 x6	7 x5	3 x0	8 x8	1 x3	3 x4	5 x9	0 x2	7 x3	4 x 1
2 x3	8 x6	0 x5	6 x1	3 x8	1 x 1	9 x0	2 x8	6 x4	0 x7
7 x7	1 x4	6 x2	4 x5	2 x4	4 x 9	7 x0	1 x2	8 x4	6 x5
3 x2	4 x6	1 x9	5 x7	8 x2	0 x8	4 x2	9 x8	3 x6	5 x5
8 x9	3 x7	9 x7	1 x7	6 x0	0 x3	7 x2	1 x5	7 x8	4 x0
8 x3	5 x2	0 x4	9 x5	6 x7	2 x7	6 x3	5 x4	1 x0	9 x 2
7 x 6	1 x 8	9 x6	4 x 4	5 x3	8 x1	3 x3	4 x8	9 x3	2 x0
8 x0	3 x1	6 x8	0 x9	8 x7	2 x 9	9 x4	0 x1	7 x4	5 x8
0 x6	7 x1	2 x5	6 x9	3 x9	1 x6	5 x0	6 x6	2 x1	7 x9

Write a letter to a friend inviting them to visit for the summer. Remember the parts of a letter: heading, greeting, body, closing, signature

Circle the word that rhymes with the first word in each row.

shower	down	tower	bowl
couch	grouch	foul	loud
sound	soup	down	pound
town	gown	mound	out
found	cookie	hound	snow
own	out	scout	grown
ouch	pouch	ounce	once
clown	frown	zoom	clam
mouth	south	mom	move
found	find	mound	huge
hound	wound	annoy	gown
gown	cowboy	voyage	frown

Lets practice just multiplication test this week☺

READING
Your other task for the day is to read a book. At this point you should be able to read for ½ hour to 1 hour each day. Look online for a variety of book lists. You can also check out my site www.plainandnotsoplain.com and see all of the books that we have enjoyed at this grade level. Write the title of the book you are reading and how long you have read for.

_____

_____

100 Multiplication facts

9 x1	2 x2	5 x1	4 x3	0 x0	9 x9	3 x5	8 x5	2 x6	4 x7
5 x6	7 x5	3 x0	8 x8	1 x3	3 x4	5 x9	0 x2	7 x3	4 x 1
2 x3	8 x6	0 x5	6 x1	3 x8	1 x 1	9 x0	2 x8	6 x4	0 x7
7 x7	1 x4	6 x2	4 x5	2 x4	4 x 9	7 x0	1 x2	8 x4	6 x5
3 x2	4 x6	1 x9	5 x7	8 x2	0 x8	4 x2	9 x8	3 x6	5 x5
8 x9	3 x7	9 x7	1 x7	6 x0	0 x3	7 x2	1 x5	7 x8	4 x0
8 x3	5 x2	0 x4	9 x5	6 x7	2 x7	6 x3	5 x4	1 x0	9 x 2
7 x 6	1 x 8	9 x6	4 x 4	5 x3	8 x1	3 x3	4 x8	9 x3	2 x0
8 x0	3 x1	6 x8	0 x9	8 x7	2 x 9	9 x4	0 x1	7 x4	5 x8
0 x6	7 x1	2 x5	6 x9	3 x9	1 x6	5 x0	6 x6	2 x1	7 x9

Write a descriptive paragraph describing what the day is like today. Topic sentence, lots of vivid words, supporting details, and then sum it all up.

_____

_____

_____

_____

_____

_____

_____

_____

_____

_____

week 35

circle the word that is spelled correctly in each row

toyle	toile	toil	toyle
powch	pouch	poush	pouche
rownd	round	rounde	rownde
goun	gowne	gown	goune
voyije	voiage	voyaje	voyage
holwing	houling	howling	whowling
nois	noys	noises	noyses
mowned	mouned	mound	mownd
anoy	annoi	annoiy	annoy
coff	cough	kough	koff
flouer	flauer	flower	flowr
froun	frauwn	froune	frown
houned	hound	hown	howned
wooned	wownd	wouned	wound
southe	south	sowth	sowthe
pound	pownd	paund	powned
grown	grone	groane	groune
thowsend	thowsand	thousend	thousand
kowboi	cowboy	couboy	kowboy
voyc	voys	voices	voyces
grouch	growch	grouche	growsh
touer	tauer	tower	touwer

545

What is the perimeter_____and area _____ of a square whose sides are 7 inch?

Round 6843 to the nearest thousand

Round 598 to nearest hundred

Round 329 to nearest ten

Round 4765 to nearest ten

Round 8333 to nearest hundred

Write 374.451 using words

30.07-3.7   46.0-12.46

Division Facts 0-9

56÷7=	15÷3=	12÷6=	8÷2=	63÷7=	0÷4=
14÷2=	42÷6=	6÷1=	16÷8=	20÷5=	49÷7=
36÷4=	64÷8=	0÷3=	54÷9=	4÷2=	48÷8=
18÷9=	3÷1=	35÷5=	8÷4=	72÷8=	6÷6=
0÷5=	42÷7=	2÷2=	36÷9=	7÷1=	12÷3=
16÷2=	30÷5=	0÷1=	28÷7=	4÷4=	40÷8=
3÷3=	32÷8=	45÷5=	4÷1=	20÷4=	15÷5=
56÷8=	5÷1=	0÷8=	6÷2=	45÷9=	0÷6=
6÷3=	21÷7=	0÷9=	7÷7=	12÷4=	18÷6=
63÷9=	18÷3=	27÷9=	24÷3=	0÷2=	28÷4=
21÷3=	16÷4=	24÷8=	10÷5=	30÷6=	1÷1=
18÷2=	27÷3=	32÷4=	9÷1=	35÷7=	40÷5=
10÷2=	8÷8=	48÷6=	5÷5=	8÷1=	24÷6=
25÷5=	9÷3=	81÷9=	24÷4=	14÷7=	12÷2=
9÷9=	54÷6=	72÷9=	0÷7=	2÷1=	36÷6=

Write a describing paragraph about your pet

_____

_____

_____

_____

_____

_____

_____

_____

READING

Your other task for the day is to read a book. At this point you should be able to read for ½ hour to 1 hour each day. Look online for a variety of book lists. You can also check out my site www.plainandnotsoplain.com and see all of the books that we have enjoyed at this grade level. Write the title of the book you are reading and how long you have read for.

_____

_____

Circle the word in the row that is spelled incorrectly

walker	calk	laws	stalk
bald	drawn	cawght	halt
strawberry	fought	caler	half
straw	small	tought	talking
awe	shawl	fallse	squall
south	porch	annoi	wallpaper
awkward	saved	hooge	cookie
worried	families	cawt	storm
funnier	huge	groop	clowns
food	shold	tasted	better
woried	ripped	huge	hole
group	caring	families	hert
discussing	laws	criminals	cawf
anoi	south	trip	caught
thaught	saved	cookie	south

Which of these letters has no lines of symmetry?

M I C R E Y

47x 26

82x 14

$5-$4.25

156 +29

284÷2

369÷3

READING

Your other task for the day is to read a book. At this point you should be able to read for ½ hour to 1 hour each day. Look online for a variety of book lists. You can also check out my site www.plainandnotsoplain.com and see all of the books that we have enjoyed at this grade level. Write the title of the book you are reading and how long you have read for.

_____

_____

Division Facts 0-9

56÷7=	15÷3=	12÷6=	8÷2=	63÷7=	?÷4=
14÷2=	42÷6=	6÷1=	16÷8=	20÷5=	4?
36÷4=	64÷8=	0÷3=	54÷9=	4÷2=	48÷8=
18÷9=	3÷1=	35÷5=	8÷4=	72÷8=	6÷6=
0÷5=	42÷7=	2÷2=	36÷9=	7÷1=	12÷3=
16÷2=	30÷5=	0÷1=	28÷7=	4÷4=	40÷8=
3÷3=	32÷8=	45÷5=	4÷1=	20÷4=	15÷5=
56÷8=	5÷1=	0÷8=	6÷2=	45÷9=	0÷6=
6÷3=	21÷7=	0÷9=	7÷7=	12÷4=	18÷6=
63÷9=	18÷3=	27÷9=	24÷3=	0÷2=	28÷4=
21÷3=	16÷4=	24÷8=	10÷5=	30÷6=	1÷1=
18÷2=	27÷3=	32÷4=	9÷1=	35÷7=	40÷5=
10÷2=	8÷8=	48÷6=	5÷5=	8÷1=	24÷6=
25÷5=	9÷3=	81÷9=	24÷4=	14÷7=	12÷2=
9÷9=	54÷6=	72÷9=	0÷7=	2÷1=	36÷6=

Write a descriptive paragraph describing what you like to do for the summer.

_____

_____

_____

_____

_____

_____

_____

_____

Circle the word in each row that is spelled correctly

butter	buter	buttur	buttor
baskit	bascet	basket	bassket
thriler	thrillir	thrillor	thriller
fassil	fossil	fossul	fassol
wiloe	wilowe	willlow	wilow
slendor	slender	slendir	slendoor
blankit	blankut	blancket	blanket
plastic	plastick	plastik	plasstik
picket	pickit	pikket	pickot
noddud	noddid	nauded	nodded
plannur	planner	plannir	plannar
swallo	swallow	swalow	swalloe
member	membir	memer	membar
summor	summer	summur	simmir
dippur	dippir	dippor	dipper
fawgy	faugy	foggie	foggy
blossom	blassom	blossum	blassum
tikket	ticket	tickit	tikkit
wellcome	welcome	welkome	welkum
witness	witniss	witnuss	witnez
market	markette	markit	marcket
dinnir	dinnor	dinner	dinnur

553

Lets work on division this week☺

READING

Your other task for the day is to read a book. At this point you should be able to read for ½ hour to 1 hour each day. Look online for a variety of book lists. You can also check out my site www.plainandnotsoplain.com and see all of the books that we have enjoyed at this grade level. Write the title of the book you are reading and how long you have read for.

_____

_____

Division Facts 0-9

56÷7=	15÷3=	12÷6=	8÷2=	63÷7=	0÷4=
14÷2=	42÷6=	6÷1=	16÷8=	20÷5=	49÷7=
36÷4=	64÷8=	0÷3=	54÷9=	4÷2=	48÷8=
18÷9=	3÷1=	35÷5=	8÷4=	72÷8=	6÷6=
0÷5=	42÷7=	2÷2=	36÷9=	7÷1=	12÷3=
16÷2=	30÷5=	0÷1=	28÷7=	4÷4=	40÷8=
3÷3=	32÷8=	45÷5=	4÷1=	20÷4=	15÷5=
56÷8=	5÷1=	0÷8=	6÷2=	45÷9=	0÷6=
6÷3=	21÷7=	0÷9=	7÷7=	12÷4=	18÷6=
63÷9=	18÷3=	27÷9=	24÷3=	0÷2=	28÷4=
21÷3=	16÷4=	24÷8=	10÷5=	30÷6=	1÷1=
18÷2=	27÷3=	32÷4=	9÷1=	35÷7=	40÷5=
10÷2=	8÷8=	48÷6=	5÷5=	8÷1=	24÷6=
25÷5=	9÷3=	81÷9=	24÷4=	14÷7=	12÷2=
9÷9=	54÷6=	72÷9=	0÷7=	2÷1=	36÷6=

Write your full name:

_____

Write your full name with middle name initial

_____

Write your 3 initials

_____

Your birthday is

_____

Your favorite food is

_____

Your favorite color is

_____

Your address is

_____

_____

_____

Your mom's phone number is

_____

The number to call for an emergency is:

_____

Circle the word that rhymes with the word in the first column.

pity	party	city	penny
diver	driver	dove	diary
spoken	bitten	bike	broken
habit	rabbit	rated	rapid
river	shave	shiver	shatter
never	clever	clover	cluster
wiper	pipe	paper	piper
easel	dull	double	diesel
cider	reader	road	rider
stolen	swallow	swollen	swimming

Lets work on division this week☺

READING
Your other task for the day is to read a book. At this point you should be able to read for ½ hour to 1 hour each day. Look online for a variety of book lists. You can also check out my site www.plainandnotsoplain.com and see all of the books that we have enjoyed at this grade level. Write the title of the book you are reading and how long you have read for.

_____

_____

Division Facts 0-9

56÷7=	15÷3=	12÷6=	8÷2=	63÷7=	0÷4=
14÷2=	42÷6=	6÷1=	16÷8=	20÷5=	49÷7=
36÷4=	64÷8=	0÷3=	54÷9=	4÷2=	48÷8=
18÷9=	3÷1=	35÷5=	8÷4=	72÷8=	6÷6=
0÷5=	42÷7=	2÷2=	36÷9=	7÷1=	12÷3=
16÷2=	30÷5=	0÷1=	28÷7=	4÷4=	40÷8=
3÷3=	32÷8=	45÷5=	4÷1=	20÷4=	15÷5=
56÷8=	5÷1=	0÷8=	6÷2=	45÷9=	0÷6=
6÷3=	21÷7=	0÷9=	7÷7=	12÷4=	18÷6=
63÷9=	18÷3=	27÷9=	24÷3=	0÷2=	28÷4=
21÷3=	16÷4=	24÷8=	10÷5=	30÷6=	1÷1=
18÷2=	27÷3=	32÷4=	9÷1=	35÷7=	40÷5=
10÷2=	8÷8=	48÷6=	5÷5=	8÷1=	24÷6=
25÷5=	9÷3=	81÷9=	24÷4=	14÷7=	12÷2=
9÷9=	54÷6=	72÷9=	0÷7=	2÷1=	36÷6=

Write an acronym for your name. Take the first letter of your name and write it down in a straight column. Then write words that describe something about YOU.

560

week 36

circle the word that is spelled correctly in each row

pielot	pilot	pillot	pilut
lemun	limon	lemon	limen
raydar	radar	rador	raidar
cabin	caben	cabbin	cabben
habet	habit	habitt	habette
limet	limnt	limit	limot
cider	sider	syder	cyder
stoalen	stolun	stolin	stolen
easel	eesall	easil	esel
talint	tallint	talent	tallent
diever	divur	divir	diver
bisen	byson	bysen	bison
levul	levil	level	levall
spokken	spokin	spoken	spoaken
pitty	pity	pittie	pitie
wiper	wipper	wipur	wipor
rivur	river	rivir	rivor
famuss	fameus	famous	faimous
promiss	promise	pramise	promisce
finesh	finish	finiche	finnesh
razor	raser	rasor	razer
nevor	nevur	never	nevir

Lets work on division this week☺

Your other task for the day is to read a book. At this point you should be able to read for ½ hour to 1 hour each day. Look online for a variety of book lists. You can also check out my site www.plainandnotsoplain.com and see all of the books that we have enjoyed at this grade level. Write the title of the book you are reading and how long you have read for.

_____

_____

Division Facts 0-9

56÷7=	15÷3=	12÷6=	8÷2=	63÷7=	0÷4=
14÷2=	42÷6=	6÷1=	16÷8=	20÷5=	49÷7=
36÷4=	64÷8=	0÷3=	54÷9=	4÷2=	48÷8=
18÷9=	3÷1=	35÷5=	8÷4=	72÷8=	6÷6=
0÷5=	42÷7=	2÷2=	36÷9=	7÷1=	12÷3=
16÷2=	30÷5=	0÷1=	28÷7=	4÷4=	40÷8=
3÷3=	32÷8=	45÷5=	4÷1=	20÷4=	15÷5=
56÷8=	5÷1=	0÷8=	6÷2=	45÷9=	0÷6=
6÷3=	21÷7=	0÷9=	7÷7=	12÷4=	18÷6=
63÷9=	18÷3=	27÷9=	24÷3=	0÷2=	28÷4=
21÷3=	16÷4=	24÷8=	10÷5=	30÷6=	1÷1=
18÷2=	27÷3=	32÷4=	9÷1=	35÷7=	40÷5=
10÷2=	8÷8=	48÷6=	5÷5=	8÷1=	24÷6=
25÷5=	9÷3=	81÷9=	24÷4=	14÷7=	12÷2=
9÷9=	54÷6=	72÷9=	0÷7=	2÷1=	36÷6=

Give me 10 adjectives that describe YOU:

1. _____
2. _____
3. _____
4. _____
5. _____
6. _____
7. _____
8. _____
9. _____
10. _____

What do you think you improved upon the most this year?_____

_____

What class did you enjoy the most this year?_____

_____

What is something you want to learn new next year?

_____

What is something you "wish" you didn't have to do?_____

_____

circle the word in each row that is spelled correctly

about	uhbout	ubowt	abowt
ketel	kettle	kettel	kettul
above	abuv	uhbove	abov
cansell	cansil	cancel	kancel
remined	remind	reemind	reemined
gathur	gather	gathir	gathor
unfolled	unfoled	unfold	unfoaled
tinnder	tender	tinderr	tendur
akshun	aktion	acshun	action
monstir	mawnster	monster	monstur
petal	petul	petall	pettal
wooman	wuman	woman	womin
weader	weeder	weder	weedur
frosty	frostie	frostee	frossty
tootor	tootur	tutur	tutor
poaster	poster	poaster	postir
behaive	beehave	behave	behaeve
reelate	relate	relait	relaite
between	betwene	bctwean	batween
chamber	chambur	chambir	chambor
cliper	clipper	clippor	clippur
egsite	eksite	excite	exsite

565

Lets work on division this week☺

READING
Your other task for the day is to read a book. At this point you should be able to read for ½ hour to 1 hour each day. Look online for a variety of book lists. You can also check out my site www.plainandnotsoplain.com and see all of the books that we have enjoyed at this grade level. Write the title of the book you are reading and how long you have read for.

_____

_____

Division Facts 0-9

56÷7=	15÷3=	12÷6=	8÷2=	63÷7=	0÷4=
14÷2=	42÷6=	6÷1=	16÷8=	20÷5=	49÷7=
36÷4=	64÷8=	0÷3=	54÷9=	4÷2=	48÷8=
18÷9=	3÷1=	35÷5=	8÷4=	72÷8=	6÷6=
0÷5=	42÷7=	2÷2=	36÷9=	7÷1=	12÷3=
16÷2=	30÷5=	0÷1=	28÷7=	4÷4=	40÷8=
3÷3=	32÷8=	45÷5=	4÷1=	20÷4=	15÷5=
56÷8=	5÷1=	0÷8=	6÷2=	45÷9=	0÷6=
6÷3=	21÷7=	0÷9=	7÷7=	12÷4=	18÷6=
63÷9=	18÷3=	27÷9=	24÷3=	0÷2=	28÷4=
21÷3=	16÷4=	24÷8=	10÷5=	30÷6=	1÷1=
18÷2=	27÷3=	32÷4=	9÷1=	35÷7=	40÷5=
10÷2=	8÷8=	48÷6=	5÷5=	8÷1=	24÷6=
25÷5=	9÷3=	81÷9=	24÷4=	14÷7=	12÷2=
9÷9=	54÷6=	72÷9=	0÷7=	2÷1=	36÷6=

Write a paragraph trying to persuade me to allow you to do something. You have to give reasons as to why you should be allowed to do it.

Title

_____

Topic sentence

_____

Points to persuade

_____

_____

_____

_____

_____

_____

Summarize your paragraph

_____

_____

Write ten of your favorite foods

1. _____
2. _____
3. _____
4. _____
5. _____
6. _____
7. _____
8. _____
9. _____
10. _____

Now number them in ABC order

Use words to write 356,320

9.36 – (4.37-3.8)

24.32- (8.61+12.5)

In three classrooms there were 18,21, and 21 students. What was the average number of students per classroom?

Skip's temperature is 99.8 degrees. Normal body temperature is 98.6 degrees. How many degrees above normal body temperature is Skips?

Division Facts 0-9

56÷7=	15÷3=	12÷6=	8÷2=	63÷7=	0÷4=
14÷2=	42÷6=	6÷1=	16÷8=	20÷5=	49÷7=
36÷4=	64÷8=	0÷3=	54÷9=	4÷2=	48÷8=
18÷9=	3÷1=	35÷5=	8÷4=	72÷8=	6÷6=
0÷5=	42÷7=	2÷2=	36÷9=	7÷1=	12÷3=
16÷2=	30÷5=	0÷1=	28÷7=	4÷4=	40÷8=
3÷3=	32÷8=	45÷5=	4÷1=	20÷4=	15÷5=
56÷8=	5÷1=	0÷8=	6÷2=	45÷9=	0÷6=
6÷3=	21÷7=	0÷9=	7÷7=	12÷4=	18÷6=
63÷9=	18÷3=	27÷9=	24÷3=	0÷2=	28÷4=
21÷3=	16÷4=	24:8=	10÷5=	30÷6=	1÷1=
18÷2=	27÷3=	32÷4=	9÷1=	35÷7=	40÷5=
10÷2=	8÷8=	48÷6=	5÷5=	8÷1=	24÷6=
25÷5=	9÷3=	81÷9=	24÷4=	14÷7=	12÷2=
9÷9=	54÷6=	72÷9=	0÷7=	2÷1=	36÷6=

Write me a declarative sentence(.)

Interrogative sentence (?)

Imperative sentence(.)

Exclamatory sentence (!)

READING
Your other task for the day is to read a book. At this point you should be able to read for ½ hour to 1 hour each day. Look online for a variety of book lists. You can also check out my site www.plainandnotsoplain.com and see all of the books that we have enjoyed at this grade level. Write the title of the book you are reading and how long you have read for.

_____

_____

circle the word in each row that is spelled correctly

sistur	sister	sistor	sisster
mayer	mayur	maier	mayor
barbor	barbber	barbur	barber
ziper	zippor	zippir	zipper
dottir	daughter	daughtor	dottor
powdor	powder	pouder	poudor
enter	entor	interr	intor
ancher	anker	anchor	anckor
tankor	tancker	tanker	tankir
chedar	cheddor	chedder	cheddar
popular	populer	poplulor	populir
pepper	peper	peppur	peppor
colar	coler	coller	collar
danjer	danger	dainger	dangor
elavater	elavator	elevater	elevator
harber	harbur	harbor	harbir
poler	polar	polor	poaler
vickter	vicktor	victor	victer
odor	oder	oader	odoor
groser	grosor	grocer	grocor
singur	singor	singer	singger
gradder	graider	grader	grador

If 2 oranges cost 42 cents. How much would 8 oranges cost?

340x9   43x33

432÷4   3912÷3

READING

Your other task for the day is to read a book. At this point you should be able to read for ½ hour to 1 hour each day. Look online for a variety of book lists. You can also check out my site www.plainandnotsoplain.com and see all of the books that we have enjoyed at this grade level. Write the title of the book you are reading and how long you have read for.

_____

_____

Division Facts 0-9

56÷7=	15÷3=	12÷6=	8÷2=	63÷7=	0÷4=
14÷2=	42÷6=	6÷1=	16÷8=	20÷5=	49÷7=
36÷4=	64÷8=	0÷3=	54÷9=	4÷2=	48÷8=
18÷9=	3÷1=	35÷5=	8÷4=	72÷8=	6÷6=
0÷5=	42÷7=	2÷2=	36÷9=	7÷1=	12÷3=
16÷2=	30÷5=	0÷1=	28÷7=	4÷4=	40÷8=
3÷3=	32÷8=	45÷5=	4÷1=	20÷4=	15÷5=
56÷8=	5÷1=	0÷8=	6÷2=	45÷9=	0÷6=
6÷3=	21÷7=	0÷9=	7÷7=	12÷4=	18÷6=
63÷9=	18÷3=	27÷9=	24÷3=	0÷2=	28÷4=
21÷3=	16÷4=	24÷8=	10÷5=	30÷6=	1÷1=
18÷2=	27÷3=	32÷4=	9÷1=	35÷7=	40÷5=
10÷2=	8÷8=	48÷6=	5÷5=	8÷1=	24÷6=
25÷5=	9÷3=	81÷9=	24÷4=	14÷7=	12÷2=
9÷9=	54÷6=	72÷9=	0÷7=	2÷1=	36÷6=

Write your address properly

Write your birthday out with all the words

Write today's date out with words

Write your full name—first, middle, and last

week 36

circle the word that is spelled correctly in each row

ridel	riddel	riddle	ridel
able	abel	aibel	aible
medle	medel	medal	medol
local	locul	lokel	loakal
pebol	pebbul	pebble	pebbel
special	speshul	speshle	spechel
buegel	bugel	bewgle	bugle
channle	channel	channul	channil
settel	settle	scettle	settol
pedle	pedal	pedel	pedol
pencil	pensil	pencel	pensel
dossile	dosul	dociel	docile
orol	orel	oral	orul
vessol	vessel	vessle	vessel
buble	bubble	bubbel	bubbul
sumble	cymbol	symbol	symbel
uncel	unkel	unkle	uncle
paddol	padol	paddel	paddle
turtle	turtool	turtul	turtel
pupul	pupool	pupil	pupol
ankel	ankle	anckel	anchol
totel	total	totle	totol

```
 28      5
 47      2
 74      4
 36      7
 91      3
 87      3
 21      5
 12      2
+14     +1
```

Sarah's first nine tests she earned these scores:

90, 95, 80,85,100,95,75,95,90
What was the average

What is the median

What is the range

What is the mode

READING

Your other task for the day is to read a book. At this point you should be able to read for ½ hour to 1 hour each day. Look online for a variety of book lists. You can also check out my site www.plainandnotsoplain.com and see all of the books that we have enjoyed at this grade level. Write the title of the book you are reading and how long you have read for.

_____

_____

100 Multiplication facts

9 x1	2 x2	5 x1	4 x3	0 x0	9 x9	3 x5	8 x5	2 x6	4 x7
5 x6	7 x5	3 x0	8 x8	1 x3	3 x4	5 x9	0 x2	7 x3	4 x 1
2 x3	8 x6	0 x5	6 x1	3 x8	1 x 1	9 x0	2 x8	6 x4	0 x7
7 x7	1 x4	6 x2	4 x5	2 x4	4 x 9	7 x0	1 x2	8 x4	6 x5
3 x2	4 x6	1 x9	5 x7	8 x2	0 x8	4 x2	9 x8	3 x6	5 x5
8 x9	3 x7	9 x7	1 x7	6 x0	0 x3	7 x2	1 x5	7 x8	4 x0
8 x3	5 x2	0 x4	9 x5	6 x7	2 x7	6 x3	5 x4	1 x0	9 x 2
7 x 6	1 x 8	9 x6	4 x 4	5 x3	8 x1	3 x3	4 x8	9 x3	2 x0
8 x0	3 x1	6 x8	0 x9	8 x7	2 x 9	9 x4	0 x1	7 x4	5 x8
0 x6	7 x1	2 x5	6 x9	3 x9	1 x6	5 x0	6 x6	2 x1	7 x9

Collin likes playing football very much. He plays football with his friends every Sunday. Last Sunday, he played football in Tuxedo Park with Evan and Greg. Collin broke his right leg when he tried to get the ball from Evan. Collin cried loudly. Greg called the police and they sent Collin to the hospital.

Now, Collin is staying in a hospital. He has to take medicine four times a day. He is unhappy because he feels lonely. He cannot walk. The boy next to him is Sam. Sam is ten years old. He likes playing basketball. He broke his arm last Friday. He always tells jokes to make Collin laugh. Sometimes they play chess together.

Answer the following questions.

Why is Collin unhappy?

_____

Does Sam like playing football?

_____

What does Sam do to make Collin happier?

_____

Is Greg in the hospital now?

_____

Did Evan break Collin's leg?

_____

can	should	can't	shouldn't	would

Fill in the blanks using the following words.

Students _____ be late for school.

It is cold. You _____ wear your jumper today.

This story book is interesting. You _____ read it.

You _____ go home on time.

Bob _____ be cruel to his pets. He _____ be kind to animals.

Tom: _____ you like something to drink?

Ann: Yes, please

Mary: _____ we stay in the classroom, Miss Smith?

Miss Smith: No, you _____. You _____ line up in the playground.

Write as numbers:

three million two hundred fifty-five thousand_____

seventy million_____

eight million two hundred thousand_____

four million eight hundred sixty-two thousand three hundred
ten_____

Round off 5, 185,924 to the nearest hundred _____

Round off 5,185,924 to the nearest thousand_____

Round off 5, 185,924 to the nearest hundred thousand_____

Buses need to be rented for 27 children going on a field trip. Each bus can take
12 children in addition to the driver. How many buses must be rented?

_____

60,000-241=

4863-376=

37x14=

100 Multiplication facts

9 x1	2 x2	5 x1	4 x3	0 x0	9 x9	3 x5	8 x5	2 x6	4 x7
5 x6	7 x5	3 x0	8 x8	1 x3	3 x4	5 x9	0 x2	7 x3	4 x 1
2 x3	8 x6	0 x5	6 x1	3 x8	1 x 1	9 x0	2 x8	6 x4	0 x7
7 x7	1 x4	6 x2	4 x5	2 x4	4 x 9	7 x0	1 x2	8 x4	6 x5
3 x2	4 x6	1 x9	5 x7	8 x2	0 x8	4 x2	9 x8	3 x6	5 x5
8 x9	3 x7	9 x7	1 x7	6 x0	0 x3	7 x2	1 x5	7 x8	4 x0
8 x3	5 x2	0 x4	9 x5	6 x7	2 x7	6 x3	5 x4	1 x0	9 x 2
7 x 6	1 x 8	9 x6	4 x 4	5 x3	8 x1	3 x3	4 x8	9 x3	2 x0
8 x0	3 x1	6 x8	0 x9	8 x7	2 x 9	9 x4	0 x1	7 x4	5 x8
0 x6	7 x1	2 x5	6 x9	3 x9	1 x6	5 x0	6 x6	2 x1	7 x9

Circle the correct answer

Mr. Maryon has a big and (expensive/more expensive/expensiver)car.

Patty is (tall/taller/tallest) than Susan.

Brooklyn has the (longer/longest/very long) hair in her class.

I can run (fast/faster/more faster) than Tom.

Autumn in Japan is (hottest/cooler/warmer) than summer.

Write one adjective for each sentence.

Do you know which is the _____? A racing car, a plane, or a
rocket?

Mary's picture is _____than Paul's picture. He can't draw at all.

Your bag is_____than mine. I can't even lift it up!

My sister doesn't like eating. She is the _____in our family.

Jadyn has the _____points in her class for being kind to others.

some	a little	a lot of

Fill in the blanks with the correct words.

We need to eat_____vegetables.

We can eat _____sweet food.

We need to eat _____rice.

We can eat _____meat.

We can drink _____soda.

We should not eat _____chips.

anything	something	everything	nothing

I have got _____to tell you, but can you keep a secret?

Do you know _____about his birthday party?

I'm hungry, I want _____-to eat.

Is there _____that I can help you with?

Calm down! There's _____--to worry about.

He is very rich. _____he has is expensive.

We didn't buy_____from China, because we lost our wallets.

There's _____left in the house. The thieves took everything.

We asked him about the news but he said_____.

Don't lie to me. Tell me _____-about the accident.

I kicked _____-when I got out of the bed. It was my cat.

The house next door was on fire last night. My neighbor has lost

_____.

The length of a rectangle is 10 meters. The width is 4 meters. What is the area?

The area of a rectangle is 20 square meters. The width is 5 meters. What is the length?

Draw me two parallel lines

Draw me two perpendicular lines

Draw a hexagon   pentagon   rectangle   star

4321 +3190=   8732-127=

100 Multiplication facts

9 x1	2 x2	5 x1	4 x3	0 x0	9 x9	3 x5	8 x5	2 x6	4 x7
5 x6	7 x5	3 x0	8 x8	1 x3	3 x4	5 x9	0 x2	7 x3	4 x 1
2 x3	8 x6	0 x5	6 x1	3 x8	1 x 1	9 x0	2 x8	6 x4	0 x7
7 x7	1 x4	6 x2	4 x5	2 x4	4 x 9	7 x0	1 x2	8 x4	6 x5
3 x2	4 x6	1 x9	5 x7	8 x2	0 x8	4 x2	9 x8	3 x6	5 x5
8 x9	3 x7	9 x7	1 x7	6 x0	0 x3	7 x2	1 x5	7 x8	4 x0
8 x3	5 x2	0 x4	9 x5	6 x7	2 x7	6 x3	5 x4	1 x0	9 x 2
7 x 6	1 x 8	9 x6	4 x 4	5 x3	8 x1	3 x3	4 x8	9 x3	2 x0
8 x0	3 x1	6 x8	0 x9	8 x7	2 x 9	9 x4	0 x1	7 x4	5 x8
0 x6	7 x1	2 x5	6 x9	3 x9	1 x6	5 x0	6 x6	2 x1	7 x9

Write your mothers full name with misses as abbreviation

Write your dads full name with mister as abbreviation

write your initials

Write all your siblings full names

write your full address like as on an envelope

READING

Your other task for the day is to read a book. At this point you should be able to read for ½ hour to 1 hour each day. Look online for a variety of book lists. You can also check out my site www.plainandnotsoplain.com and see all of the books that we have enjoyed at this grade level. Write the title of the book you are reading and how long you have read for.

_____

_____

Write me a book report about a book you just read.

Title_____

Author_____

Settings_____

Characters_____

Main point of the book_____

_____

Give a small summary of the book_____

_____

_____

_____

_____

_____

_____

READING

Your other task for the day is to read a book. At this point you should be able to read for ½ hour to 1 hour each day. Look online for a variety of book lists. You can also check out my site www.plainandnotsoplain.com and see all of the books that we have enjoyed at this grade level. Write the title of the book you are reading and how long you have read for.

_____

_____

100 Multiplication facts

9 x1	2 x2	5 x1	4 x3	0 x0	9 x9	3 x5	8 x5	2 x6	4 x7
5 x6	7 x5	3 x0	8 x8	1 x3	3 x4	5 x9	0 x2	7 x3	4 x 1
2 x3	8 x6	0 x5	6 x1	3 x8	1 x 1	9 x0	2 x8	6 x4	0 x7
7 x7	1 x4	6 x2	4 x5	2 x4	4 x 9	7 x0	1 x2	8 x4	6 x5
3 x2	4 x6	1 x9	5 x7	8 x2	0 x8	4 x2	9 x8	3 x6	5 x5
8 x9	3 x7	9 x7	1 x7	6 x0	0 x3	7 x2	1 x5	7 x8	4 x0
8 x3	5 x2	0 x4	9 x5	6 x7	2 x7	6 x3	5 x4	1 x0	9 x 2
7 x 6	1 x 8	9 x6	4 x 4	5 x3	8 x1	3 x3	4 x8	9 x3	2 x0
8 x0	3 x1	6 x8	0 x9	8 x7	2 x 9	9 x4	0 x1	7 x4	5 x8
0 x6	7 x1	2 x5	6 x9	3 x9	1 x6	5 x0	6 x6	2 x1	7 x9

Give me an example of a fiction book

Give me an example of a nonfiction book

Do you know what a biography is?

Do you know what an autobiography is?

What is a dictionary?

What is an atlas?

What is a thesaurus?

Use a ruler to draw a line segment for each measurement

1 ½ inch

3 ½ inch

4 ½ inch

5 inch

---

1 foot=12 inch
1 yard= 3 ft or 36 inch
1 mile= 5280 ft

1 pint= 2 cups
1 quart= 2 pints
1 gallon= 4 quarts

1 minute=60 seconds
1 hour=60 min
1 day=24 hours

6 cups_____pt

3 ft_____in

4 pt_____qt

8 min_____sec

2 yd_____in

8 qt_____gallons

5 hours_____min

5 ft_____in

8pt_____cups

3 days_____hours

7 yd _____ft

10 gal_____quarts

10 min_____seconds

2 mile_____ft

16 quarts_____pt

24 hours_____min

1 mile_____ft

1 gallon_____quarts

7 days_____hours

1 foot_____inch

1 yard_____feet

1 quart_____pints

1 pint_____cups

Also included in this book are 21 weeks of vocabulary words that every 4th grader should know. I would suggest you copy them onto index cards at the beginning of the week and have your child practice saying them and knowing what they mean by the end of each week.

Week 1	week 2	week 3	week 4	week 5
its	piece	however	reached	vowel
questions	usually	happened	listen	fable
reference	friends	adaptation	amendment	genre
citation	heard	camouflage	document	metaphor
bibliography	accuracy	carnivore	consitution	simile
book	acute	herbivore	preamble	mystery
newspaper	across	early	morning	categories
since	become	remember	himself	true
index	computations	whole	several	hundred
caption	quiz	behavioral	cover	against
complete	obtuse	enemy	jury	pattern
problem	computation	ominivore	representative	numeral

week 6	week 7	week8	week 9	week 10
composite	biosphere	legislative	alliteration	decided
diameter	ecosystem	executive	street	course
probability	ecology	phony	nightmare	surface
quadrant	muscle	congressional	quickly	produce
radius	environmental	English	shown	potential
tessellations	ground	finally	verb	kinetic
biome	judicial	analogy	inches	yet
south	conjunction	quotations	convex	thermometers
notice	travel	proofread	exponent	crazy
cried	certain	interjection	parallelogram	mechanical
voice	figure	correct	vertex	thermal
slowly	I'll	wait	nickname	chemical

week 11	week 12	week 13	week 14	week 15
government	system	equation	cholesterol	insensitive
object	clause	inequality	carcinogen	spiteful
among	brought	ratio	translucent	vidictive
cannot	understand	volume	husband	disagreeable
revenue	hyperbole	equilateral	cardiovascular	worthless
annex	idiom	digits	hostile	forlorn
boycott	superlative	carefully	aggravated	lonesome
immigrant	thousands	scientists	belligerent	ostracized
paragraph	language	known	arrogant	alienated
immigration	though	island	callous	dejected
machine	explain	constellation	obnoxious	depressed
plane	quarantine	eclipse	resentful	estranged
week 16	week 17	week 18	week 19	week 20
humiliated	humane	difference	present	finished
obsolete	energy	probably	beautiful	discovered
depression	subject	written	edge	beside
suddenly	region	length	sign	million
direction	believe	dictatorship	asserted	lie
anything	exercise	monarchy	cautioned	perhaps
divided	ecstatic	anarchy	bellowed	imperialism
general	enthusiastic	aristocracy	interrupted	fascism
amiable	elated	autocracy	responded	communism
altruistic	gratified	democracy	taunted	patriotism
charitable	vivacious	theocracy	demanded	captialism
empathetic	developed	reason	complained	socialism

week 21
weather
instrument
third
include
built
glossary
aquaphobia
homophobia
claustrophobia
astraphobia
optophobia
amaxophobia

Master Spelling List for Teacher

week 1
ache
admit
animal
April
bacon
bathroom
camera
flap
grateful
happiness
manage
navy
plane
radish
waste

week2
bedtime
being
beverage
cedar
decoy
elegant
female
jelly
lemon
medicine
meteor
rectangle
recycle
secret
skeleton

week3
blindfold
cinnamon
dentist
giant
history
imagine
island
minus
pirate
principal
rifle
silence
skid
spinach
whine

week 4
auto
bobbin
bony
closet
cobra
doctor
elbow
frozen
hotel
knot
object
poetry
solemn
solve
total

week 5
amuse
bubble
budding
budge
computer
customer
duty
humor
hungry
husky
Jupiter
number
sundown
summer
usual

week 6
already
balcony
country
deny
early
envy
February
greedy
hydrant
hymn
library
reply
satisfy
skyline
syllable

week 7
afraid
aide
bay
break
chain
delay
failure
great
maize
payment
prey
refrain
reain
stain
waist

week 8
agree
between
breathe
disease
eagle
easel
greenery
greetings
meek
people
preach
season
wheat
wheel
yeast

week 9
account
aloud
amount
boundary
couch
county
doubt
foul
fountain
hound
mountain
noun
ounce
pound
south

week 11
balloon
bruise
canoe
cartoon
choose
cougar
drew
group
lieutenant
loose
movable
route
shoot
through
troupe

week 12
appointment
avoid
choice
destroy
employer
enjoy
join
loyalty
moisture
poison
rejoice
royal
soybean
voice
voyage

week 13
beige
believe
conceited
eight
field
fiend
freight
friend
height
leisure
neighbor
receive
sleigh
thief
weigh

week 14	week 17	week 20	week 23
alphabetize	anxious	airport	bicycle
arise	ax	barefoot	bifocals
concise	boxes	birthday	bimonthly
enterprise	coax	cardboard	binoculars
justice	example	downstairs	quadrangle
memorize	except	earthquake	quadruplet
office	excuse	farewell	triangle
police	exercise	flyswatter	tricep
price	Mexico	forenoon	tricolor
prize	saxophone	iceberg	tricycle
service	sixteen	landlord	trio
surmise	sixth	northwest	tripod
surprise	taxes	scarecrow	unicorn
twice	Texas	teakettle	unicycle
wise	toxic	throughout	uniform

week 15	week 18	week 21	week 24
coffee	across	batteries	discolor
cough	afford	cowboys	dislike
different	battle	delays	disobey
elephant	goddess	donkeys	distrust
elf	copper	gravies	nondairy
enough	difference	ivies	nonfat
graph	difficult	ladies	nonsense
half	message	Mondays	unbreakable
laughter	gallon	pennies	uncertain
oneself	official	ponys	unfair
photo	recess	stories	unfold
rough	success	trays	unfriendly
sniffle	suppose	Tuesdays	unhappiness
telephone	terrible	valleys	unlucky
tough	traffic	Wednesdays	unselfish

week 16	week 19	week 22	week 25
argue	bare	prearrange	beliefs
beautiful	stair	predict	calves
beauty	pane	preface	chiefs
cue	hall	prepay	cliffs
feud	bury	preview	cuffs
few	groan	reappear	elves
hue	bear	rebuild	halves
mew	stare	recover	knives
newt	raise	redecorate	leaves
pew	haul	refill	lives
queue	weight	reform	loaves
review	pain	reload	roofs
view	grown	remodel	scarves
you	berry	repaint	shelves
Yule	wait	restore	wives
	rays		

week 26	week 29	week 32
ailment	biggest	accepted
attention	brighter	admiring
basement	clumsiest	captured
celebration	crazier	choking
movement	cruelest	dining
employment	earlier	dozed
germination	firmer	fanning
limitation	flattest	guarded
measurement	greener	hoping
disappointment	noisiest	invited
multiplication	prettier	pledged
statement	quietest	practicing
subtraction	simpler	proving
treatment	tastiest	rearranged
vacation	widest	squeezing

week 27	week30
aren't	bass
couldn't	bowl
doesn't	close
hasn't	cobbler
he'd	does
I'd	file
she's	flounder
should've	grave
they'll	hawk
wasn't	list
weren't	minute
what's	object
who'd	paddle
won't	present
you've	sow

week 28	week 31
scheme	board
scholar	bored
school	coarse
schooner	course
scratch	council
scream	counsel
screw	creak
scrimmage	creek
scrub	knot
straight	not
strainer	lead
strength	led
string	wring
stripe	ring
struggle	who's
	whose

Due to the size of this book, I was unable to put the answer key with it. You can goto www.plainandnotsoplain.com under homeschooling resources and download a PDF for free with the answers.

Made in the USA
Middletown, DE
10 May 2020